a

OLAVUS PETRI AND THE ECCLESI-
ASTICAL TRANSFORMATION
IN SWEDEN 1521-1552

THE MACMILLAN COMPANY
NEW YORK · BOSTON · CHICAGO · DALLAS
ATLANTA · SAN FRANCISCO

MACMILLAN & CO., LIMITED
LONDON · BOMBAY · CALCUTTA
MELBOURNE

THE MACMILLAN CO. OF CANADA, LTD.
TORONTO

Olavus Petri
and the
ECCLESIASTICAL TRANSFORMATION IN SWEDEN
[1521-1552]

A Study in the Swedish Reformation

by

CONRAD BERGENDOFF

✠

New York
THE MACMILLAN COMPANY
1928

All rights reserved

Copyright, 1928,
By THE MACMILLAN COMPANY.

Set up and printed.
Published May, 1928.

SET UP BY BROWN BROTHERS LINOTYPERS
Printed in the United States of America by
THE FERRIS PRINTING COMPANY, NEW YORK

TO

MY FATHER AND MOTHER

FOREWORD

THIS work is a result of researches conducted in the University Libraries of Uppsala and Lund, in the Royal Library at Copenhagen, in the University and Royal Libraries of Berlin. With gratitude, the author recalls the many acts of kindness of which he has been the recipient in these libraries. He is mindful, too, of the distinguished friend who suggested this subject, and whose kind and unfailing interest has been a source of constant encouragement in the pursuit of these studies, namely, His Grace, Nathan Soderblom, Archbishop of Uppsala. It is the author's earnest desire that this treatise may have shed some additional light on a man and a period known too little outside of his native country, and in this country hardly at all.

CONTENTS

CHAPTER		PAGE
I.	THE ECCLESIASTICAL TRANSFORMATION, 1521-1531	1
II.	THE YEARS OF PREPARATION	62
III.	OLAVUS PETRI AND THE FIRST LITERARY PRODUCTIONS OF THE SWEDISH REFORMATION	86
IV.	THE POLEMICAL WRITINGS	112
V.	THE LITURGICAL WORKS	147
VI.	THE HOMILETICAL WORKS. THE THEOLOGICAL THOUGHT OF OLAVUS PETRI	178
VII.	THE LEGAL AND HISTORICAL WORKS	209
VIII.	THE SUBORDINATION OF CHURCH TO STATE, OLAVUS PETRI AND THE EVANGELICAL MOVEMENT, 1531-1552	220
	BIBLIOGRAPHY	252
	INDEX	259

OLAVUS PETRI AND THE ECCLESI-
ASTICAL TRANSFORMATION
IN SWEDEN 1521-1552

OLAVUS PETRI AND THE ECCLESIASTICAL TRANSFORMATION IN SWEDEN 1521-1552

CHAPTER I

THE ECCLESIASTICAL TRANSFORMATION
1521-1531

THE decade 1521-1531 witnessed some of the most important, if not the most important, events in Swedish history. This was the period of the foundation of the modern Swedish State, which has its beginnings in the reign of Gustavus Vasa. During these years, too, came the transformation in language and literature, for the literary productions of this period determined the cultural character of the new nation. And that which is the subject of this investigation, the nature of the Swedish Reformation, can be understood only against the background of these years. This decade saw the transformation of the Church from a wealthy and powerful organization, obedient and loyal to Rome, into a body dependent upon the king for its support and authority, and in matters of doctrine pledged to preach an evangelical faith. The period is full of dramatic interest, and its leading personalities are virile. Our study centers in the man who gave the new nation its spiritual training, and influenced its religious and cultural destiny. But his work would have been impossible without the king, who built a new State and remodeled the ecclesiastical structure. Though the king's policies during this decade were destructive to the Church, they made possible, at the same time, the constructive labors of the Reformer. To understand the latter, it is necessary first to trace the policy of Gustavus Vasa in regard to the Church and see its effects upon both State and Church.

The fifteenth century [1] in Sweden was the era of the union between the three Scandinavian kingdoms, effected at Kalmar in 1397. The dominant power in the Union was Denmark, and its kings sought continually to increase their power in Sweden, at the expense of Swedish independence. But their efforts met repeated resistance from both ecclesiastic and lay powers. In order better to meet the attacks of the nobles and peasants, the Danish kings adopted the policy of treating the Swedish Church with consideration and generosity, winning thereby the prelates to an attitude favorable to the Union. For example, in 1434, in the Engelbrekt uprising, the Church seems to have fomented, or at least favored, the anti-Danish rebellion. But after 1436, when the king, Eric of Pommerania, had guaranteed privileges to the Church, and especially during the archiepiscopate of Nicholas Ragvaldi (1438-1448), the ecclesiastical leaders tended toward alliance with the foreign master. In the Kalmar Recess of 1483 the Church again received guaranties of freedom. But the growth of ecclesiastical power, coupled with the strengthening of foreign

[1] L. A. Anjou, *Svenska Kyrkoreformationens Historia,* Chap. I; K. B. Westman, *Reformationens genombrottsår i Sverige,* Chaps. III, V; H. Hildebrand, *Sveriges Historia,* I, 2, pp. 313ff.; E. Hildebrand, *Sveriges Historia,* IV.

domination, made the position of nobles and peasants unbearable. The anti-union party gathered increasing strength. Though it was unable, under Karl Knutsson, to establish again an independent kingdom, it could, in 1471, defeat Christian I's purpose of making Sweden his vassal state. The truce that followed, while it made dependence upon Denmark more endurable, further divided the country. In 1514 Christian II became king of Denmark, but the Swedes, under the director of the kingdom, Sten Sture, delayed his reception as their king. Sture had won his position at the expense of Eric Trolle, father of the new archbishop, Gustav Trolle, and a feud sprang up between the director and the archbishop, immediately on the latter's return from Rome, in 1515. The archbishop favored the acceptance of Christian II, but his conduct won him enemies, and, in 1517, deposition, at the hands of a Swedish Diet. His castle at Uppsala was destroyed, and he was kept under surveillance. The result was open war with Christian II. Though at Brännkyrka, south of Stockholm, in 1518, the Swedish forces were successful, the king succeeded, by deceit, in carrying off six hostages to Denmark, among whom was Gustavus Vasa, a scion of the Sture family. In 1520 the Danish king returned and completely subdued the country. He celebrated his triumph in a manner that has never been forgotten nor forgiven. In the Massacre at Stockholm, over eighty persons perished, among whom were two bishops and a large number of the foremost nobility. The people were left leaderless, and opposition had presumably been crushed by the cruel tyrant. That his ally, Archbishop Trolle, gave ecclesiastical sanction to the massacre—in fact it was formally based upon the Nationalists' deposition of the archbishop—and that the Church had favored the Union which now produced such a catastrophe, created a sentiment against the prelates which the events of the following years could capitalize.

Gustavus Vasa escaped from Danish imprisonment and by way of Lübeck returned to Sweden, in May, 1520. His aim now was to free Sweden from the Danish power. In Dalarne he found his first army, and during 1521 the larger part of Sweden gave him allegiance. By the end of 1522 all of Sweden, except Stockholm, Kalmar, and Älfsborg, was won. Gustavus needed foreign aid, however, and this he negotiated in Lübeck. Kalmar fell at Pentecost, and Stockholm on June 21, 1523. In June the Swedish Parliament elected Gustavus king, and on June 4 he assumed the name. The crown he would not take until he felt that both the foreign and internal affairs of the State were permanently ordered. He had to wait until 1528. During these years he developed the policy toward the Church which resulted in its thorough transformation.

The Swedish Church at the opening of the third decade of the sixteenth century [2] had behind it a history of some seven hundred years. Ansgarius had first begun missionary work in 829 A.D., and his labors were continued by Frankish and English missionaries. Primacy over the new Church was vested first in Hamburg, after 858 in Bremen, and in 1103 in Lund, where now an archbishopric was created. The complete organization of the province under Rome was effected at the Council in Skeninge, in 1248. An archbishopric in Uppsala was granted by Alexander III, in 1164—by the middle of the fifteenth century it considered itself primate over the Swedish Church. By the latter

[2] Anjou, *op. cit.*, Chap. I; Westman, *op. cit.*, Chap. IV.

date episcopal sees had come into existence in Linköping, Skara, Strengnäs, Vexiö, Vesterås, and Åbo (in Finland). Of the many orders and monasteries that had found a home in Sweden the most famous was St. Birgitta's, at Vadstena. Gustavus Vasa declared in 1527 that the Crown and the nobility jointly had hardly one-third of the wealth concentrated in the Church. His statement is generally considered as exaggerated, but that the Church was the most united, the most powerful, and the wealthiest body in the country at the opening of the sixteenth century cannot be doubted.[3] In 1520 it had suffered a crippling blow through the massacre of two of its bishops, Vincent of Skara and Matts of Strengnäs. Its archbishop, moreover, had been deposed as a traitor, and the attitude of the Nationalists was hostile. In 1522 Bishop Otto of Vasterås died, and in the same year the bishop in Finland, Arvid of Åbo, drowned in his flight from Finland to Sweden. Bishop Ingemar of Vexiö was of advanced age, and had no political power. Successors to the martyred bishops were elected in 1522—in Strengnäs, Magnus Sommar, in Skara, Magnus Harraldson. In 1523 Peder Jakobson was elected to succeed Bishop Otto. The confirmation of these bishops-elect became one of the factors in the Swedish Reformation. The only remaining regularly confirmed

[3] Of 107,589 *hemman* (homesteads) in the kingdom at this time, 13,738 were the property of the Church, a percentage of 12-13 percent. But this sum does not include the parsonages in the 1700 churches of the kingdom. About one-quarter of the land of the Church belonged to monasteries, one-quarter to the diocesan centers, and one-half to the parishes. The center of Church wealth lay in Östergötland, Vestergötland, Småland, Öland, where the property of the Church included one-fourth of all the homesteads. (Westman, *op. cit.*, pp. 73-4, following H. Forssell, *Sveriges inre historia från Gustav den förste*, I.)

bishop was the able Hans Brask, in Linköping. He stood practically alone before the advance of a new government and a new teaching. When his cause was lost, he fled to the Continent (1527).

At the beginning of his campaign to unite the nation with himself against the foreign king, Gustavus had promised Brask (July 25, 1521) to "defend and protect all the privileges, persons, and possessions of the Holy Church." [4] In his and the royal council's proclamation at the end of the year, the regent (until 1523 he used the title *riksföreståndare* or director of the kingdom) defended the rebellion against Christian II before foreign powers, and among other accusations held the Danish king guilty of putting to death "servants of God's Word, bishops and priests, contrary to the Holy Church and all Christian Ordinances." [5]

Whatever may have been the attitude of Gustavus originally to the Church as a spiritual institution, there is little doubt as to the position he soon came to hold as against her temporal claims. He may have been influenced by German soldiers, of whom the chronicler P. Swart says that "many came daily," [6] but this can hardly apply to the men from Lübeck. The Council's manifesto of June, 1523, tells us that among these were "the learned, the wealthy, and the most powerful of the Lübeck burghers," [7] and Lübeck's influential class during this time was actively anti-Protestant.[8] That the soldiers had influence on the common people, most of all the townsmen, seems evi-

[4] *Gustav I's Registratur,* Vol. I, p. 3.
[5] *Ibid.,* p. 23.
[6] *Krönika, utg. av Nels Eden,* p. 54.
[7] *GR* I, 77-78.
[8] Westman, *op. cit.,* p. 44, following H. Schreiber, *Die Reformation Lübecks.*

dent from the efforts of Olavus Magni, the last Catholic pastor in Stockholm, and of Bishop Brask, to counteract Protestant activities as early as 1522.[9] In that year the bishop had placed a ban on Lutheran books. In May, 1523, he complained of the Lutheran preaching in Strengnäs,[10] where Olavus Petri was teaching. And it was here, rather than through the German merchants and soldiers, that Gustavus found impetus for an action against the Church, which had undoubtedly been long in his mind.

At Strengnäs, in June, 1523, the representatives of the nation had elected Gustavus as their king. And as their king he was confronted at once with the necessity of coming to terms with the other power that wielded authority over them—the pope at Rome. Through the Council, a letter was addressed to Rome in which the pope was advised that only the singular grace of God had prevented the extinction of the ecclesiastical authority in Sweden. The deeds of the deposed archbishop, Gustav Trolle, had brought about a condition that needed speedy reformation, and the pope was requested to give Johannes Magnus the power to effect reforms.[11] Before he left Strengnäs, the king made the acquaintance of the archdeacon at the cathedral church, Laurentius Andreae, and of Olavus Petri, who had been teaching in the Cathedral School since his return from Wittenberg and the death of his bishop, in the Stockholm Massacre, 1520. The chronicler Swart tells us that especially that part of the new teaching impressed the king which declared that there was no Scriptural foundation for the tem-

[9] *Ibid.*, p. 148; *cf.* G. Carlson, *Kyrkohistorisk Årsskrift*, 1922, p. 78.
[10] *Handlingar rörande Skandinaviens historia*, XVII, 118; also, p. 171.
[11] *GR* I, 88-89.

poral power of the Church.[12] The calling of Olavus to Stockholm the following year, to serve as preacher there, testifies to the readiness of the king to hear and have proclaimed this new interpretation of the Church. And in making Laurentius Andreae his chancellor, he gave to the Protestant teaching a protection which was to have immeasurable consequences.

Before the month was over (June 29), the king took a step which indicated the direction of the future. He demanded, through the Council, a loan of treasures and money that churches and cloisters could spare;[13] in the open letter to the kingdom explaining this measure he expressed his intention to repay this loan "rather in excess, than reduced."[14] Johannes Magnus, the papal nuntius, assured Brask that toward heresy the king would use his royal authority, but wished that suppression should be "with moderation and without violence, that it may not cause further disturbance."[15] The nuntius had not yet left for Rome, and the king was still favorable toward peace with Rome. At the same time his need of funds carried him in the direction he was inclined to go—toward a subordination of the property of the Church to his political ends.

In September, while Johannes was still in Stockholm, three additional letters to the pope were given him from the king and his chancellor. The first, dated the tenth, renewed the request for the authorization of Johannes to reform the Church, so that *"S. Sedis Apostolice auctoritas in perpetua gloria conservetur."*[16] The second, two days later, breathed the

[12] *Krönika*, p. 84.
[13] *GR* I, 100-101.
[14] *Ibid.*, p. 126 (Sept. 8).
[15] *HSH* XVII, 157.
[16] *GR* I, 131.

same tone of devotion to the Apostolic Father.[17] The third, of September 14, requested confirmation of the bishops-elect—Johannes Magnus in Uppsala, Magnus Harraldson in Skara, Magnus Sommar in Strengnäs, Petrus Magni in Vesterås (instead of Peder Jakobsson, whose election the king had annulled, for political reasons).[18] The pope was told that the poverty of the land did not permit the payment of the annates, instead *"maius obsequium Sanctitati vestri"* was promised.[19]

But meanwhile the pope had acted most unfortunately for himself. He had rewarded Francesco de Potenza, on his return from a mission to Denmark, with the bishopric in Skara, and had taken the part of the deposed Gustav Trolle, whom he ordered reinstated under penalty of ban.[20] The reaction on the king soon made itself evident. In reply to the pope's support of Trolle, he declared that if the pope continued in this policy, he himself would order in regard to the Church and Christian religion in his country *"secundum quod Deo et omnibus Christianis principibus placere credamus."* [21] And in a similar letter of October 4 (the first was addressed to the College of Cardinals) the pope was clearly told that the king would oppose him in this matter *"sanguine nostro, si opus fuerit."* [22] Even more threatening was the attitude of the king when he learned of the Skara appointment. He declared that he would not tolerate the

[17] *Ibid.*, 132-4.
[18] Westman, *op. cit.*, pp. 174-5.
[19] *GR* I, 139-140. Westman, p. 177, estimates the sum due Rome, in modern terms, at c. 134,000 Kr. (= $36,000). The entire income of the State, ten years later, was c. 640,000 Kr.
[20] Westman, *op. cit.*, pp. 177-178.
[21] *GR* I, 145-6 (Oct. 1).
[22] *Ibid.*, p. 148.

appointment of a foreigner. And if on account of the refusal of the payment of annates confirmation of the bishops-elect should be refused, thus causing the Church to suffer continued harm, he would have them confirmed *"a solo et summo pontifico Christo."* [23]

The severance of the Church in Sweden from Rome can in reality be dated November, 1523. For the position of the king was immovable, and Rome remained uncompromising; official relationship with the Curia ended with the letter just quoted. Whether a different course of events might have reconciled the king to Rome is a useless question. After this date the king was more concerned with the relationship of the Church to the Crown than to the Vatican.

The following year, 1524, drew the king further in the path he had already entered. At its beginning, he ventured the suggestion to Johannes that the latter might confirm the bishops-elect. As grounds for his request, he cited the Councils of Nicaea and Basel, and Christ. *"Christus summus sacerdos noster—non a papa sed a christo christiani nominamur et sumus."* [24] According to the "new teaching," the fees to Rome were not Scriptural, while France furnished precedents for non-papal confirmation. But even more remarkable was the letter of Laurentius Andreae, in February, to the monks at Vadstena who had complained over the forced loan taken by the king. The chancellor explained to the monks that the Church was the communion of believers, the people, and the possessions of the Church were, in fact, the property of the people. Scriptures contained examples of the use of temple money for the welfare of the people. And as for any

[23] *GR* I, 173-174 (Nov. 2).
[24] *Ibid.,* pp. 178-181.

"new doctrine" that might be supposed to underlie the king's policy, he wished that the monks would study the writings of Luther and condemn them according to the Scriptures.[25]

Brask soon found occasion to combat this exegesis, for he wrote to the king [26] that the people, on this principle, refused to give to the Church its due, because they owned the Church's property. Further, he wished the king to prohibit the reading and sale of Luther's books in the kingdom, as well as to refuse protection to Luther's disciples.[27] The answer of the king was not encouraging. He could not accede to Brask's request, as long as no impartial tribunal had rendered judgment upon Luther's books. And since anti-Lutheran literature circulated in the kingdom, it was wise to hear both sides before coming to a decision against Luther. Nor could he refuse protection to any of his subjects except on valid accusations against them.[28]

At the meeting of the Royal Council at Vadstena, in October, 1524, the position of Gustavus became apparent. Laurentius Andreae had prepared an agenda for the meeting, wherein it was proposed that the matter of the confirmation of the bishops-elect should be discussed. "They have waited long enough for the confirmation of the Pope, which before God is unnecessary, and entails a waste of money." The complaint that a new doctrine was abroad was ungrounded, but since this charge might have ill effects on the common people, it was proposed that those who raised this cry out of malice should be silenced,

[25] *HSH* XVII, 205-212.
[26] *GR* I, 305 (April 14).
[27] *Linköping Biblioteks Handlingar*, I, 163 (May 22).
[28] *GR* I, 232.

and that the best remedy against false doctrine would be to order "the preaching of the Gospel and the Word of God alone."[29] Also, it was proposed to discuss the need of quartering horses in the monasteries, "as in Denmark."[30] But the king seemed not to have been willing to go as fast or as far as "Master Lars." In his propositions as finally presented to the Council, the problem of the confirmation of the bishops was presented, but the matter of the new teaching did not occur, and the cloister measure was motivated by the large income of the monasteries, though these were occupied by few brothers. And, finally, in the answer of the Council to the king's propositions,[31] and in the resolutions of the meeting,[32] neither the confirmation of the bishops-elect nor the new teaching was mentioned, while the quartering of horses in the monasteries was deemed unwise. The situation, then, at this time, seems to have been that the party whose leader was Laurentius Andreae was committed to a rapid change, the Council was conservative and probably had many opponents to any change, while the king occupied a mediating position, with sympathies for the former group, but biding his time because of the influence and power of the latter party.

Brask's correspondence of 1524 indicates the fear he was beginning to feel concerning the inroads of the new doctrine. We have noted his plea to the king to prohibit the sale of Lutheran literature. The same day (May 22) he had written to Ture Jönsson, a powerful member of the Council whose sympathies were with Brask, that he realized that he was not in

[29] *Ibid.*, p. 254.
[30] *Ibid.*, p. 255.
[31] *Ibid.*, pp. 261-265.
[32] *Stiernman, Alla Riksdagars och Mötens Besluth*, I, 31.

good standing with the king, due to the influence of some of Luther's party near to the king. The growth of the "Lutheran party" was such as to fill him with forebodings of coming heresy.[33] Before the king had answered his letter, Brask had addressed an open letter to his diocese against the "Martinianos." Söderköping, an important trade center,[34] was especially addressed. "On account of the confusion and false ideas," Brask wrote, "which the followers of Martin Luther have spread in this country for several years (*några åar*) in order to cause a great division in Christendom, and to blind half-educated and simple Christian men in regard to the sacraments and many other points in the holy Christian faith, therefore, we cause it to be declared publicly, both from pulpit and through this open letter—that no one may sell or buy in this diocese any of the aforementioned Luther's writings—or perniciously spread these among our Christian laity, imperiling their soul's salvation and well-being, until a Council shall have been held concerning this Martin Luther's false teachings about the holy Christian Church." We are informed that "it happens daily that many foreigners come into this diocese with these heretical books and teachings."[35] But the alert bishop could not hope much from his prohibition. Toward the end of the same month he wrote Johannes Magnus, since the previous summer archbishop-elect in Uppsala,[36] that the disturbance caused by the foreigners increased *"non obstante nostra prohibitione."*[37] The

[33] *Link. Bib. Hand.*, I, 164-165.
[34] It had received special trade privileges from Gustavus, June 10, 1523 (*GR* I, 83).
[35] *Link. Bib. Hand.*, I, 166-167 (June 2).
[36] Westman, *op. cit.*, p. 173.
[37] *HSH* XVIII, 236 (June 20).

Uppsala prelate could comfort his brother in Linköping, that in his parts only a *"fatuus germanus mercator"* had caused any trouble, and he had been examined and bonded."[38]

Brask could feel himself and his cause still further threatened by the course taken by two men whose religious convictions were similar to his own. Peder Jakobsson and Master Knut Michaelis (the one canon, the other dean in Vesterås) had been prominent supporters of the Sture regime, and after the liberation from Denmark had seen prospects of advancement, the former having been elected as bishop in Vesterås, the latter as archbishop in Uppsala. The king, however, had annulled the election in both cases. In the fall of 1524 the two prelates were in Dalarne,[39] and rumors of trouble reached the king, who suspected treason. The king managed to placate the querulous province, and the offended churchmen sought refuge in Norway. The grounds of their dissatisfaction were political and personal; they compared the Vasa regime with that of their former master, Sture, to the disadvantage of the present king. Nor could they likely forget their hopes which the king had disrupted. Thus, while the religious situation was not the cause of their sedition, their deeds further weakened the power of the Church to withstand the advance of those who favored the new doctrine and the subordination of the Church to the State.

What the king could not gain at Vadstena in October, 1524, he did win at Stockholm in the following January. Here, at the meeting of the Council, it was decided that horses might be quartered at the monas-

[38] *Ibid.*, p. 248 (Aug. 28).
[39] Westman, *op. cit.*, p. 209.

teries, and further, that the tithes of the Church should devolve to the king, except as much as was needed for purchase of the sacramental elements.[40] Brask did not attend the meeting, and before he could reply to its action he had received further bad news. Olavus Petri, who had been transferred to Stockholm in 1524 as its preacher, had not stopped with the preaching of Reformation doctrine, but in February, 1525, had translated one of those doctrines into action, by entering the matrimonial state. The letter of the Linköping bishop to the king in March was not of the most friendly tone. He had cause to complain— the cloister measure, the disposition of the tithes, and the scandalous marriage of Stockholm's preacher. In regard to the latter, he mildly rebuked Gustavus. "There is much murmuring in the kingdom, that such a thing should happen in Your Majesty's capital, just where His Majesty is daily present."[41] The king, however, did not mince his words to the bishop. To the latter's complaint, that the cloister proposition was a "foreign" measure, the king considered that "you ought to know well that foreign methods are not altogether useless. One can take of them as much as reason and necessity demand—you are aware that necessity breaks law, not only that of man, but occasionally also that of God."[42] Furthermore the churchman had complained that the monastery services would be affected. The king replied, "perchance so, if nought else were service unto God but to support a crowd of hypocrites, and a great part of them in a loose life. As if it were not also a godly service to consider

[40] *GR* II, 29-30.
[41] *Link. Bib. Hand.,* I, 175-179 (March 26).
[42] *GR* II, 84 (April 4).

the common welfare, so that the kingdom and its inhabitants be cared for." And Master Olof needed not be attacked. "In our humble judgment it seems strange that one should be banned for the sake of marriage, which God has not forbidden. Whereas among your ecclesiastics one is not banned according to papal law for whoredom, rape, and many other such crimes which God has forbidden. For this and other similar reasons it is rumored that the papal laws are being despised in foreign lands."[43] A week later, the king had still other "foreign rumors" to relate. On the Continent there was an unholy war, and the French king had been captured by the emperor. Therefore there was increased peril from the latter's relative, Christian II, and the cloister measure was justified.[44]

As a further step in his combat against the incoming tide of heresy, Brask published, Easter Eve, April 15, a strong manifesto against the new teaching. It was directed to his clergy, and written in Latin. He enumerated the false teachings of the Lutheran heresy, which he would call "Luciferan." He could no longer be silent, as were certain others, of whom one might justly expect action in this crisis. The heresy was not new; rather it was a resuscitation of heresies long condemned by the Church. He did not doubt the final outcome, but he urged his clergy to penitence, to prayer, to increased faithfulness.[45]

From other quarters, too, came attacks on the royal policy, which the king was quick to defend. The dean at Uppsala, Jöns Laurentii, had written that the people complained of the reduction of the episcopal

[43] *GR* II, 86.
[44] *Ibid.*, p. 90 (April 12).
[45] *HSH* XVIII, 303-309.

retinue in Vesterås. Gustavus replied that he could not understand the disaffection of the people, but he could guess that it offended "you and several others who do not know or do not want to know otherwise, than that the office of bishop was instituted as some great lordship, forgetting the Scriptural teaching that the bishops are the servants of the people—this office they can better fill when they have few, than when they have many, at their court. Such was the practice in early Christendom, when the true bishops lived, who did not fulfill the functions of their office with weapons in hand, but by suffering, and who would rather receive blows for the sake of God's Word, than they would give any. If you or others are disaffected, is is a sign that you do not, or do not want to, know what is the character of a true bishop." [46] The king was also convinced that some of the cloister brethren did not know their rightful duties, for soon after he wrote to the vicar general of the preaching brethren that some of his monks were stimulating the rebellion in Dalarne, wherefore he ordered all foreign monks in his cloisters out of the kingdom by the Day of John the Baptist. If they did not comply, other measures would be taken; "that you may give them fully to understand." [47] The king even felt it necessary to guard one of his liegemen, Gudmund Pedersson, against possible influence from one of these lord-bishops—Brask in Linköping. He feared that the bishop might use the Peasant Uprising in Germany as an argument against the Reformation. "If the bishop tries to give you or others any other interpretation, so that the evangelical doctrine, which he calls Luther's

[46] *GR* II, 94-95 (April 23).
[47] *Ibid.*, p. 127.

heresy, should not have any success, then he is only telling his own opinion and how he would want things."[48] And in a letter of September 8 he made a definite distinction between his party and that of the bishop.[49] Also to the bishop-elect in Skara the king indicated his attitude toward the old and the new, in a letter of November 11, the same year: "What you write that many ill customs have arisen, we also admit, and we would gladly cooperate with you and other good men to the end that they be corrected. Yet it can perchance be that some customs have long been considered good, that have the appearance of being such, yet in fact have no foundation in the law of God. And some are indeed so clearly contrary to God's law that in regard to them there is no doubt.— We appreciate your good advice and intention in suggesting that some pledge be given that such ill customs should be abolished and God thus be pleased. Yet in our feeble understanding we know of no promise that might be more acceptable to God, than that which we have already promised when we accepted the Christian faith, namely, that we abide in His Law, and forsake such customs as are contrary to His Commandments and have no foundation in His Law."[50]

To 1525 belongs another measure adopted by the king, whereby he suggested to the prelates a program more in harmony with their office than the one they were wont to pursue in competing for temporal authority. He urged upon the archbishop-elect a translation of the Bible into Swedish. The resulting letter of the primate to those concerned gives us the

[48] *Ibid.*, p. 138 (June 3).
[49] *Ibid.*, p. 214 (to Gudmund Pedersson).
[50] *Ibid.*, p. 244.

reasons that the king had advanced. *"Omnes nationes per totum orbem"* had translations not only of the New but, in many cases, also of the Old Testament. The times were so full of religious controversy that Christians needed the Scriptures in their own language if they were to judge wisely. Moreover, the illiteracy and inability of the clergy prevented the proper instruction in the Word. The king, too, had declared this to be the responsibility of the clergy, if they were to be considered as true shepherds. *"Quibusquidem rationibus tam manifestis certe non potuimus contradicere";* therefore he was writing to learned prelates in churches and monasteries, assigning to each a definite part for translation. The work was to be ready in September, when the translators would meet in Uppsala.[51] The letter was sent in June. The following January, at the Council meeting in Vadstena, we find the work still unfinished, though still contemplated. The twenty-third of the same month, Brask, who had not been in favor of the plan,[52] had so far progressed with his assignment (Mark, I and II Corinthians) as to be able to dispatch his cantor, Magister Eric, to Uppsala, with the work.[53] Beyond that the proposition seems not to have developed. A half year later the Protestant translation came from the press.[54]

The Council meeting at Vadstena in January ushered in a new year and an accelerating pace in the progress of the king's ecclesiastical policy. In December Gustavus had visited the wealthy monastery at Gripsholm; and, declaring that it had been given the brethren by his grand-uncle, Sten Sture the Elder,

[51] *HSH* XVIII, 297-300 (June 11).
[52] *Ibid.*, pp. 300-303, letter to Peder Galle (Aug. 9).
[53] *Ibid.*, pp. 315-316.
[54] See Chap. III.

under pressure, he, as his heir, reclaimed the property. It was a bold move, and was sure to raise criticism. But the Council ratified the act.[55] Further, in view of the obligations to Lübeck, which were a constant source of worry, it was decided that a tax be laid on all cities, and that two-thirds of the parish tithes, as in the previous year,[56] be granted the royal treasury.[57] The coming summer the king hoped to celebrate his coronation.[58]

The following months showed the results of these decisions, and, in general, were trying days for the king. The two fugitive churchmen were still busy in Dalarne, raising dissatisfaction, and had complicated the king's position by seeking the cooperation of the Norwegian archbishop, Olof of Trondhjem,[59] who had granted them refuge in his country. The loyal churchmen at home were not too enthusiastic in furnishing the king with the revenue due from their parish tithes. In March the king wrote one of his men, Måns Brynteson, that the clergy had taken their share first and left the king's part to the good-will of the people.[60] A month later the bishop-elect in Skara was told that little of the revenue had come in.[61] The confiscation of Gripsholm had produced widespread murmuring. In April the defendant sought to placate opinion in letters to Dalarne, Vestergötland, Östergötland, and Småland.[62] A similar letter to electus in Skara, Thure

[55] *GR* III, 24-25.
[56] In 1525 the tithe had been granted, except what was needed for the sacraments.
[57] Stiernman, *Riksdagars och Mötens Besluth* I, 39 (Jan. 11, 1526).
[58] *GR* III, 20.
[59] Westman, *op. cit.*, p. 211.
[60] *GR* III, 95-6 (March 20).
[61] *Ibid.*, p. 109 (April 12).
[62] *Ibid.*, pp. 101-102 (April 6).

Jonsson, etc., contained a reference to conditions in
Denmark, where churches and cloisters had been taxed
80,000 Gulden, and half of the tithes.[63] In Norway,
so the archbishop-elect had notified Gustavus, the
Swedish loyalty to the True Faith was a subject of
public prayer. The king had no objection to this
kindness, though he ventured the suggestion that "the
greater part of them (the Norwegians) have a meager
conception of what a true Christian Faith is." [64] He
believed that the fugitive prelates had spread rumors
in Norway. Nor was he certain of his own electi. To
the above-mentioned Måns Brynteson he divulged a
suspicion that these had in mind to let themselves be
confirmed without his knowledge, "holding, after they
are confirmed, that they owe us no allegiance, but
only the pope in Rome." [65] Meanwhile, in Uppsala,
an evangelical preacher, Master Michaels, had caused
protest at the Mart, and the king was blamed for this.
The king defended himself to the archdeacon in
Uppsala, and hoped that "God may forgive them that
cast so many reflections on the conduct of others, and
pay no attention to their own, which needs first attention." [66] In June came further pressure from Lübeck,
regarding the payment of the debt.[67]

The king, harassed by difficulties from many sides,
called another meeting of his Council, at Stockholm.[68]
Here, in August, he showed his persistent will to overcome opposition. Master Knut was condemned of

[63] *Ibid.*, pp. 108-109 (April 12).
[64] *Ibid.*, p. 112 (April 15).
[65] *Ibid.*, pp. 95-96 (March 20).
[66] *Ibid.*, pp. 100-101 (March 28).
[67] *Ibid.*, p. 173 (June 18).
[68] *Ibid.*, pp. 188-190. (The king gave as motive the information he had received from Frederick of Denmark, regarding the movements of Severin Norrby, the ally of the deposed Christian.)

treasonable alliance with Peder Jakobsson, and both Council and king requested the delivery of the traitors from Norway.[69] From the churchmen the sum of 25,000 marks was demanded; 15,000 was agreed upon as a compromise. Also the cities and peasantry were taxed, and a scheme of military service was enacted.[70] Another result of the meeting was a Tractate with evangelical Prussia regarding commercial relationship.[71]

Positive advances of the evangelical cause, coupled with further crippling of the Catholic forces, helped the more to transform the situation in favor of the new regime. In February, the first Protestant book had been published—*An Useful Teaching,* and in August the translation of the New Testament was ready. In their quiet but increasingly strong influence on public opinion, these books laid a foundation in public opinion on which the king continued to build a new State and a new Church-order. At the same time, the old regime continued to lose ground. Johannes Magnus had courted the ill grace of the king by his lordly manner on a visitation tour early in the year, and at the time of the meeting with the king at Uppsala.[72] Gustavus suspected an intrigue between his archbishop-elect and the archbishop of Norway— the two seemed to have met, on the former's tour.[73] In June, Brask had heard the rumor that Johannes was in confinement in Stockholm.[74] During the summer he was intended to serve on an embassy first to

[69] *Ibid.*, pp. 220-224.
[70] Westman, *op. cit.*, p. 281.
[71] *Ibid.*, pp. 290-292.
[72] *Ibid.*, pp. 262, 271.
[73] *GR* III, 193-194.
[74] *HSH* XVIII, 341.

Poland, then to Russia, but neither materialized, and finally he was allowed to depart to Prussia.[75] He never returned to Sweden, and the archbishopric at Uppsala had lost its last Catholic occupant.

Meanwhile Brask was continuing his losing battle against the Reformation. He had translated the bitter reply of Duke George to Luther, and with his press at Söderköping was planning to counteract the influence of Lutheran literature. But the king rudely shattered his hopes, for he ordered his printing plant closed,[76] and discountenanced his circulating such tracts. Instead he invited Brask to send learned men to Uppsala to a disputation, to decide what was false, and what true.[77]

In harmony with his plan of a disputation to settle the religious controversy within his kingdom, Gustavus sent before the end of the year a letter to "learned men throughout the kingdom," asking for written replies.[78] The questions that they were asked to answer were those that the Reformation had raised, and the king wanted the opinions of his churchmen on them.[79] Brask seems not to have been consulted in this matter. And as to a disputation, he claimed that all his clergy "have no such doubt concerning the holy Christian faith which has hitherto been accepted in Christendom, that they need to dispute further about it than the holy fathers of the Church have disputed in all these years."[80] To this letter the king replied that neither "we nor others up here have

[75] Westman, *op. cit.*, pp. 292ff.
[76] *GR* III, 311 (Nov. 6).
[77] *Ibid.*, pp. 313-314 (Nov. 9).
[78] *Ibid.*, pp. 331-333 (Dec. 4).
[79] For the origin and history of these questions, see Chap. IV.
[80] *GR* III, 425 (Dec. 27).

doubts as to the Faith, that it is certain and true as it was taught by Christ, but it might well be argued which party rightly has the Faith, and if it be true, as you seem to believe, that here a new Faith is preached." The king also was to be consulted before the bishop issued any letters such as Duke George's.[81] On the same day as Brask wrote in reply that he was but preaching the Truth as it had been determined by "apostles, saints, church fathers, and ecumenical Christendom's councils," and urged the king to follow in the holy footsteps of Sweden's sainted King Eric,[82] the king directed another reply to Brask, deploring the spread of false rumors as to a new Faith, accusing "some of the church's men" as the source, and promising that a meeting was to be called to decide the matter.[83]

At the beginning of the year 1527 matters seem to have come to a climax. In the tone of the king was a suggestion of decision. Within a few months the crisis actually did come, and the result of the events of the preceding years became apparent. The storm area was again the obstreperous province of Dalarne. Around a new uprising there the decisive factors converged, as by centripetal force. Out of the rapids of the early months of 1527 the stream of national policy emerged, pointing in a new direction and compelling in its further course.

The activities of Peder Jakobsson and Master Knut in Dalarne had come to a bitter end. The archbishop of Trondhjem had denied them further refuge, and the two had fallen into the hands of the king. In

[81] *GR* IV, 3-4 (Jan. 4, 1527).
[82] *Ibid.*, pp. 400-402 (Jan. 7).
[83] *Ibid.*, pp. 12-13 (Jan. 7).

February, 1527, they were tried, and executed.[84] But meanwhile a usurper had appeared, a Jöns Hansson, who had persuaded the malcontents in Dalarne that he was the son of Sten Sture the Younger, and the rightful heir to the throne. In fact he was an adventurer, and his role as much the result, as the cause, of disaffection among the peasants, who complained of heavy taxes and a new religion.[85] The latest phase of their independence was the more ominous, as a religious motive now was added to an economic one. Gustavus seems to have realized the possibilities of a new threatened revolt—such is the interpretation that the coming events suggest.

Reiterated and growing rumors of a new religion in the country irritated the king increasingly. Of this the letters of the first months of the year abundantly testify. To Nils Olson, his liegeman at Stäkeborg, he wrote: "We have perceived that there is talk and discontent among the people concerning the Gospel that is preached and taught here (Uppsala). Use your utmost diligence to find out, if possible, where it has its source, and inform us in writing." [86] A few days later he wrote to Brask: "We have learned that more and more the rumor is spread throughout the kingdom, against ourselves, our court, and Stockholm city, to the effect that we have accepted some new faith. We know well that some of the church's men have given rise to it." He was intent on a meeting for the settling of the controversy.[87] Another letter, of the same date, revealed more fully the king's mind. To the whole kingdom he declared the rumors of a new faith false,

[84] Westman, *op. cit.*, pp. 327-329.
[85] *GR* IV, 418.
[86] *Ibid.*, p. 5 (Jan. 4).
[87] *Ibid.*, pp. 12-13 (Jan. 7).

"though here, as elsewhere, one is of the opinion that many ill customs ought to be discarded, such as have arisen in Christendom to the oppression of the common people by the prelates of the Church, contrary to the law of God." The greed of these prelates, not a new faith, was the cause of the present rumors. In vain the king had waited for a general Church Council; therefore he would arrange for one in the kingdom. "The crux of the controversy is in regard to the dominion which the high officers of the Church—the pope, the bishops and their following—to this day have exercised over the laity, contrary to seemliness and God's law." They have weakened kings so that these could not defend their realm. The pope had gone to war with the emperor on funds gathered through the sale of indulgences, which were intended for war against the Turks. And now the emperor had seized and imprisoned the pope. "When good, reasonable men begin to talk of these things and would see such unseemly conditions eliminated then the churchmen spread false rumors of a new faith."[88] Insofar as these rumors had ground in "fantastic" preaching by a German, Melchior Hoffman, in Stockholm, during the winter months of 1526-1527,[89] the king was willing to remove the cause, for he deprived the too-enthusiastic Lutheran of the privilege of preaching in public.[90] The king understood the dangers to his left, as well as to his right. About the same time he proceeded more effectually to silence Brask, whom he suspected of having had literature published in Copenhagen,

[88] *Ibid.*, pp. 18-20 (Jan. 7).
[89] H. Lundstrom, *Undersökningar och Aktstycken*, pp. 13-40.
[90] *GR* IV, 25 (Jan. 13).

when the Söderköping press was suppressed. Since the readers of such propaganda could no more judge correctly than "the blind can distinguish colors," the bishop was forbidden to circulate anything among "simple folk" unless censored by the king, until the proposed provincial council had been held.[91] Still another step was taken when the king ordered Brask to recall a ban he had placed on a party which had broken a cloister vow.[92] To the province of Vestergötland, the king repeated his discountenancing of false rumors which he had addressed to the kingdom. "We give you to understand that in these parts (Uppsala) nothing else is preached than the clear and pure Gospel and Word of God which Christ Himself has commanded and the Apostles have preached." Again the abuses of the churchmen were mentioned, by which the common people suffer. The revenue from indulgences impoverished the kingdom, but aided the prelates to "wealth, great power, and proud bearing toward nobles and kings."[93] From a letter to Ture Ericsson, we learn that also the nobles' unjust treatment of the Church was charged against the king in public opinion.[94] His attitude toward votive chapels he revealed in forbidding the building of one, and by the curt commentary "such foolishness shall cease."[95]

If the ecclesiastical situation irritated the king, political complications now entered to spur him to action. From Prussia, with whom a treaty had been

[91] *Ibid.*, pp. 42-43 (Feb. 2).
[92] *Ibid.*, p. 54 (Feb. 15).
[93] *Ibid.*, pp. 74-76.
[94] *Ibid.*, p. 80.
[95] *Ibid.*, p. 78 (Feb. 26).

negotiated a half year earlier, came encouragement to the king to continue his Protestant policy.[96] But internal conditions may have been sufficient to dictate the development of that policy. For the Lübeck debt was pressing, and its payment was an internal matter. Most difficult was the question of consolidating and appeasing public sentiment. Since 1523 progress had been slow, but steady. But now the discontent in Dalarne was threatening to overthrow all that had been accomplished. When signs appeared, indicating that the ill-will might spread, Gustavus became uneasy. At the close of March he wrote to Måns Brynteson, that "Bishop Hans in Linköping, Ture (Jönsson) and Electus in Skara have been together and addressed the people, advising simple and innocent folk under no conditions to accept the evangelical doctrine." The king wished immediate confirmation of this gathering by secret message.[97] To these powerful council members in the southern part of his kingdom, the king sent a letter a few days later describing the difficult circumstances of the kingdom, and asking them for advice. He felt that he alone was bearing the responsibility of rule.[98] In informing Brask of his proposed trip to Finland to meet a Russian embassy, regarding a Russian treaty, he asked that his absence from the kingdom be kept a secret.[99] He felt compelled to meet the Russians in Finland, he wrote to Electus in Skara, because of the possible effect of the trouble in Dalarne on the foreigners if they came to Sweden.[100]

But between April 14 and April 23 the program of

[96] Westman, *op. cit.*, p. 390.
[97] *GR* IV, 111-112 (March 29).
[98] *Ibid.*, pp. 113-116 (April 2).
[99] *Ibid.*, pp. 127-128 (April 7).
[100] *Ibid.*, pp. 138-140 (April 14).

the king had been radically changed. By the latter date, the proposed trip to Finland was canceled, and the Russians were requested to come to Sweden. What is more, the king had issued a call for a diet at Söderköping. Instead of sailing for Finland at Easter time (April 21), he wanted a Parliament at Pentecost; "because of disloyalty and trouble appearing in the kingdom time upon time, we are doubtful if we care any longer to bother about the government." [101] We may place the time of this decision even a day earlier, for in a letter of April 22 to Olavus Magni, who was on a mission in Lübeck, the king spoke of soon meeting with representatives of the kingdom.[102]

Between the fourteenth and the twentieth Gustavus had come to Stockholm, and met with some of his councilors.[103] They had advised the change of plans. But their advice may have been only confirmation. The king was undoubtedly the planner. What could the cause have been? It cannot be fully ascertained. Probably the situation in general is sufficient explanation. Still, a passage in the letter of April 14 to the Electus in Skara and Ture Jönsson is worthy of remark. The king has "in these days" had his scouts in Dalarne. Among other things they reported that the usurper had claimed to have the support of "both bishop-elect and Ture and some others in the kingdom." The king did not suspect them, yet he wanted them to write a disclaimer to the people in Dalarne.[104]

A careful reading of the available documents does leave the impression that the king suspected some rela-

[101] *Ibid.*, pp. 147-148 (April 23).
[102] *Ibid.*, pp. 143-145 (April 22).
[103] The call for Parliament mentions the names of four (*GR* IV, 147, April 23).
[104] *Ibid.*, pp. 139-140

tionship between the threatened churchmen of the old regime in the south, and the uprising in the north, of his kingdom. In fact, the king expressly said so, in a letter of a month later, to Jöns Nilsson, in Brask's diocese. "The root" of the trouble in Dalarne is to be found in "some of the ecclesiastical persons" who inspired the people "that here a new faith is being accepted to the suppression of Christianity." They knew that this was not true, but because "we occasionally speak of their deceit, through which they have risen to power over nobles and kings and common people," they wanted to set the people against the king *"and drive us from the government."* The head of this party in rebellion was in the diocese of Linköping, and the aim was to recall Archbishop Trolle and then King Christian.[105] The charge that the usurper was a tool for Christian and other foreigners was repeated a few days later.[106]

The conclusion seems warranted that the king felt himself in peril and that the suggestion of quitting the kingdom concealed the fear that conditions made his throne uncertain. Not that he really intended to abdicate, but he deemed the boldest move to be the safest. The correspondence from these critical days shows no slacking up of interest for the future ordering of the State, both internally and in foreign matters. But either the kingdom must follow his rule, or—we do not know what the alternative might have been. His course for the present was clear. The uprising must be quelled. The Church was fomenting the uprising. Therefore the Church must be dealt with. In the preparations for—and, not least in the sequence

[105] *Ibid.*, pp. 175-176 (May 16).
[106] *Ibid.*, p. 179 (May 19).

Ecclesiastical Transformation in Sweden

—of the Diet it becomes clear that not the foreign debt, nor the peasant trouble, was the "root" to be attacked, but, in the king's own words, "the ecclesiastics." The king would not be crowned until he could be sole king in his realm.

The call to the Diet requested the presence of all the nobility, six peasants from each legal unit (*lagxago*), the mayor and one councilman from each city, and two or three of the most learned of each chapter, "in order that an agreement might be reached in the religious dispute which has arisen here as well as in the rest of Christendom—and if it be not peaceably settled in time, it can be understood what ill effects may follow.[107] The place of meeting was changed from Söderköping to Vesterås, which lay nearer the seat of the uprising, and the time, from Pentecost to Trinity.[108] To his council members the king wrote asking that the matter of the trouble in Dalarne be not made common talk, and he wanted them to come to the meeting adequately armed.[109] The desire of Ture Jönsson to be excused from the meeting could not have quieted the king's suspicions, nor did he permit his absence.[110]

Meanwhile the king strove to bring the men in Dalarne to their reason. He wrote them concerning the coming Diet, and claimed that he was willing to leave the government, rather than be the cause of internal dissensions.[111] He desired that men from Vesterås should visit their neighbors, and use their influence to bring them to loyalty again. They were informed that men from Lübeck would also be at the

[107] *Ibid.*, pp. 147-148 (April 23).
[108] *Ibid.*, pp. 162-163.
[109] *Ibid.*, pp. 166-167 (May 14).
[110] *Ibid.*, pp. 183-184 (May 20).
[111] *Ibid.*, pp. 159-161 (May 5).

meeting, and their demands would be the more difficult in view of lack of inner concord.[112] Through representatives, the malcontents had summarized their grievances in twelve points, which the king answered in conciliating terms, promising further reply at Vesterås. Some of the complaints Gustavus promised to investigate or remove their cause—matters of coinage, of injustice suffered from the king's subordinates. To some charges the king declared himself not guilty—high prices, new fashions. Some criticized measures were defended as necessary—taxes, quartering of horses in monasteries. The twelfth point referred to "Lutheranism." The king replied that he had only commanded the preaching "of the Word of God and the Holy Gospel." He did not want that the priests in their greed should, as formerly, have power over people and rulers. The accusers were a crowd of monks and priests who looked to their own, not the kingdom's, welfare. "It would be well if the common people could realize that the policy of the king was to their benefit."[113] Again, when at Uppsala, the king had men sent to Dalarne to seek to bring the dissatisfied to a better reason,[114] while he wrote in friendly tone, promising all possible alleviation.[115]

While, in the foregoing, we note a tone of compromise in regard to the peasants, there was no change of attitude toward the churchmen. In the reply to the complaints, as well as in the instructions of the Uppsala conciliators, the prelates were charged with treasonable intentions. The king was willing to conciliate the people, but not the ecclesiastics. The people

[112] *Ibid.*, pp. 163-165 (May 14).
[113] *Ibid.*, pp. 169-174 (May 14).
[114] *Ibid.*, pp. 177-180 (May 19).
[115] *Ibid.*, pp. 181-182 (May 20).

Ecclesiastical Transformation in Sweden 33

did not understand the nature of their own complaints
—"monks and priests have suborned them." [116]

The Propositions presented by the king, through
Laurentius Andreae, when the estates had gathered in
Vesterås in June, were a logical outcome of the king's
policy as it had been developing for several years and
was now openly declared. First, the message [117]
described conditions as they existed when Gustavus
consented to assume the rule of the kingdom. Steady
progress toward unification and security had been
achieved, though foreign aid had had to be obtained.
Then the repeated uprisings in Dalarne were touched
upon—"Dalarne's men seem to think that they may
set up and cast down whomever they please in the
kingdom's government." Then followed a rebuttal of
the charges and complaints emanating from this province, much similar to the reply already given the complainants a month before. Toward the Church the
attitude was unchanged. Rumors of a new religion
came from men high in the Church, "who wish to
remain secure in their great power, dominion, and
arrogance." But many "now here, as in other countries, have begun to realize how in many things the
Crown, the nobility, and the common people have
been deceived and oppressed by the ecclesiastics—who,
with self-invested religious offices, which God never
commanded, or through mortgage, sale, force, etc.,
have brought it to pass that the Crown and the nobility together hardly have one-third of what priests and
monks, churches and cloisters, have." [118] When it was
said that the king "does not want any priests in the

[116] *Ibid.*, p. 174.
[117] *Ibid.*, pp. 200-215.
[118] *Ibid.*, p. 209.

kingdom," it was falsely reported, for the king was desirous of supporting "rightful pastors and teachers, insofar as they fulfill their duties," but he wanted the advice of the estates as to correct treatment of "the others, who do not abide in the duties of their office, or are of no service to the community"; he found no brief for them in Scriptures.[119] Once more we hear of the king's readiness to abdicate, and the Propositions close with a summary of the most fundamental defects in the government—the income to the Crown was not sufficient for defense, for the expenses of the court, for the rebuilding of castles, for a royal wedding. The holdings of the Church left nothing with which to endow the nobility. The mines were closed. Complaints were heard as to marketing. The kingdom suffered from uprising.

The chronicler, Peder Swart, has related the story of the sessions of Vesterås in a manner not entirely in agreement with other sources. Modern scholars have had to correct his version of the order of events.[120] But some of the events themselves are not improbable as he relates them.[121] Swart described the tenseness of the situation, following Andreae's presentation. Only Brask and Ture Jönsson ventured to oppose the inevitable. Then the king burst into an angry attack. "I may labor for your welfare to the utmost of my ability, either in spiritual or temporal matters, and still have nothing else to expect as reward than that you would gladly see the ax on my neck, only you yourselves do not want to wield it." He demanded recompense for the expenses which he had

[119] *Ibid.*, pp. 210-211.

[120] H. Hjärne, *Reformationsriksdagen i Vesterås;* S. Tunberg, *Vesterås Riksdag 1527;* Westman, *op. cit.*

[121] *Krönika*, pp. 110-121.

incurred for the kingdom, abdicated his position, and retired to the castle.

The progress of events during the following days is not clear; the results, however, are not in doubt. Each of the estates drew up their reply to the Propositions; these are preserved in the records. The answers of the Peasants agree in the main with those of the Townsmen and Miners. Rebellion was not to be tolerated. Since monks had much to do with stimulating rebellion, they should be confined to their monasteries, except for stated leaves. The prelates were to warn the clergy against sedition. Cloister-quartering was necessary. Certain Stockholm churches might be torn down, as they weakened the city's defenses. The religious controversy "goes over their heads," but they desired that a disputation should be held before they closed the meeting, and that it should determine what ought to be preached. The Council was empowered to decide as to the restoration of Church property to the Crown. The king might have the episcopal castles until the others were rebuilt. "No bishops shall send to Rome for confirmation after this day."[122] It is probable that the lower estates were the easiest to be won to a policy of meeting the king's demands, and that the real battle was fought in the Council and nobility, where Brask and Ture Jönsson opposed the king.[123] Finally, even here, probably under pressure from the other estates, resistance was broken, and the demands of the king were granted. The rebellion in Dalarne would at once be put down. The king might retain Gripsholm. Quartering was to be permitted in the monasteries, "though in such manner that the clois-

[122] *GR* IV, 220-222.
[123] S. Tunberg, *op. cit.*, I, 23-24.

ter members receive their support, and the cloisters be not destroyed." All property given to the Church since 1454 was to be returned to the rightful heirs; if the property had been bought by the Church, recompense was to be given. Concerning the bishops, "it shall be so ordered that they shall come to an agreement with the king, how strong His Majesty wants their retinue to be; what remains of their income they shall give to the king in money, in amount agreeable to the king." For the present at least, the king might have their castles. A similar course was permitted as against the wealth of the cathedral churches. The complaint about a new faith should cease. "The pure Word of God shall be preached, everywhere, according to God's commandment, and not uncertain wonders, human inventions and fables, as has been much the practice hitherto. Good, old Christian customs shall abide." [124]

Gustavus was satisfied, and again assumed the power. The estates as a whole agreed to a common formula, the Vesterås Recess, adopted June 24. In this the estates promised (1) to put an end to the uprising in Dalarne; (2) to grant the king the income of the churches, bishops and canons (above what was necessary for their support), the episcopal castles, and the management of the monasteries; (3) to return to the heirs all goods given to the Church after 1454; (4) to quiet complaints against a new faith, on the condition that the Word of God be preached in

[124] *GR* IV, 216-220. Westman, *op. cit.*, p. 436, cites similar wording regarding preaching of the "pure Word of God" in the Prussian Constitution, 1525, and the Danish Recess, 1536. To these might be added the resolution of the Town Council of Basle, 1528-29, forbidding the clergy to preach aught but the pure Word of God. See P. Smith, *Erasmus,* pp. 389-390.

purity.[125] The latter measure was passed after a disputation had been held, as requested. Evidently the "new" preachers had proved that their preaching was not "new."[126]

Of the same date is Vesterås *Ordinantia*, which according to a letter of the king[127] was the decision of "ourself and our beloved Council." In this the Recess was practically applied, and the new policy of the Crown toward the Church was defined. The bishop was to provide suitable preachers in his churches; if he failed to do this, the king could intervene. The bishop was to give an account of his income to the Crown, whereupon he would receive his allotted share (many fines and revenues formerly paid to the bishop were transferred to the Crown). The clergy were to be ruled by the civil law. With proper consent, the monks might make begging tours during a period of ten weeks—five in winter, five in summer. Improper pressure by clergy over laity through ban and refusal of sacrament, or in making of wills, was prohibited. The Gospel was to be taught in all schools. The ordination of a pastor was to depend upon his ability to preach God's Word.[128] A Latin rescript[129] of the *Ordinantia* contains several additional items, among which is a prohibition of fees to Rome or any foreign center, and a stipulation that the election of bishops should be confirmed by the king.

The decisions of Vesterås were a complete triumph

---

[125] *Ibid.*, pp. 226-231; *cf.* H. Holmquist, *Svenska Reformationens Begynnelse, 1523-1531*, pp. 100-102.

[126] *Ibid.*, pp. 230-231.

[127] *Ibid.*, p. 309 (Aug. 26).

[128] *Ibid.*, pp. 241-243.

[129] According to E. Hildebrand in *Kyrkohistorisk Årsskrift*, 1914, pp. 31-36, a later version; *cf.* Westman, *op. cit.*, p. 421.

for Gustavus, and an ominous defeat for Brask and his party. Before he left, the friends of the bishop had to give the king a bond for the loyal conduct of Brask, pledging that the latter would not act traitorously through "messenger, letter, word, or deed, secretly or openly." [130] Later in the summer Gustavus visited Linköping, and translated the Vesterås decision into practice, depriving the bishop of much of his income and his castle. Brask submitted, and even received a written guarantee of the king's friendliness.[131] But while on a visitation tour to Gottland, which the king had sanctioned, the bishop made use of the opportunity, and proceeded to the Continent, forever leaving Sweden. The news of the flight soon reached Gustavus, and only confirmed his previous suspicions. He wrote to Ture Jönsson, "he (Brask) is not altogether as innocent in regard to the trouble that was incited in Dalarne as he made believe and asserted at Vesterås. He probably feared that the truth would be revealed and proved against him, which the usurper's chancellor has confessed concerning him, that he should have given support in money sent through one of his men, Peder Helsing." [132] Lacking evidence of Brask's actual participation in any seditious movement against the king, we cannot take the king's words without reservations. But, on the other hand, there seems to be sufficient evidence that the king *thought* that Brask was involved. Not what may have been the fact, but what the king thought to be the fact, prompted his decision to summon the estates to Vesterås for a final test of power. The king was

[130] *GR* IV, 259.
[131] *Ibid.*, pp. 287-288 (Aug. 2).
[132] *Ibid.*, pp. 327-328 (Sept. 26).

convinced, during those important days of April, that Brask and his followers were involved in the Dalarne uprising, and that unless their power was broken at once the result might be the loss of his throne to the exiled Christian II. His decision and power of will won him the day, and in four months his place was immensely strengthened, while Brask was a fugitive. With his departure the Catholic party had lost its leader, if not its hope.

A hostile and influential bishop with freedom of action in Danzig was not to the advantage of Gustavus' foreign policy in general, and Danish relationships especially. Therefore he sought to induce him to return and defend his conduct.[133] But Brask kept his distance,[134] only to receive from the king a most severe denunciation for his desertion. The letter of Gustavus is a curious document. It charged Brask with treason, oppression, and unfaithfulness in office. Christ's charge to a shepherd was that the flock should be fed—Brask had "sheared the wool and cut the necks of his sheep." At great length the king defended his church policy. Luther's teachings had not been condemned by any council "because they are nothing else but the true and pure Word of God." It was false that the king "does not believe Christ to be true God, but merely man"—the king believed what "Christ and His Holy Apostles and Disciples have taught us, and the twelve Articles of the Holy Christian Faith contain." As for his oath to defend the Church, the king had no qualms of conscience, for the Church was not, as Brask held, "walls and buildings and church rents,"

[133] *GR* V. pp. 29-32 (Jan. 25, 1528).
[134] In Dantzig, Brask was protected by Poland's king. He died in the monastery of Landa, in the diocese of Gnesen, 1538 (E. Hildebrand, *Sveriges Historia* IV, p. 143).

but "all right-minded Christian people." A Christian church, unlike the Hebrew temple, was "the house in which we come together, and have to do with the Word of God, the sacraments, etc." And Christian service was not confined to one place—"all of man's life should be a true service unto God."[135] Although the letter set forth the king's idea of the function of the Church, i.e. an institution for the instruction of the people, it can hardly be considered as solely his own composition. It abounded with citations from David, St. Paul, the Letter to the Hebrews, from Ambrose, Jerome, Gratian, St. Bernard, and referred to *De Investitura*, Leo VIII, and Charlemagne. It marked the end of a correspondence with Brask that had extended over many years and that in itself had been a battle between the old and the new. Brask was in many respects a true patriot, and had rendered Gustavus valuable State service. But when he placed the temporal estate of the Church above the national welfare, he crossed swords with a man who had a new conception of both State and Church on his side. Brask thought that the Crown should depend for its power upon the Church and the nobility.[136] Gustavus Vasa was convinced that Church and nobility should derive their privileges from the Crown. The Parliament at Vesterås was the beginning of the modern age in Sweden.

The king was not slow to pursue the consequences of the decisions of Vesterås. The letter of the Council to the Kingdom, announcing the actions of the Diet, informed the people that "we want of course that there shall be bishops, yet not so mighty that kings

[135] *GR* V, 165-179 (undated).
[136] Westman, *op. cit.*, p. 218.

Ecclesiastical Transformation in Sweden 41

or the kingdom shall be in any peril from them—they can the better care for the Word of God." [137] One by one, agreements were reached with the bishops, the cathedrals, and the monasteries, whereby the Crown secured the income of these above what was necessary for their support. In Linköping, a procurator was appointed to supervise the temporal affairs of the diocese.[138] In the diocesan centers the king advised as to the number of clergy it was necessary to have.[139] For the monasteries administrators were appointed. In general, there was a sharpening of the king's tone. He reminded the bishops that the Vesterås meeting had given him the power to "tell the bishops how mighty we want to have them." [140] The clergy in Uppsala [141] and Norrland [142] were strictly commanded to put an end to false rumors and seditious utterances. Before his departure, Brask had been enjoined from receiving candidates into the convent at Vadstena without the king's consent,[143] and Ture Jönsson was informed that there was a sufficiency of monasteries.[144] Because their monastery served a needful purpose as an inn, the Brothers of St. Anthony were given an extended time for purposes of soliciting alms,[145] but the Abbess of Sko Convent received a biting denunciation because she had "bribed" the king's niece to take on the "pharisaical habitum" of the convent before her death. "There is no more holiness in your garment

[137] *GR* IV, 252-256.
[138] *Ibid.*, p. 290 (Aug. 2).
[139] *Ibid.*, pp. 317-318 (Linköping), pp. 319-320 (Vexio).
[140] *Ibid.*, p. 268 (July 4).
[141] *Ibid.*, pp. 269-270 (July 4).
[142] *Ibid.*, pp. 271-272 (July 4).
[143] *Ibid.*, p. 289 (Aug. 2).
[144] *Ibid.*, pp. 306-308 (Aug. 26).
[145] *Ibid.*, pp. 320-321 (Sept. 7).

than in any other," the Abbess was told, "though she and others had made use of such deceit as a baited hook, in order to catch goods and money." [146]

One result of the new policy had probably not been anticipated by the king. When the people learned that the power of the bishops was broken, and that they were not to receive the income they had previously enjoyed, they became slack in paying the bishops even the share allotted to them. Consequently, both now and later, the king found it necessary to admonish the kingdom as a whole, or special localities, that this was not the meaning of the *Ordinantia*. He wanted the clergy "supported with proper means," so that they could "render the community the service that they ought, with preaching and other functions that belong to their office." [147] Also the stipulation in the Recess that permitted heirs to claim property from the Church was abused. "We have truly investigated and learned how everybody, peasants as well as nobles, in all the dioceses of the kingdom, snatch to themselves property, estates and lands, grazing land, fisheries and other possessions from cathedral churches, clergy and parish-lands, which they have little, or rather, no right or reason to claim." Hereafter the king's consent was to be obtained for such claims. [148]

Over four years had elapsed since Gustavus Vasa had been elected to the throne. During this period he had often been reminded of the necessity of a coronation. But Gustavus had wanted to make sure that the crown would stay on his head, before he had

[146] *Ibid.*, pp. 359-360 (Oct. 30).
[147] *Ibid.*, pp. 309-310 (Aug. 26), *GR* V, 23-25 (Jan. 21, 1528), 154-155 (April 10), 156-157 (April 10), 161-162 (Nov. 25).
[148] *GR* V, 87-88 (May 26, 1528).

it placed there. Now, after his policy had triumphed at Vesterås, and his position of king was real, not merely fictitious, he planned to be crowned. The date was set for Epiphany, 1528,[149] and the unconfirmed bishops-elect were bidden to arrange for their consecration before that time. The Electus of Skara was informed that popular sentiment demanded "anointed bishops, though such anointment in truth is of little need." In case the candidate demurred, he would not be compelled—the king would find someone else.[150] A letter of Laurentius Andreae to the bishop of Strengnäs indicated what the reason for hesitancy might be. The chancellor wrote that the king wanted evangelical, not papal bishops, and that no more would be demanded of them than God required. An appended formula for the consecration revealed that the new bishops owed allegiance to the king, and not to Rome.[151]

When the Council met in Uppsala, previous to the coronation, Gustavus once again canvassed the situation before assuming the crown. He wanted some definite statement as to what was to be done regarding the troublesome Dalarne, and he wanted to know what complaints could be made against him. The Council answered that the Vesterås Recess would be fulfilled, and, if necessary, they themselves would proceed to quell the disaffected province. As to complaints, they suggested to the king that monks and nuns be not mistreated, and that they be not permitted to run away from monasteries, or into marriage. Also that the masses be allowed in accordance with "good old customs." Finally, that the king would punish "the

[149] *GR* IV, 334-335 (Oct. 7).
[150] *Ibid.*, pp. 368-369 (Nov. 7).
[151] H. Lundstrom, *Undersökningar och Aktstycken*, pp. 7-12.

eating of meat on Fridays or Saturdays, concerning which, most of all, the complaints arise in the kingdom."[152]

Gustavus did not think these complaints unsurmountable obstacles, and on January 12, 1528, the crown of the kingdom was placed on his head. The preacher of the day was Olavus Petri, and in clear, almost stern, language he read the law of obedience to the people, and the law of responsibility to the king. Five years earlier, at Strengnäs, when Gustavus Vasa had been elected king, he had heard Olavus Petri proclaim the Lutheran doctrines. Since then the king had put some of those doctrines into practice, and on this day an evangelical preacher preached the coronation sermon for an evangelical king in the archiepiscopal church of Sweden.

Gustavus I was wise enough to perceive that his coronation did not solve the troubles of the State. It did not of itself pacify Dalarne, nor did it pay the debt to Lübeck.[153] Nor was all opposition to the evangelical party yet crushed. The work of uniting and consolidating the kingdom must go on.

The usurper in Dalarne had extended his operations across the Norwegian frontier, and succeeded in securing the support of a powerful churchman, Vincent Lunge, who sent him troops and attempted to hinder the church revenue in the border province of Jemtland from going to Uppsala.[154] A series of ominous letters from the king and Council,[155] and a meeting of the

[152] *GR* V, 5-8 (Jan. 11).
[153] In 1529 the amount of the debt was fixed at 114,515 Lübeck marks, of which 68,696 were still unpaid (Hildebrand and Stavenow, IV, *Sveriges Historia*, 182).
[154] *GR* V, 220-221 (Jan. 5), 231 (Jan. 31).
[155] *Ibid.*, pp. 17-18 (Jan. 17), 232-234, 39-41 (Feb. 14).

Ecclesiastical Transformation in Sweden

king and the province at Tuna, February 18, at which the leaders were tried and executed, finally brought the malcontents to their senses, and by the end of February the king could announce to the kingdom that peace had been restored in Dalarne.[156] Through Frederick, king of Denmark, Vincent was influenced to give no further aid to the enemies of Gustavus,[157] and was forgiven.[158] During the summer the usurper had fled to Rostock.[159] The archbishop in Trondhjem, Olof, was also under suspicion, and received the reproaches of the Swedish king.[160] But in general the relationship between the kings of Sweden and Denmark at this time was friendly, for both feared the return of the dreaded Christian, and were pledged mutually to aid each other in case of any attempt by Christian to return to power.[161] As the uprising in Dalarne was connected in the mind of Gustavus with the intrigues of Christian, he looked to Denmark to refuse any assistance to his enemies in Norway. Though no great help was given, Gustavus had succeeded in bringing to an end the stubborn resistance in Dalarne.

In February, 1529, the representatives of the Church gathered at Örebro for the first meeting under the new order effected at Vesterås. Some forty churchmen are mentioned in the preserved records. The Catholic bishops of Skara, Strengnäs, and Vesterås were present, but the "president" was Laurentius Andreae, the king's "authorized representative." The character of

[156] *Ibid.*, pp. 52-53 (Feb. 28).
[157] *Ibid.*, p. 235 (Feb. 2).
[158] *Ibid.*, pp. 147-148 (Aug. 26).
[159] *Ibid.*, p. 124 (Aug. 7).
[160] *Ibid.*, pp. 158-160 (Nov. 1).
[161] *Ibid.*, pp. 135-140 (Aug.).

the dominant party at the meeting is apparent from the nature of the resolutions.[162] The duty of the churchmen, these confessed, was "to proclaim, propagate, and advance the Word of God." In the cathedrals and schools at least one *lectio* should be given each day in the Scriptures, "with good and rightminded interpretation." The clergy were admonished to attend these readings. The bishops should provide the deacons with "the New Testament books in Latin," and see to it that learned men were appointed to the city churches. In monasteries, too, there should be instruction in Scriptures. Preachers were prohibited from "haranguing each other from the pulpit." Sermons were to expound the Lord's Prayer, Credo, Ave Maria, "for the good of young and simple folk, and the Ten Commandments one or two times a month. Prayer shall precede and follow the sermon." The deacons were to be strictly supervised, so also the monks. In cases where the canon law, but not God's law, prohibits marriage, the authorities might give dispensation, yet in such a way "that one avoids criticism as much as possible." Penitents should be penalized as might best suit the case and serve the community. There were too many holidays. Those of Our Lord, the Virgin Mary, the Apostles, and Fathers were declared sufficient—others should be omitted, as conditions might permit. One pastor (*kyrkioherre*=head pastor) shall be in charge of all the churches of a city. Then followed a series of

[162] The attitude of the Catholic party before and after the meeting may be inferred from an entry in Vadstena Monastery's Journal, to the effect that on January 26 three brothers departed for Örebro, at the king's request *"versus concilium Örebroense contra Lutheranos."* They returned *"perturbati."* (Cited by Anjou, *Svenska Kyrkoreformationens Historia*, II, 74.)

Ecclesiastical Transformation in Sweden 47

explanations of current customs which were Catholic in themselves, but, if they were to remain for the present, should be understood in an evangelical light. Such were the consecration of water, and the use of images, palms, candles, oil—all were signs to remind of things holy, but in themselves had no peculiar sanctity. Church bells and church buildings were practically useful, not intrinsically holy. "The people ought to be taught to give their candles to the poor, rather than place them before images." Fasting and holidays were of assistance to Christian living, not anything meritorious before God. Pilgrimages were unnecessary —"God is just as much present in one place as in another."[163] From another source, a Vatican document, probably the notes of a Catholic member of the meeting,[164] we learn that Laurentius Andreae would have gone still farther, particularly as to communion in both kinds, but the condition of the people made a slower progress necessary. As it was, the Council was sufficiently revolutionary for the Roman party, who could not but feel themselves dictated to by the king through his chancellor, and who were compelled to write their names under the above resolutions. "For the constitutional development of the Swedish Church, this transformation of the medieval Church Council organization into an agency of the evangelical reformation was to be of supreme importance."[165] The king had given the Church a certain freedom in matters pertaining to itself, but it was nevertheless a freedom derived from the State, and not from itself. It was no longer a Church above the State, nor even

[163] Hildebrand-Alin, *Svenska Riksdagsakter*, I, 118-122 (dated Feb. 7, 1529).
[164] *Meddelande och Aktstycken, KÅ,* 1903, pp. 87-88.
[165] Holmquist, *Svenska Reformationens Begynnelse*, pp. 125-128.

a Church beside the State, but a Church within the State.

The result of the enforcement of the Vesterås decisions and, more recently, the Council at Örebro, was a new revolt, this time in the southern part of the kingdom. The mayor of Jönköping, Nils Arvidsson, had raised the cry of rebellion in Småland, and the news of the murder of the king's officer and the capture of the king's sister soon reached Stockholm. The king guessed the cause of the trouble, and defended his course "in the evangelical matter and toward bishops, monks, and cloisters."[166] The leaders of the uprising sought to inveigle the other provinces and make the revolt general. But Gustavus was quick to act, decisive and persuasive. To the country as a whole, but also the several provinces and certain cities, letters were at once dispatched.[167] The neighboring province of Vestergötland joined the men of Småland, but the king succeeded in keeping Östergötland, Uppland, and Dalarne quiet. The leaders of the revolt gave the Church question as the motive of their action. The king had introduced the Lutheran heresy, despoiled cloisters and churches, degraded and debased the sacraments, "as is sufficiently proven by the books that he has permitted this past winter to issue from the press concerning the sacraments." He had demanded unlawful taxes, driven away men of the Church "in order that he might take their property, tithes, and all their other possessions." Heretics and renegade

[166] *GR* VI, pp. 27-29 (April 4, 1529).

[167] Östergötland, April 4 (*GR* VI, 27-29), again April 14; Linköping, Uppland, Småland, Jönköping, Dalarne, April 16-20 (*ibid.*, pp. 37-48); Dalarne, April 24 (p. 50); Kalmar, May 5 (pp. 74-77).

monks had been given influential positions, and these had "led us into false doctrine and discarded all that belongs to true worship."[168] They further charged that the king ate meat in Lent and influenced others to do likewise; that the mass had been changed so as to be held in Swedish; that they were forbidden "confession, consecration of priests, unction, confirmation"—so that "we will soon become heathen." The officers of the king were criticized for their severity.[169] To this list of complaints the allies in Vestergötland added a couple. The king considered the Virgin Mary "as no better than other mortal women," and had forced "monks, priests, and nuns to marry."[170] In his letters the king promised that wrongs would be corrected, and expressed astonishment that such a course as revolt should be pursued when these matters could be remedied peaceably.[171]

Undoubtedly Gustavus was uneasy at the prospects. Among his first steps was to call the nobility of Uppland to Stockholm.[172] To his brother-in-law, Count John of Hoja, whose wife was in captivity, he wrote, "We fear that the treason is of so great proportions that we soon will not know whom to put confidence in."[173] He had quickly perceived that there were other leaders in the background, and that these were the powerful Ture Jönsson, and the bishop of Skara. The former he now described as one of King Christian's sworn men "who has concealed himself so

[168] *Ibid.*, pp. 356-358 (April 4).
[169] *Ibid.*, pp. 358-359 (April 8).
[170] *Ibid.*, pp. 361-362 (April 20).
[171] *Ibid.*, pp. 30-33 (April 14).
[172] *Ibid.*, p. 39 (April 16).
[173] *Ibid.*, pp. 67-69 (April 29).

long in the kingdom, but nourished treason in his heart."[174] His representatives in the affected territory informed him that Ture was "the head of the revolt, and that the people complained most of all about Master Laurentius and Master Olavus and others who have gone over to the evangelical party"; Laurentius was considered the cause of the king's ecclesiastical policy.[175]

Ture Jönsson, however, did not succeed in winning others to his cause, and in a few weeks the uprising died down. On the advice of his representatives, the king offered a general amnesty to all who before a certain date renewed allegiance to him, and loyalty to the decisions of Vesterås.[176] His authorized spokesman, Holger Karlsson, had counseled the king to let the people remain in their "old and Christian customs," even claiming that the common people "will never go under the teaching which now for some time has been expounded by some, unless they are by force compelled to do so," and placing the root of the complaints in the new preaching and new books.[177] The people, accordingly, were instructed that they might retain their ancient customs, that "each one may preach and believe what he thinks good," and that monks and nuns might continue in their ways.[178] But the king was careful to define "God's pure Word and good old Christian customs" as that which "the Recess resolved in Vesterås" contained.[179]

Meanwhile, the arch-conspirators, Ture Jönsson and

[174] *Ibid.*, p. 54 (April 24).
[175] *Ibid.*, pp. 366-368 (April 25).
[176] *Ibid.*, pp. 372-373.
[177] *Ibid.*, pp. 370-372 (April 29).
[178] *Ibid.*, pp. 86-88 (May 8).
[179] *Ibid.*, p. 84 (May 6).

Bishop Magnus, had followed the course of Johannes Magnus and Brask—they had left the kingdom. In Denmark refuge was afforded them, despite the protests of Gustavus.[180] From the Danish Council, Tyge Krabbe wrote explaining that the intention of the government was not hostile; rather, he hoped that the king might be reconciled with the fugitives, advising Gustavus, furthermore, to forsake the Lutheran heresy "which has no prospect in the future."[181] The king, in fact, preferred to have the couple in Sweden, and tried to induce them to return, but the stumbling-block was Vesterås Recess. This the two considered to be the cause of all the trouble, and they "have no intention to agree or yield to it."[182]

With the rest of the leaders the king dealt at the Diet at Strengnäs, in June. Here, too, he defended his course since Vesterås, two years previous. As far as the king was aware, no new teaching beyond that then authorized had been preached. Only as far as the needs of the kingdom had necessitated had he weakened the Church, which was not to be confused with its prelates. The fugitive bishops had fled; he had not driven them away—strife between bishops and kings antedated any reformation. The Council had consented to all confiscation of Church property. In regard to the monasteries, too, Vesterås Recess had been followed. Of means received from them some had been used for furthering the education of certain young men. Mass in Swedish had neither been commanded nor prohibited, but freedom had been permitted, and the Latin mass still remained. If the

[180] *Ibid.*, pp. 105-107 (May 22).
[181] *Ibid.*, p. 383 (May 22).
[182] *Ibid.*, pp. 388-390 (May 30).

king's followers had ridiculed the saints, it was not with the king's consent. He had sanctioned only such books as were Christian—nor did one need to read what one did not like. Eating of meat in Lent injured no one; it was quite common in other lands, where there was more knowledge of Scriptures; even in Rome it was not uncommon. All taxes had been agreed to by the Council. He could not forbid priests, monks, and nuns to marry, as long as the Word of God permitted marriage. Foreigners had been called in only for purposes of the State. His proposed marriage to a foreigner was also of advantage to the kingdom. His oath to protect the Church had not been violated— the Church was the community of all Christian people; these he had protected.[183] Thus the actions at and since the Vesterås Diet were defended at length. Now, as before, the king considered the duties of the government to be clear, so also those of the Church. "The king is bound to hold the bishops to their rightful duties, because the function of the king is to uphold that which is right and punish that which is wrong."[184] The representatives of the kingdom were completely subordinated and reaffirmed the Vesterås resolution. Three of the leaders in the revolt who had refused amnesty, denying guilt, were tried and condemned. The property of the two fugitives was confiscated.[185] From Strengnäs, Gustavus emerged even stronger than before.

The position he had now attained made the king confident of his right and power to intervene where he wished in the matters of the Church. In Uppsala,

[183] *Ibid.*, pp. 141-152.
[184] *Ibid.*, p. 154.
[185] *Ibid.*, pp. 162-179.

a Doctor Hans had been indiscreet in the time and place, as well as the enthusiasm, of his evangelical preaching. The king wished that more moderation be exercised "in the reformation of some things which with good reason have hitherto been observed."[186] That the change was being made too rapidly in Stockholm, also, an incident from this year testifies. When the representatives came back from the Örebro meeting in February, the German element thought that regression rather than advance had characterized the meeting, and Olavus Petri had to defend his position before the City Council, of which he was secretary. He recorded there: "Then Gudmund and Peter and the mayor began to speak severely to the Germans, that they should not cause any tumult here in the city, and they were told that one has to proceed slowly with the people in this country."[187] Even more than Olavus, the king knew the necessity of a gradual transformation, and he used his power on his followers as well as his opponents. That he was consciously proceeding as an evangelical king can hardly be doubted. In a letter to a member of the Danish Council he affirmed that, unlike the Swedish fugitives in Denmark, he has "through the mercy of God consented to the preaching of the Gospel in our kingdom, and to the effecting of some transformations—such as generally follow upon the preaching of the Gospel."[188] It may be that he was more interested in the consequences of the Gospel than the Gospel itself, but he saw, nevertheless, the relationship between the Gospel and the consequences. The policy he advised the bishop of

[186] *Ibid.*, p. 208.
[187] H. Lundstrom, *Undersökningar och Aktstycken*, p. 35.
[188] *GR* VI, 315-316 (Oct. 19).

Finland, Mårten in Åbo, to follow was pretty much his own method. The king had advised Mårten "to promote and favor the holy evangelical doctrine which belongs to your office," and had received the reply that "many feel that the new teaching is peculiar," whereupon Gustavus wrote, "Thus we counsel and demand of you, that you pay not too much attention to the protests of your chapter, but follow the right interpretation and spirit of the holy Gospel."[189] The same bishop was also advised that the king's pleasure should be consulted in the election of archdeacon and canons.[190] Naturally, the election of bishops was closely watched. Dean Sven in Skara had been elected as successor to the fugitive Magnus, but had declined. But he was acceptable to the king, who saw in his unanimous election "the will of God," and urged his acceptance. As to consecration, he was told, "you might just as well at once be consecrated along with the Electus of Linköping."[191] The Electus of Linköping was Dean Jöns Magni, who agreed to the king's propositions as to the administration of Brask's diocese.[192] Bishop Peder of Vesterås had been too eager to inform his diocese concerning the meeting at Örebro, and was placed under the supervision of his archdeacon, Nils Andreae.[193] On the death of Ingemar in Vexio, Jöns Boethius was elected, and accepted by the Crown.[194] The vacant see was now Uppsala. In the spring the chapter there, and "some of the royal

[189] *Ibid.*, pp. 104-105 (June 3).
[190] *Ibid.*, pp. 118-119 (June 7).
[191] *GR* VII, 15 (Jan. 13, 1530).
[192] *Ibid.*, pp. 13-14 (Jan. 13).
[193] *Ibid.*, pp. 58-60 (March 27).
[194] *Ibid.*, pp. 194-195 (Nov. 11).

Ecclesiastical Transformation in Sweden 55

Council," had elected the bishop in Finland to this position,[195] but he had refused the call.

Even in the internal affairs of dioceses the king intervened. He forbade the administrator of Uppsala diocese to issue a proclamation, as the bishop of Vesterås had done.[196] The parish of Orsa had chosen a pastor whom the king did not favor—a new election was ordered.[197] The parish of Kuddby complained of their pastor's marriage. The king instructed them that "men, wise and learned in the Holy Scriptures, had recently determined that the marriage of clergy was Scriptural"; therefore he could not hinder it.[198] The pastor in Sätila lost his thumb, whereupon some would have forced him from his office. If this were the papal law, replied the king, "we pay little attention to it," for such an accident was no Scriptural bar to the office.[199] Monasteries at Enköping and Stockholm had become deserted—the one was ordered transformed into an asylum, the other into an hospice.[200] The condition of the schools bothered the king. Their decline was "a great and irremediable injury to the kingdom"; the bishops should strive to improve them.[201] The Electus of Skara was admonished to provide for a certain student who wished to study in Germany, and the student was advised to study "imperial law and other arts" that could be of service to the kingdom.[202] At Strengnäs, Gustavus had expressed his opinion of

[195] *Ibid.*, p. 103 (June 5).
[196] *Ibid.*, pp. 56-57 (March 27).
[197] *Ibid.*, pp. 102-103 (June 5).
[198] *Ibid.*, pp. 205-206 (Dec. 6).
[199] *Ibid.*, pp. 209-210 (Dec. 8).
[200] *Ibid.*, p. 83 (April 26), pp. 252-253 (Jan. 27, 1531).
[201] *Ibid.*, p. 70 (April 10, 1530).
[202] *Ibid.*, p. 137 (June 29).

the relative merits of monks and students, the one he would discourage, the other favor. To the Electus in Skara the king confided that if he could so order it that "without much clamor the monastery could be entirely abolished" the king would have nothing against it, "rather would we gladly see it."[203] But in judging the interference of the king in the internal affairs of the Church as a whole, it is necessary to keep in mind both the continued, persistent opposition of the old to the new, and the weak, unorganized attempts of the new to displace the old. Perhaps the supervision of the king was as much a matter of necessity as of desire.

The Church Council at Örebro and its consequences, as well as the results of the enforcement of the Vesterås decisions in general, testify to the slow and stubbornly resisted progress of the evangelical transformation. In 1531 came another exercise of royal prerogative over the Church, followed by a distubance which only brought the new order of things yet a few steps onward.

At the opening of the previous year, the royal Council had levied a tax on all chapels, churches, and cloisters in the cities, in the form of a bell—the next largest that each possessed. The reason was, again— the Lübeck debt. But it was considered inadvisable to extend the tax to the country churches.[204] A year later, the condition of the debt was such as to cause the Council to forget its scruples or hesitancy, for then the demand was made upon all the churches of the realm.[205] Precedents were not far to seek—the king

[203] *Ibid.*, pp. 211-212 (Dec. 13).
[204] *Ibid.*, p. 12 (Jan. 6).
[205] *Ibid.*, pp. 238-242 (Jan. 25).

had only to point to the other Scandinavian kingdoms.[206]

Again the northern provinces showed signs of disloyalty. The tax-gatherers received blows instead of bells. Some of the parishes which had turned over their bells reclaimed them. Dalarne was the center of the movement which soon spread to Vestmanland, Nerike, Helsingland. The additional grievance of the celebration of mass in Swedish was used as incentive to revolt. The king tried to appease the troublemakers by asserting the need of the tax as its motive, as against the confiscation of Church property. The bells could be retained, if a sum equal to their value was paid. Mass in Swedish he had not commanded, and would not further allow, except where it was specially requested.[207] "We are not altogether as afraid of them as they think," he wrote to one of his councilors,[208] but he was averse to civil strife and suspected, as always, the hand of Christian.[209] Therefore he tried by peaceful means to allay the dissatisfaction. In some cases he reduced the taxes as a reward for loyalty.[210] He half-promised that this would be the last assessment on churches.[211] He pointed to the obedience of the rest of the country.[212] When the men of Dalarne announced a meeting in Arboga, the king called the Council, and representatives of that province, with others, to Uppsala for the same date.[213] The result of the Uppsala meeting was a general call

[206] *Ibid.*, pp. 274-275 (Feb. 22).
[207] *Ibid.*, pp. 292-294 (March 24-25).
[208] *Ibid.*, pp. 318-319 (April).
[209] *Ibid.*, pp. 280 (March 18), 301 (March 31).
[210] *Ibid.*, pp. 304, 305, 316-317.
[211] *Ibid.*, pp. 311-312 (April 12).
[212] *Ibid.*, pp. 312-313.
[213] *Ibid.*, pp. 318-319.

to the discontented sections to remain loyal, and not prepare the way for foreign invasion, which the fugitives were favoring.[214] The opposition demanded another Diet, but this was deemed unnecessary.[215] On promise of being forgiven by the king, the men of Dalarne and Helsingland finally complied, and paid the tax.

Gustavus was not in martial mood these months, for invitations had already been issued for his wedding. At the beginning of the year the king and Council had decided in favor of a royal marriage with the daughter of the ruler of Sachsen-Lauenburg.[216] A contract had been drawn up [217] and the marriage was planned for the summer. In July the bishops-elect, Sven in Skara, Jöns Magni in Linköping, and Jöns Boethius in Vexiö, were invited to be present, but it was desired that before the event they should have received their consecration.[218] As yet nothing had been done to find an archbishop for Uppsala, since the bishop of Åbo had declined. In October, 1530, Laurentius Andreae wrote to Sven of Skara: "As yet nothing has been done to provide for Uppsala. Probably it is wise to wait until we hear what may be determined and resolved at the Diet of Augsburg. I do not know if it is on account of this or other reasons that you are not in haste with your consecration; but I suppose that this and other things contribute thereto. However that may be, it would be well if the Uppsala church did not need longer to be deprived of the comfort of a shepherd, though I perceive that here this

[214] *Ibid.*, pp. 338–340 (May 18).
[215] *Ibid.*, pp. 365–367 (June 18).
[216] *Ibid.*, pp. 256–261.
[217] *Ibid.*, pp. 284–290 (March 19).
[218] *Ibid.*, p. 376 (July 6).

matter is taken to heart very little."[219] Among the complaints of the people of Helsingland during the bell-uprising was the vacancy of the archbishop's seat in Uppsala. The king had answered that, in view of what the realm had suffered from the archbishopric, he had not been constrained speedily to have it filled, but he would now take the matter into consideration with the Council.[220] In the invitation to the bishops-elect, it was requested that they be accompanied to Stockholm by "the best and most intelligent of their chapter for the sake of some important matters which then will be transacted." Besides the marriage of the king, the program included the consecration of bishops and archbishop. Peder Swart, the chronicler, describes the election of archbishop as having taken place in June, and as resulting in 150 out of 170 votes for Laurentius Petri.[221] But his chronology is not dependable, and of the time, as well as of the nature of the elective body, there are no certain records. More probably, the election of archbishop took place after the bishops and their followers had come to Stockholm in August.[222] To Bishop Magnus of Strengnäs and Peder of Vesterås fell the lot of consecration. On the tenth of August they swore to a secret protest, in the presence of Peder Galle and prebendary Torgams, that they had been forced to agree to the change in the Church. They deplored the mass in Swedish, the distribution of the sacrament, the taxation of the clergy. They confessed their obedience and loyalty to their spiritual mother—the Church of Rome.[223] And on the twenty-

[219] Uno von Troil, *Skrifter och Handlingar* I, 358.
[220] *GR* VII, 324-326 (April 30, 1531).
[221] Quoted by Anjou, *op. cit.*, II, 92-93.
[222] See *Svenska Riksdagsakter*, I, 170-172.
[223] *GR* VII, 543-544.

seventh of the same month, the prospective consecration was again the object of a secret protest. In this the bishops-elect of Skara and Vexiö were included, and they promised to seek confirmation from Rome, *"dum tempus et occasio fuerint oportuna."* [224] Thus fortified, the bishops ordained the bishops-elect, and on September 22 the new archbishop. Through Bishop Peder of Vesterås, who had been canonically ordained in Rome, May, 1524, the ordination of Laurentius has been considered as preserving in Sweden the apostolic succession.[225] The first act of the new archbishop was to officiate at the marriage of the king, which took place two days later. "Sweden had received its first clearly evangelical bishop and archbishop, and its first evangelical royal couple, married by the archbishop. A return to Rome was henceforth impossible." [226]

Thus, in a decade, Sweden had undergone a transformation of overwhelming significance. At the beginning of this period the nobility had been weak, and the ruler a foreigner, while the Church was strong and independent. At the close, a native king had laid strong foundations for a new dynasty, and attained supreme power in the kingdom. The nobility had been increased and enriched. The Church, on the contrary, had been sundered from Rome, its allegiance transferred to the king, its bishops and archbishop made subservient to the Crown, its wealth confiscated. Even the function of the Church had been redefined, and its goal made evangelical. Before England had broken with Rome, while Denmark and Norway were still

---

[224] Lundstrom, in *Historisk Tidskrift*, 1897, pp. 63-64.
[225] Lundstrom, *KÅ*, 1906, pp. 266-268.
[226] Holmquist, *Svenska Reformationens Begynnelse*, p. 153.

struggling with strong Roman hierarchical parties, while the fate of Germany was still undecided, and Calvinism was but in the making,[227] Sweden had, through its leaders, pledged itself to an evangelical Church within an independent State. True, the transformation had been to a great extent political, and the changes effected had transformed the body rather than the soul of the Church. Had only the will of Gustavus Vasa been the cause of the change, it is a question how long it may have endured. But in the background was a less conspicuous, a silent, but creative personality, whose preaching, whose books and translation, whose personal influence, carried the Reformation into the ranks of the clergy and the masses of the people. Olavus Petri educated the mind and nourished the spirit of the evangelical movement. The spiritual change took much longer than a decade, but it was more thorough and abiding. The king made possible the beginnings of the religious transformation. The Reformer made permanent the transformation of the character of the new Church and State.

[227] Anjou, *Svenska Kyrkoreformationens Historia,* II, 98.

CHAPTER II

THE YEARS OF PREPARATION

In one of the oldest of Sweden's communities, the town of Örebro,[1] in the diocese of Strengnäs, Olavus Petri was born, January 6, 1493.[2] The situation of Örebro had determined its character as an important military and commercial center. Lying between the eastern and western divisions of the kingdom, Svea and Göta, it often witnessed the passage of armies, and the town itself was dominated by its castle, historic already in the sixteenth century. Foreign traders, too, found Örebro a strategic center, and tradition tells of merchants of Lybeck erecting a church before the city church of St. Nicolai was built. The latter traces its beginnings to the fourteenth and fifteenth centuries, and contains the tomb of one of Sweden's noblest patriots, Engelbreckt Engelbrecktson, who had lost his life in the uprising against Danish oppression, half a century before Olavus was born. The father of Olavus was a smith, and an echo of the boy's impressions from his father's shop is found in the son's writings, thirty-five years later, where he asserted that "to preach the

[1] J. F. Bagge, *Beskrivning om Upstaden Örebro;* H. Hofberg, *Nerikes Gamla Minnen.*

[2] *Works,* Vol. IV, p. 560. An earlier tradition, based on Hallman, *The Tvenne Brödher—Mest. Oluff Petri Phase—Mest. Lars Petri* (Sthm., 1726), set the date 1497. H. Schück, in *Samlaren,* 1888, has discussed the dependability of the two records given in *Själfbiografiska Anteckningar, Works,* IV, 560ff.

Word of God is the duty of the clergy, just as to forge is the duty of the smith."[3] Of the father, Peter Olaffson, or the mother, Christina Laurentii, hardly more than the names are known, and the facts that the former died in 1521, the latter in 1545. Nor is much known of the early school days of Olavus, or his brother, Laurentius. In Örebro was a Carmelite monastery, one of the two of the Order of Sweden. It had existed since 1418; its building had probably been occupied by some other Order before that date, as the Örebro Cloister was older, and had previously borne the names of Vår Fru (Our Lady) and St. Olof. It seems not to have been very large, and its school in the days of the Petri brothers could not have been above the ordinary. But evidently it was here that Olavus received his earliest instruction in the language and customs of the Church. In the lower schools of Sweden at this time the curriculum was confined to reading and writing, and memorizing of Pater Noster, Ave Maria, Symbolum Apostolicum, and the Seven Psalms. Training in the ceremonies and music of the ritual was also given.[4] We can judge that the methods and character of instruction were no better in the North than on the Continent, before the Reformation. The textbooks were the same, e.g. Alexander de Villa Dei's *Doctrinale* (Latin Grammar), and Donatus (Grammar), while the ferule was as much the schoolmaster's symbol in Örebro as in Eisleben.

Olavus has told us no more about his days in Uppsala than of those in the cloister school, and we can only gather from other sources what Uppsala had to offer its students in the first decade of the sixteenth

[3] *Works*, I, 241.
[4] K. F. Karlson, *Blad ur Örebro Skolas Äldsta Historia*, p. IX.

century.[5] Until 1348 Swedish students had sought higher instruction in Paris; from that date to 1409, Prague was the attraction; thereafter Leipzig, Erfurt, Rostock, and Greifswald became the most frequently visited centers.[6] In 1477 the pope granted the prelates of Sweden the right to establish a university, similar in its privileges to the University of Bologna. During the same year, the archbishop Jacob Ulfsson and his six bishops, together with the director of the kingdom (*Riksföreståndare*), Sten Sture, and twenty-three of the Council, issued letters granting the new University all the temporal privileges enjoyed by the University of Paris. In October, 1477, the University was solemnly opened. Its economic as well as its scholastic bases, however, were insecure, and with the resignation of Archbishop Ulfsson in 1515 and the ensuing conflict in the nation between the national party and the Danish king, the University seems to have ceased to function. During its earlier and happier days it provided the courses common to medieval universities, Aristotle, Thomas of Aquinas, Euclid, and the Canon Law furnishing the major contents. It is uncertain whether students stayed beyond the baccalaureate degree. The many *Baccalaurei Upsalienses* at German universities indicate rather that from Uppsala they proceeded to foreign schools for the higher

[5] The more detailed, and less reliable, autobiographical (alleged) record states that Olavus studied in Örebro from his seventh to his thirteenth year, and that he was at Uppsala until 1506. There is manifestly an error, for his thirteenth year would be 1506. As the first certain record of Olavus in Germany is 1516, the Uppsala years must be thought of as falling within the years 1506-1516.

[6] For the history of Uppsala, see C. Annerstedt, *Uppsala Universitets Historia,* I, Ch. I.

degrees. The scarcity of manuscripts in Sweden, the high cost of books, the distance from centers of learning, made the progress of studies difficult in Uppsala. On the other hand, the high positions attained to by Swedish students at the foreign school gives reason to believe that their instruction at Uppsala was of a high standard, as judged by other medieval universities. But Olavus Petri seems to have decided to seek even his baccalaureate degree at a German university.

Rostock, founded in 1419, became the favorite school of fifteenth-century Swedish students. A large number of the leading names of the Church at the beginning of the Reformation are found in the rolls of that university two or three decades earlier. Thus of the bishops, we find Otto in Vesterås, Vincent in Skara, Hans Brask in Linköping, and Magnus in Skara, enrolled at Rostock between 1480 and 1504.[7] The powerful chancellor, Laurentius Andreae, matriculated there in 1498. Occasionally we find Swedish students at Greifswald, more frequently at Leipzig and Cologne. Between 1483 and 1516 thirty students from Sweden enrolled at Leipzig; between 1503 and 1520, twelve at Cologne—among these the last two Roman archbishops of Sweden, Gustav Trolle (1511) and Johannes Magnus (*magister artium*, 1517).[8] Rostock clung to the old faith in the early days of the Reformation, and its work came almost to a standstill. The Swedish students forsook it for Wittenberg. But after the new religious thought had transformed the school, it again became a favorite center, and between 1540-1573 drew

[7] Annerstedt, *op. cit.*, I, 44.
[8] *Ibid.*, p. 45.

over one hundred Swedish students, while in the same period Wittenberg claimed hardly seventy-five.[9]

A search of the University *Matrikel* of Greifswald, Rostock, Leipzig, and Wittenberg fails to reveal any trace of Olavus Petri at these schools before 1516.[10] In the summer of that year, we find *"Paulus Phase de Schvecia"* enrolled at Leipzig.[11] Who or what led him here we do not know. Swedish students may have influenced him. In 1512 *"Michael Langerbeyn de Strengyss"* was enrolled there, and two years later a group of Swedish names was entered on the *Matrikel* during the summer term—*"Petrus Schwenn de Upsalia, Caspar Johannis de Abo, Petrus Brask de Lencopia regni Schwecie, Thuro Benedicti de Hendelin regni Schwecie."* Three of this quartet reveal the peripatetic nature of medieval students. Petrus Brask we first find at Rostock in 1510, as a baccalaureus of Uppsala. At Rostock he earned a master's degree during the winter term, 1510-11. In 1514 he was at Leipzig. In June, 1516, he enrolled at Wittenberg, whence he received a master's degree the following February. Thuro Benedicti seems to have been his companion. He too is at Leipzig in 1514, and at Wittenberg in 1516-17, earning the master's title at Wittenberg, February, 1517. Michael Langerbeyn received his master's

[9] Anjou, *Svenska Kyrkoreformationens Historia* III, 17.

[10] In the University Matrikel of Rostock II, 53, is a *"Nicolaus Petri de civitate Strengnensi,"* enrolled June 15, 1513. Five days later, June 20, *"Olaus Magni de Swetia Lincopensis dioc. et civitatis"* was entered (p. 54). Both were promoted to baccallaurei in 1513-14 (p. 56). Could Nicolaus Petri be Olavus Petri? At Leipzig, Olavus called himself Paulus. The longer autobiographical record states that Olavus studied at Rostock and Wittenberg (it does not mention Leipzig). (*Works*, IV, 560.)

[11] *Die Matrikel der Univ. Leipzig*, I.

degree at Leipzig in 1513, and in July, 1514, was at Rostock.[12]

At Leipzig Olavus did not remain long. For before the semester was completed he had moved to Wittenberg, where, together with *"Olaus Brunes ex Suecia,"* he was enrolled as *"Olaus Phase ex Suecia Sweignen dio."*[13] Petrus Brask and Thuro Benedicti had been there since June and remained at least till the following February, when they were promoted to magistri. Shortly afterwards (April) Olavus was made baccalaureus, so also Olavus Brunes, in October. In February, 1518, *"Joanne Ferreo Montano Artium magistro et theosophie baccalaureo tunc artium facultatis decano,"*[14] *"Olaus Vase de Suecia"* received the *insignia magistri*.[15] The following November Olavus returned to Sweden.

The period between 1516-1518 was eventful not only in the life of this Swedish student but in the history of the world. A mere outline of the principal happenings in Wittenberg these years suggests the character of the period. In 1516, and again in February, 1517, Luther preached against the purchase of indulgences, whose falsity he had by this time come to perceive. On October 31 the ninety-five Theses appeared on the church door at Wittenberg. In July, 1518, Luther was accused of heresy by the papal fiscal

[12] Matrikel Univ. Leipzig, Rostock, Wittenberg. Also *"Die Baccalaurei und Magistri der Wittenberger Philosophischen Fakultät, 1503-1517"* in *Osterprogramm der Univ. Halle-Wittenberg, 1887*.

[13] *Album Acad. Vitebergensis*, I, 62.

[14] The autobiographic notes have *"Magistrum Johannem Ferreum Hessum."* Cf. H. Schück, in *Samlaren*, 1888, p. 21.

[15] *Osterprogramm der Univ. Halle-Wittenberg*, 1888, p. 16.

Mario Perusco, and in August was commanded by Silvester von Prierio, general auditor for processes of the Apostolic Chamber, to come to Rome within sixty days, an order that the cardinal legate to the Reichstag at Worms, Thomas Cajetan, was authorized to execute by force, if necessary. When both emperor and elector refused Luther's extradition, Cajetan attempted, in October, to persuade Luther to recant, especially Thesis 58, which concerned papal authority. Refusing both threat and favor, Luther left Augsburg, and in November (28) appealed, in Wittenberg, from pope to Council. The same month (November 9), the pope had declared indulgences authorized and recommended by the Church.[16]

Such were the principal outward events which must have made deep impression on the students of Wittenberg, among whom was Olavus Petri. But, naturally, the attention of this prospective baccalaureus and magister would be occupied, at the same time, with the duties of a student. It is possible to give quite a full picture of the life of the University at this time, thanks to a document of the University authorities in reply to a query from the elector Frederick as to the organization and work of the faculty.[17] The communication describes conditions in 1516. The schedule of the Arts department (in which Olavus received his degrees) was as follows:

> 6 A. M. in winter = 5 in summer. Licentiate Amsdorff, in Aristotelian Logic, according to Scotus. Simultaneously, Magister Bruck, Aristotle according to Thomas.

[16] K. Müller, *Kirchengeschichte*, II, I, 226-231.

[17] In Walter Friedensburg, *Urkundenbuch der Universität Wittenberg, I,* 1502-1611, pp. 77ff.

Ecclesiastical Transformation in Sweden

7 A. M. Magister Feltkirchen, in Natural Physics, according to Scotus. Magister Joh. Gunckele, do. according to Thomas.

8 A. M. Magister Fach, in Poetics (Virgil).

12 M. Licentiate Sebastianus, in Peter Hispanius, via Scotus. Magister Staffelsteyn, do. via Thomas.

12 M. Magister from Augustinian Cloister, in Ethics.

2 P. M. Magister Czorbig, in Astronomy and Mathematics.

3 P. M. Magister Otto Steckman, in Grammatica. Magister Premsel von Torgau, in Metaphysics.

4 P. M. Magister Fach, in Rhetoric.

During the winter five new magistri were added, with the following subjects: Aristotle's Logic, *"textualiter secundum novum translationem"*; Aristotle's Physics and Metaphysics, *"textualiter ibid."*; Aristotle's *"De animalibus"* and Quintilian (alternate years); elementary instruction in Latin, Greek, Hebrew, Grammar, etc. (by two of the five magistri).

The great attraction at Wittenberg, however, was not in the Arts faculty, but in that of Theology. It can hardly be doubted that a Wittenberg student would be left untouched by the activity of this branch of the University. At 1 P. M. Doctor Martin Luther lectured on the Bible, and this may be one reason why the Arts schedule had no one-o'clock subject. At 4 P. M. Licentiate Amsdorff (in place of the regular professor, Doctor Carolstadt) instructed, in Gabriel Biel. Every Friday a disputation took place, under Doctor Peter Lupinus. The summer of 1518 saw another brilliant star added to the Wittenberg group, namely, Philip

Melanchton. John Böschenstein also began instruction in Hebrew—a textual study of the Seven Penitential Psalms—but his stay was brief.[18] Certainly there was much to occupy the minds and hours of the Wittenberg students of 1516-1518.

In Luther's development these years are of the greatest significance. His Swedish disciple revealed in future works that he had taken impress from the position Luther had attained to, in this period. Nothing is more difficult to trace than the extent of a teacher's influence upon a pupil. Nor is this the place for a study of Luther's influence on Olavus Petri. But it is in place to sketch briefly the work and teaching of Luther in Wittenberg during these years while Olavus was there as a student. In how far these had effect on the Swedish student, the work of his later years can best make manifest.

In this period falls Luther's ever widening divergence from Aristotle, along with which grew a suspicion of Erasmus' standpoint. In a letter of October 19, 1516, to Spalatin, Luther disagreed with the conception of Erasmus in regard to *"justitiam,"* and explains *"Non enim, ut Aristoteles putat, iusta agendo iusti efficimur, nisi simulatorie; sed iusti fiendo et essendo operamur iusta."* [19] The following February he sent Lang a tract against Aristotle and the Scholastics, to be sent to Truttfetter. He stated that he was intent on writing a commentary on Aristotle's *First Book of Physics,* and went so far as to say that were not Aristotle human, he would be tempted to see in him the devil himself, so baneful was his influence on theology.[20] Again, in

[18] *Ibid.,* pp. 87-89.
[19] E. L. Enders, *Briefwechsel,* I, 63, 64.
[20] *Ibid.,* I, 85.

March, Luther wrote Lang, this time regarding Erasmus. Luther read him, and liked his censures upon the unlearned clergy, but feared that Erasmus did not understand Christ nor the grace of God. *"Humana praevalent in eo plus quam divina."* He further warned Lang to read Erasmus with discernment. A man is not a wise Christian because he is a Greek or a Hebrew scholar. The judgment of one who attributed something to the will of man was bound to differ from that of one who knew nothing beyond grace.[21] That these letters reveal something more than mere speculation on the part of Luther, that they expressed an activity on the part of the writer that was transforming the University, a letter of May 18 bears witness: "Our theology and Augustine are here making the best of progress, and, with the help of God, already have become supreme at this University. Aristotle is losing his foothold; his downfall is pending, and when he falls, it will be forever. It is really a wonder, how the Sentences are now despised. As a rule, no one can hope for an audience who does not treat, in his lectures, with our Theology, that is, the Bible and Augustine, or some other of the old Church Fathers."[22]

The open break with Aristotle came in September. In his *Disputatio contra scholasticam theologiam*, a result of Franz Günther aus Nordhausen's disputation *um die Wurde eines biblischen Baccalaureus zu erwerben*, on September 4, 1517, Luther definitely opposed the influence of the Greek philosopher in Christian theology. In the 97th Thesis of this *Disputatio* he denied the freedom of the will and affirmed that neither man's nature nor the works of

[21] *Ibid.*, pp. 87-88.
[22] To Lang, Enders, I, 86.

the Law, but only the grace of God can sanctify man. Köstlin considers this blow of Luther as shaking the foundation of the whole building of medieval philosophy. In Erfurt the Theses were condemned, but in Wittenberg they found ready acceptance.[23] The emancipation of Biblical theology from Greek philosophy as applied in medieval Scholasticism was one of the most revolutionary of the movements of the Reformation. For the life of Olavus Petri, the fact that he was at Wittenberg at the time when this struggle reached its climax cannot have been without result. A later work revealed his own attitude toward the "doctrines of the heathen Aristotle." [24]

To this period belongs, further, Luther's public approval of the doctrines contained in *Theologia Germania*. In December, 1516, he sent Spalatin *Ein geistlich, edles Buchlein,* which he had himself edited and for which he had written a preface. At this time Luther had but a portion of the book and considered its author to be Tauler. The contents he called *"puram, solidam, antiquae simillimam theologiam,"* and gave it the highest praise—*"neque enim ego vel in Latina, vel nostra lingua theologiam salubriorem et cum Evangelio consonantiorem."* [25] In this booklet are contained some of the highest expressions of German mysticism. "The best should be the most beloved, and in this love nothing should be considered as profitable or unprofitable, advantageous or disadvantageous, gain or loss, glory or dishonor, laudable or unpraiseworthy, or the like. But what in truth is the noblest

[23] *WA* I, 221-228.
[24] *Works*, I, 185.
[25] Enders, *op. cit.*, I, 74.

and best, that should be the most loved, and for no other reason than that it is the best and noblest."[26] "God must be incarnated in me, that is, He takes onto Himself all that is in me, within and without, so that nothing may remain in me that might withstand God or hinder His work. In this salvation and betterment I neither can nor may do anything, but only purely permit it, so that God alone does and works while I allow Him and His work and His Will."[27] "What is it, then, that is, and to which one should hold? I answer: One thing only: that one knows God. That is true obedience to the Truth. So it is in the blessed Eternity. Therein is nought sought or thought or loved save this one thing; and so is nothing prized except this. Herein one may understand what disobedience is: that man considers and prizes himself as something; he thinks himself to be, to know, and to be capable of something; he seeks himself and his own in things and has love to himself."[28] The true Christians "live in such a state of freedom, that they have lost all fear of pain or hell, as well as hope of reward or heaven. They live in pure dependence on and obedience to the eternal good, out of a free love."[29] Of such a mysticism we find little trace in the writings of the Swedish Reformer. It is not foreign to him— he speaks often of the mystical union of Christ and the Christian—but we may safely conclude that his mysticism is mediated through Luther, who, despite his fulsome praise of *Theologia Deutsch,* transformed its teachings, as far as he was concerned, from a sub-

[26] *Theologia Deutsch,* Chap. VI, Par. 1, hrsg. von H. Mandel, "Quellensschriften zur Geschichte des Protestantismus," VII, 14-15.
[27] *Ibid.,* Chap. III, Pars. 3, 4, pp. 11-12.
[28] *Ibid.,* Chap. XIII, Par. 1, pp. 31-32.
[29] *Ibid.,* Chap. X, Par. 2, p. 23.

lime Quietism to an eager, conquering Life in the fellowship of God.[30]

Undoubtedly the most impressive, as well as the most dramatic and effective of the teachings of Luther between 1516-1518, were those in regard to indulgences. In 1516 and in 1517 he had warned the people against the false trust that many placed therein. A sermon,[31] probably preached on the day of the Theses, but printed in February, 1518, enables us to know what the students of Wittenberg heard those days concerning indulgences: "From no Scripture can one show, that God's justice demands or exacts suffering or satisfaction from the sinner. He only requires sincere and true contrition and conversion, and the resolution (on the part of the sinner) hereafter to carry the Cross of Christ and to do the aforementioned (alms) works, though not decreed by anyone." "It is a great error for anyone to think that he can make satisfaction for his sin, since God always freely forgives, out of infinite mercy, and but requires that henceforth we live righteously." "If souls can be rescued from purgatory by indulgences, I do not know, nor do I believe it, whatever some doctors say. It is, however, impossible to prove, and the Church has not so decided." "In these points I am not in doubt, and am well grounded in Scripture. You, too, should have no doubt therein. Let doctors scholastici remain scholastici. All of them, with all their opinions, are not able to substantiate a single sermon."

A Lenten sermon of 1518 [32] marks the development

[30] *Cf.* Karl Holl, *Gesammelte Aufsätze zur Kirchengeschichte*, pp. 81ff.
[31] *"Eyn Sermon von Ablass und Gnade,"* WA I, 243-246.
[32] WA I, 271, 272.

to which Luther had come, while the Swedish disciple was still in Wittenberg. "The healing of the Cross is so holy and so high, that it cannot be contained in any Monstrance of gold or silver. It requires a living, eternal Monstrance. For the healing is living, as is the soul of man." "Those that say, Ah, I have done all I could; I have done enough; I hope God will be merciful to me—they set an iron wall between themselves and the grace of God. But when you experience within yourself: Ah, I will call upon God, pray, and knock, etc., then the grace is already present. Call then on God and thank Him.—God is perfect in all creatures, in all secret places; He is before and behind thee. Or do you think that He is in Heaven, asleep on a cushion? He is awake, knows your needs and sorrow."

During 1517-1518 the first of Luther's writing in German began to appear. In April, 1517, *Die sieben Buss psalmen* were published, *"die erste von Luthers Schriften, die er selbst dem Druck übergeben."* [33] From June, 1516, to Lent, 1517, Luther preached a series of sermons on the Ten Commandments. An abridgment of these sermons was published as *Kurze Auslegung der zehn Gebote Gottes, ihrer Erfüllung und Ubertretung,* in 1518.

What had Olavus Petri received in Wittenberg from 1516 to 1518? We cannot know. But it is hard to believe that Luther had not left enduring marks on his development. He must have lost faith in Scholasticism and come to see in the Bible the only source of spiritual truth. His eyes had been opened to the abuses existing in the Church, and the events of 1518 had shaken the doctrine of the supremacy of the pope. Above all,

[33] *WA* I, 154.

he had heard of a righteousness of God that is given
freely to those who believe, and cannot be earned by
any number or kind of good works. At the same time,
it should be remembered that he had heard of no
division of the Church. The problem was not one of
breaking away from the Church; it was rather one of
restoring what had been lost or forgotten during the
development of abuses and foreign doctrines. Throughout his career Olavus held that in Sweden there had
been no falling away from the Church. When, ten
years later, he wrote, "We will always claim to be part
of that Christian communion which is not limited only
to Rome, but exists throughout the whole earth," [34]
he was consistent with what he had heard and learned
in Wittenberg.

The reasons causing the return of Olavus to Sweden
in 1518 to 1519 we do not know. Student life in Wittenberg had its difficulties. In 1516 the pest harried Wittenberg, and about two hundred of its students left
the University during 1517-1518. Thereafter the
stream of students into the city became so great that it
was difficult, even impossible, for faculty as well as students to secure rooms. Prices for food naturally rose
in the overcrowded city.[35] But of none of these things
do the writings of Olavus speak, and we must be content to record the meager notice, among his autobiographical remarks, that in 1519 he returned from
Germany to Sweden.

Again in his homeland, Master Olavus turned his
steps to his native diocese, whose bishop-seat was in
Strengnäs.[36] It was an old religious center, tracing

[34] *Works*, I, 342, "*Itt Fögho Sendebreff til Paulum Helie.*"
[35] *Urkundenbuch*, pp. 82, 147-148.
[36] L. Hallman, *Det Gamla och Nya Strengnäs*.

its history back to the days of the English missionary, St. Eskil, from whom a neighboring community, Eskilstuna, had its name. Its cathedral had been dedicated in 1291, and was richly endowed. At the time of Olavus' early childhood, one of its most renowned bishops, Doctor Conradus Rogge, a Doctor Utriusque, of Perugia, had occupied the episcopal chair. His successor was Mattias Gregorii, commonly called Bishop Matts, who in 1513 added to his religious duties the political one of Chancellor to the King. By him, Olavus was ordained a deacon in September, 1520, and about the same time he became the secretary, or chancellor, of the bishop.

The autumn of 1520 was one of the most critical and disastrous seasons in the history of Sweden.[37] When Christian II, in September, made his fatal visit to Sweden, Bishop Matts of Strengnäs was one of his active supporters, and his secretary, Olavus Petri, received commissions which gave him a part in the negotiations between the contending parties. Of his bishop, Olavus wrote in the *Chronicle* that "of the Swedes, no one did so much for the king, as he."[38] In November, Christian, after a brief trip to Denmark, returned to Stockholm, and there met with the Council, the nobility, and the leaders of the Swedish nation.

It was a fateful assemblage. November 8 the king established a court of trial, and proceeded to reckon with all who might be counted powerful to oppose him. The occasion for judgment was found in the deposition of Archbishop Trolle, who now had opportunity to accuse his enemies. But the king went

[37] Olavus' own account of these events, in *"Krönika," Works,* IV, 272ff; *cf.* E. Hildebrand, *Sveriges Historia,* Vol. I. Also, *ante,* p. 3.
[38] *Works,* IV, 287.

beyond the list that Trolle would make, and included in the number of victims even those who had aided his cause. The bishop of Strengnäs, in fact, was the first to be beheaded, along with the bishop of Skara. When the day's work was done, no less than eighty-two of the foremost men of Sweden lay dead on the Great Market Place. The executions went on the following day, and later, in other parts of the kingdom. The Danish King added one more "blood-bath" to the world's melancholy list of similar events. It marked the beginning of the final dissolution of the Kalmar Union.

Though tradition has it that Olavus and Laurentius Petri also came near to losing their lives in Stockholm,[39] the fact cannot be proved. Olavus has made no mention of the danger. But his detailed description of the events of those November days, and his position as secretary to Bishop Matts, make likely that he was an eyewitness of the trial and massacre. Men less closely connected with political affairs than himself fell victims to the executioner, for no apparent reason, so that the Strengnäs chancellor was not out of peril. That these crimes should be sanctioned in the name of the Church could not but have raised many questions in the mind of the young magister, recently returned from Wittenberg.

As successor to the episcopate in Strengnäs, Christian II placed one of his tools, Johannes Beldenack, who, however, soon followed his master to Denmark. The duties of the office fell automatically on the archdeacon Laurentius Andreae.[40] He was about ten years

---

[39] J. G. Hallman, *op. cit.*, Chap. II.

[40] Biography by Bishop C. H. Rundgren, in *Svenska Akademiens Handlingar ifrån År 1886*, Part VIII, 1893, pp. 45ff.

older than Olavus, had studied in Rostock, earned his magister degree, and spent considerable time in Rome. Hither he had made three trips, and spent part of his time vainly trying to win back the St. Birgitta Hospis from the pope to the Vadstena monastery. As a *publicus apostolica auctoritate notarius* he was evidently trained in law, and as early as 1505 he had rendered valuable service to the civil rulers. In Strengnäs, after 1520, he was highest in administration. Probably he it was that appointed Olavus as scholasticus of the Cathedral School and permitted him to preach.[41] The new bishop, Magnus Sommar, was elected in 1522. Between the archdeacon and the teacher sprang up a friendship and alliance which was to have far-reaching results.

The preaching of Olavus soon attracted attention. From a document of the dean of Strengnäs we learn the theological position of the deacon in 1523. Dr. Nicholas Benedicti had detected errors in his subordinate, and listed them along with his own refutation of the Lutheran heresies.[42] The errors of Olavus were found in his assertions, that

(1) No place in Scripture teaches that St. Anna was the mother of the Virgin Mary.

(2) Joseph, the husband of Mary, was a young, not an old man.

(3) The true Faith has not previously been preached here.

(4) The Mendicants should not be permitted, for they are in violation of Deut. xv.

(5) No one ought to trust in man, as in the

---

[41] *Cf.* Swart, *Krönika,* p. 84.
[42] *HSH* XVII, pp. 135ff; *cf.* Westman, *op. cit.,* pp. 163ff.

Virgin or any other saint; our trust should be in God alone, according to Jer. xvii.

(6) The office of preaching is the principal one in the Church of God, and greater than that of celebrating the mass.

(7) Confraternities of the Psalter of the Blessed Virgin and of other saints ought not to be allowed, for they are fruitless, and without authority of Scripture.

(8) Confession should be to God alone, secretly (mentaliter), and not to priests.

(9) The Epistle of James is not authentic, so that public confession can be proved by it.

Allowing for the prejudices and partisanship of the critic of Olavus, we can nevertheless perceive in these "errors" the tendency of the "Lutheran" teacher. There is an appeal to Scripture, which the older man could not understand—in his refutation he defends the practices of the Church by references to Aquinas, Lyra, Antoninus, the Legends, Collects, etc. The disciple of Luther had seen with his teacher that the Church was subordinate to the Word on which it was founded. He was beginning to apply the principle in Strengnäs. Here, in 1501, Bishop Rogge had founded a fraternity for the Virgin, which should perform the Rosary service five days a week, from Easter till Advent.[49] Such fraternities Olavus branded *"frivole,"* and unbiblical. But he extended his attack still further. To him the popular faith in the Virgin and saints as a whole was false. In God alone man should trust. The personal relationship of man and his God, which Luther had so clearly taught, now found utter-

[49] L. Hallman, *op. cit.,* pp. 63-64.

ance in his disciple. It remained one of the cardinal teachings of the Swedish Reformer.

The attitude of Olavus to the function of the Church, moreover, is evident in these "errors." He had begun his criticism of the mass. The prime purpose of the clergy was to preach, not to celebrate a sacrifice. On this point hinged the whole public worship of the Church. To attack it meant a blow at the medieval structure in its entirety. That the dean did not understand the significance of the "new" teaching in his church is evident from the fact that his main defense is directed against Olavus' preaching concerning confession. To the Roman it seemed the most dangerous point, because it concerned the practices of every man and woman in the Church. It was dangerous enough, inasmuch as it might affect obedience to the Church. In reality, the question of the mass was the more vital. It affected the doctrine and nature of the Church.

Intimately connected with the denial of the traditions and practices of the Church as against Scripture, and with the redefining of the function of the clergy, was the attack on the Orders. Throughout his later writings Olavus was bitter in his denunciation of the Mendicants in special, but also of the monastic life in general. The whole movement was to him "a devil's business," [44] and "God has let the world be plagued with toads and grasshoppers." [45] The Scriptures knew nothing of these organizations—the Church should prohibit them; so the Swedish Reformer taught, as clearly as the German.

If a letter that Bishop Brask had received from

[44] *Works*, I, 502.
[45] *Ibid.*, p. 504.

Uppsala [46] correctly reported Olavus' statements, the latter had also begun his attacks on the worldly wealth of the Church, while preaching "Lutheran heresy," *"contra decreta sancte Romane ecclesie ac ecclesiasticam libertatem."* So much, nevertheless, is certain— that the preaching of Olavus was being rumored abroad, and new things were being uttered about man's approach to his God, the authority of Scripture, the abuses of the Church, the mass, the monks, and the truth of Christianity. That Olavus was conscious of the novelty of his teaching, Doctor Nicholaus' third item indicates. Olavus would hardly go to that extreme, saying Christianity had never before been preached in Sweden. But doubtless he did assert that the full truth had not been preached since Roman abuses had come to overshadow the Gospel brought to those parts by Sts. Ansgar and Sigfrid.[47]

The teaching of Master Olof these years in Strengnäs School cannot be accurately described, in the absence of records. But the words of the chronicler Swart may not be far from the truth, when they relate that "'he read passages from the Old and New Testament for those who desired to hear him, among whom were, first and foremost, *M. Laurentius Archidiaconus ibidem,* and several young men from among the prebendaries and canons."[48] Though Laurentius was the older and more experienced, Olavus was the clearer in the perception of the Biblical teachings, and the course of later events points back to these years in Strengnäs as the period in which the convictions and beliefs of both men ripened into principles and pur-

[46] *HSH* XVII, 143.
[47] *Works,* I, 340.
[48] *Krönika,* p. 84.

Ecclesiastical Transformation in Sweden

poses. The older, judicial mind saw the implications of the newly discovered truths on the systems of government in Church and nation. The younger, contemplative man concerned himself with the bearings of these truths on the personal experience of faith and on the worship and life of the spiritual Church. The contribution of each to the Church and State was to be of lasting value.

In Strengnäs, at Pentecost, 1523, the estates met and elected Gustavus as king of Sweden. Master Laurentius seems already to have served the State before this event;[49] after it he became the secretary in the Royal Council. The chronicler[50] tells us that the king once heard some of Olavus' disciples preach, the novelty of whose doctrines both interested and pleased him. On inquiring of Laurentius as to the value of this new doctrine, the king received a reply much to his liking. For "Laurentius instructed him thoroughly, in regard to many points—how Doctor Martin Luther had begun this thing and for what reason, how he had undermined the foundations of Pope, Cardinals, and the mighty Bishops, having proved that they could not adduce a single letter of Holy Writ to show that their great power and authority rested on the commandment of God—and much else of like nature." Gustavus had doubtless heard of Luther before this time, but it is not probable that he understood the nature of the Wittenberg controversy any better than did Emperor Charles. It is likely, therefore, that Laurentius Andreae first made Gustavus cognizant of the bearing of the new teachings on the problems which were uppermost in the king's mind, problems of recon-

[49] *Cf.* Westman, *op. cit.*, p. 151, note 1.
[50] *Krönika*, p. 84.

structing Sweden into a unified, independent State. And the king was so far convinced that for the next five years he allowed his chancellor to guide him in the transformation of the structure and spirit of the Church.

For Olavus the king had greater need in Stockholm than in Strengnäs. In 1524 the Strengnäs scholasticus became secretary in the City Council of the capital, and on April 27 made the first entry in the *Tänkebok*, or Record, which he was to keep until 1531. He tells us that the king requested his release from the bishop-elect of Strengnäs, for this new office. At the same time he served as preacher in the city church, St. Nicholas by name.

Stockholm,[51] first named in the records in the year 1252, had on account of its location as a key to the interior of Sweden, become the political and commercial center of Sweden in the later Middle Ages. Its castle and its church occupied, one the most strategic, the other the most conspicuous, spot on the tongue-shaped island, whence, in time, the city spread to the north and south shores of the mainland. The Dominicans and Franciscans each had their monastery, the latter Order also being represented by a cloister for sisters of the Rule. Near the St. Nicholas church lay the Council-house, where Olavus recorded the decisions of the Council. The pulpit in the church was small and placed high above the floor, wherefore "Olav in the basket" became a popular designation of the new preacher. The pastor of St. Nicholas between 1520-1523 had been Olavus Magni, who in the latter year became dean of the Cathedral Church in Strengnäs. About the time of the arrival of Olavus in Stockholm,

[51] H. Hildebrand, *Sveriges Historia*, I, Part 2, Intro., pp. 26-30.

St. Nicholas received as its new pastor Nicolaus Stecker,[52] the German secretary of Gustavus. Stecker was a German, born in Luther's native city, Eisleben, and a former student of Luther at Wittenberg in 1520. Thus both the pastor and deacon-preacher of St. Nicholas, after 1524, were anti-Roman. The presence of a German as pastor of the church is explained by the fact that half of the burghers of the city were of that nationality. The city had lost heavily in the struggles and plagues of the fifteenth century, and in 1524 could count but 770 taxable citizens.[53] Recalling the influence of the German merchants in the spread of the Reformation, we can understand the situation in Stockholm in 1524 and immediately succeeding years—it furnished a congenial atmosphere for the continuation of the work of Olavus Petri and Laurentius Andreae; it proceeded much faster in the transformation of preaching and cult than the rest of the kingdom; in fact, at times seemed to go too fast. Here Olavus Petri was to accomplish the task of his life, for which the preceding years and experiences had been the preparation.

[52] G. Carlsson, in *KÅ*, 1922, pp. 77ff.
[53] H. Schück, *Svensk Litteraturhistoria*, I, 216.

CHAPTER III

OLAVUS PETRI AND THE FIRST LITERARY PRODUCTIONS OF
THE SWEDISH REFORMATION

In February and in August, 1526, appeared the first printed Reformation literature in Sweden. *"Een nyttwgh wnderwijsning wthwr schrifftenne om menniskiones fall/och hurwledhes gwdh henne wprettadhe ighen/Hwilken mykit nyttugh är allom christinom meniskiom ath wetha/besynnerligha eenfålloghom prestom/som sådant plichtoghe äre theras almogha ath lära"* (An Useful Teaching from the Scriptures concerning the Fall of Man, and his regeneration through God, which it is very necessary that all Christians know, especially unlearned pastors, whose duty is to teach the common people) came from Richolff's royal press in Stockholm, St. Sigfrid's Eve, February 14, 1526. From the same press, on the fifteenth day of August, 1526, the New Testament in Swedish was given to the Swedish people. Royal approval was signified by the king's coat of arms, printed on the last page.

Neither of these books bore any name to reveal their authorship. And into modern days their authorship has been a disputed question. Olavus Petri and Laurentius Andreae have, since the sixteenth century, each been credited with the New Testament translation. Nor have there been wanting those who would credit Laurentius Andreae also with *An Useful Teaching,* though this has received less attention and been more generally conceded to Olavus Petri. The problem is both the more complicated and interesting because there appears to be a connection between the two books that has hitherto been slightly more than noticed. Since our approach to the question is from the side of Olavus Petri, we may formulate the problem thus: (1) Did Olavus Petri write *An Useful Teaching?* (2) What is the relationship between *An Useful Teaching* and the Testament translation? (3) Did Olavus Petri translate the New Testament?

But before we attempt an answer to the first query, we feel it necessary to give some description of the first evangelical book that was produced in Sweden. Its contents were indicated in its opening pages:

> The noble estate in which man was created
> How man forfeited this estate
> How God, through Moses, gave man the Law, through which he might realize his sin and evil condition
> The Ten Commandments, and how these are kept or broken
> The Credo, its 12 articles, what each contains and requires
> Prayer, with an exposition of Pater Noster and Ave Maria
> The Magnificat [1]

[1] A. Andersson, *Skrifter Utgifna af Svenska Litteratursällskapet,* II, 3, pp. lxxxiff., has found a proof copy of an older edition's first section, in which the Magnificat and the Seven Psalms are not listed in the Table of Contents. It consists of but eight pages, which have been slightly corrected in the later edition. Circumstances in the printery were such that at most only a month could have separated the two printings.

A right observance of Our Lord's suffering and death
An exposition of the Seven Psalms

Since 1893 the theory has been accepted that the Swedish book was based on Luther's *Betbuchlein*.[2] But as against Bang, who considered the entire work as a more or less literal translation of an edition of the *Betbuchlein* of 1524, A. Andersson [3] has pointed out striking differences. The first two sections, on man's creation and fall, are altogether independent; so also is the introduction to the Lord's Prayer. The conclusion of the latter section resembles passages in Luther's *"Sermon von dem Gebet."* The Magnificat is not found in the *Betbuchlein* in any edition prior to 1526. Nor are the Seven Psalms found in the various German editions of the work. The parts of the *Useful Teaching* that do follow *Betbuchlein* agree in many respects with a Hamburg edition of 1523. But, as a whole, "more than one half of the book is independent of the *Betbuchlein*—no edition of the *Betbuchlein* gives the same selection of contents—in no edition are the sections treated in the same manner as in the *Useful Teaching*." [4] The purpose of the book, then, could hardly have been to give in Swedish a translation of this devotional book of Luther that bears in itself the seeds of his later Catechism. As Luther, so did the Swedish author wish to make available for Christian people, and especially the clergy, an easy exposition of the main doctrines of the Christian religion as interpreted evangelically. But

[2] A. Chr. Bang, *Dokumenter og studier vedrorende den lutherske katekismus' historie i Nordens kirker*, Univ. Program, I, p. 91.

[3] Andersson, *op. cit.*, II, p. xliff.

[4] *Ibid.*, p. xlii.

Ecclesiastical Transformation in Sweden

the independence of the Swedish work suggests that there must be some other motive than translation that prompted the production of an evangelical book of Christian teachings.

I am inclined to believe that that motive is related to the appearance of another book of devotions in Swedish, namely, the *Tideboken* (*Horae*), a Catholic work which was printed sometime "after September 26, 1525, by Richolff in Uppsala."[5] It has indeed been pointed out that this work might have "influenced the author in the matter of the selection of material, which his book should include,"[6] but the influence, I believe, is more than one of form. *Tideboken* was the first religious book printed in Swedish. Its compiler is unknown, but it is clearly a strictly Catholic work. On the first page appears Pater Noster. Then follow:

Ave Maria
Magnificat
Hours of the Holy Spirit
Hours of the Cross, *"Herre wij hedrom tith kors Och wy dyrkom thina ärofulla pino"* (Lord we honor Thy Cross, and we adore Thy praiseworthy suffering)
The Seven Psalms, *"Oc äre ganska nyttoghe at läsa fore syw dödheligha synder"* (And are very useful to read before the Seven Deadly Sins)
List of Saints
Prayers to Christ and Saints
Credo—Commandments
The Seven Deadly Sins
Prayers

[5] *Ibid.*, p. iv.
[6] *Ibid.*, p. xli.

The influence of *Tideboken* upon *An Useful Teaching* is further evident when we find a very close resemblance between the two in the translation of Pater Noster and Credo. And in the Seven Psalms it is too much to say that the translation of *Tideboken* is "altogether different" (*"alldeles olik"* [7]) from that of the evangelical book. Undoubtedly the latter is a more scholarly and faithful translation, based upon Luther and Bugenhagen, but in point of language there are many resemblances. In fact the words and phrases are in numerous places identical. One is led to believe that the author of the Protestant book had the Catholic *Horae* before him. Considering, further, that the contents of the evangelical work are parallel to what the Catholic work presented, from its side, we feel drawn to the conclusion that the book of February, 1526, was intended as an answer to that of the fall of 1525. In both are: Pater Noster, Ave Maria, Magnificat, the Credo, the Commandments (without explanation, in the Catholic book), the Seven Psalms. The "Hours of the Cross" are matched with a *"right* observance of Our Lord's Suffering and Death." Of course the treatment in each varies greatly, as greatly as the faith of the respective authors differed. And it is clear that the Protestant drew much, if not most, of his material from Luther. But the point we wish to make is this, that Luther was for him a means and not an aim. His goal was not to translate Luther, but to use Lutheran writings to show how the evangelical teaching differed from the Catholic, to combat the effect of *Tideboken* by presenting the *Biblical* view of cardinal Christian doctrines as against the Catholic.

[7] *Ibid.*, p. xli.

Reference to the political and religious situation during the latter half of the year 1525 also confirms the opinion that a Catholic book of devotions in Swedish was not looked upon with favor by the king or his chancellor, and that it should at least not occupy the field alone.[8] This view of *An Useful Teaching* in no way detracts from the scholarly work, the independent spirit, and the literary qualities evident in the book. It but helps us to understand why the book appeared when it did, and why it had such a form as it possesses. The first literary production of the Swedish Reformation is not a copy of Luther, but an independent work, whose aim is to be found in its relationship to the Catholic *Tideboken,* and in its reference to the character of the Swedish Reformation in its earliest years. It hoped, not to suppress Catholic doctrines, but to supplant them.

Who was the author of this first evangelical writing? The editors of the *Works* of Olavus Petri have included it in their collection, and most scholars in the period (Schück, A. Andersson, Linderholm) speak of it as the work of this Reformer. Especially since the discovery in 1898 by O. Ahnfelt [9] of a hitherto unknown work by Olavus Petri, which is based upon and in places

[8] This view is further strengthened by a passage in Swart's *Krönika,* pp. 91-92, which Tegel included in his *History of Gustav I* (1622), p. 118. Swart relates that in the early part of 1526 the king reproached the archbishop-elect because "here in Sweden are absolutely (*platt inga*) no books produced in our Swedish tongue, except the Danish *Horae,* in which was mixed up much falsehood, contrary to the true teachings and sense of the Holy Scriptures." *Klemming, Sverges Bibliografi 1481-1600,* p. 152, note, in quoting Tegel's notice, says that the king believed the Swedish *Horae* to be a translation of the Danish of C. Pedersen—in reality it was modeled upon the almost contemporary Latin *Horae* printed by Richolff in Uppsala.

[9] "*Om Menniskans Ärliga Skapelse Fall och Upprättelse*," *Skrifter Utgifna Af Svenska Litteratursällskapet* (1898), II, 7.

is identical with the book of 1526, it has been less questioned that the earlier work is also from his hand. But as early as 1894 R. Steffen declared against O. Petri's authorship,[10] and has remained sceptical in later editions of his *Litteraturhistoria*. And N. Lindqvist, in his study (1918) of the language of the New Testament,[11] has not considered this work as sufficiently proved to be that of Olavus Petri. The most important argument against his authorship rests on the language of the *Useful Teaching*. In some respects it differs from the language known as the Reformer's own in the records of the court in Stockholm, where Olavus Petri was secretary from 1524.

But I believe that on a closer study of the variations of language even this argument falls. An acceptance of the conclusions of Lindqvist as to the forms used by Olavus Petri in 1525 in itself helps to prove the possibility of his authorship of the *Useful Teaching*. Among the principal forms in question are:

min, sin (mine, his), which O. Petri usually wrote *myn, syn*
wor (our), which O. Petri usually wrote *war*
noghon, -ot (some, any), which O. Petri usually wrote *naghon, naaghon, -ot*
såå (thus), which O. Petri usually wrote *saa*
åår (year), which O. Petri usually wrote *aar*
vid, vidh (with, beside), which O. Petri usually wrote *wijd*
wore (pret. were), which O. Petri usually wrote *waare, ware*.[12]

---

[10] *Samlaren, Extra Häfte*, 1893, "Våra första reformationsskrifter och deras författare," p. 7.

[11] *Reformationstidens Bibelsvenska*, p. 6.

[12] This list includes only forms concerned in *An Useful Teaching*.

Ecclesiastical Transformation in Sweden

N. Lindqvist's aim has been to establish the *"normal språk"*—the normal, or basic language of the New Testament translation of 1526. In this connection he has studied the language of Olavus Petri, and found that it underwent a change, in many respects a great change, in the months preceding the appearance of the New Testament in August, 1526. The cause of that change he finds in the work of translation and printing, and believes it to have been the influence of the language of Laurentius Andreae.[13] Though in many respects the evidence bears up these conclusions, I believe that *all* the changes cannot be attributed to such an influence. For many of these changes had become established by November, 1525, or December. This is particularly true of the forms listed above.

Of *sin* and *min*, Lindqvist says that they appear first in the Stockholm minutes, November 10, 1525, but do not gain ascendancy over the *y* form until March, 1526.[14] But I find no *y* forms between November, 1525, and March, 1526, whereas *i* forms occur December 11 and 18, February 12 and 28. Consequently the *i* form can be dated back to November, 1525.

War had become *wor* in April, 1525.[15]
Na(a)ghon changed to *noghon*, in June, 1525.[16]
Saa and *aar* became *såå* and *åår* in November, 1525.[17]

Widh, according to Lindqvist, supplanted *wijd* definitely in February, 1526,[18] but I find *vid*, November 8 and December 11, and *widh*, December 18, 1525.

---

[13] *Reformationstidens Bibelsvenska*, pp. 119-120.
[14] *Ibid.*, p. 113.
[15] *Ibid.*, p. 112.
[16] *Ibid.*, p. 113.
[17] *Ibid.*, p. 114.
[18] *Ibid.*, p. 113.

If any month should be selected as giving evidence of influence on the writer, it would appear to be November. By that time, also, he had settled on forms that later appeared in the book published February, 1526. In other words, the language of the *Useful Teaching* was the language of Olavus Petri during November, 1525. This is further witnessed by such forms as *haffde* (had), *ey* (not), *sidhen* (since). On the other hand, the forms *ecke* and *effther*, that occur in the printed work and not in the written, Lindqvist, in regard to the Testament translation, traces to the printer.[19] Since the printer was the same for the February and the August works, the statement would also apply to these forms in the *Useful Teaching*. Also the adjective ending *-ugh* in the printed work, as against Olavus Petri's more common ending *-igh*, can be attributed to the printer, who in his previous work, *Tideboken*, a few months before had used this form.

As a result of these observations, it would seem that little indeed is the ground for denying the authorship of *An Useful Teaching* to Olavus Petri. To the arguments in his favor can also be added one, alluded to by H. Schück,[20] from the *Chronicle* by P. Swart, that Olavus Petri "also wrote several small books very useful for instruction and introduction into the Word of God and had them printed."

Significant is the change of the language of Olavus Petri during the closing months of 1525. The probable cause was the preparation of his first manuscript for the printer. Apart from a probable later influence

[19] *Ibid.*, pp. 189-191.
[20] "*Våra Äldsta Reformationsskrifter och Deras Författare*," *Historisk Tidskrift* 14 (1894), p. 108.

the following year, no external influence on the language of the Reformer need be assumed. And from these changes we can deduce that in November he was busy preparing the work which was to counteract the Catholic production of the previous months. Consequently we would say that Olavus Petri wrote *An Useful Teaching* during November and December of 1525. During these months Richolff's printery in Uppsala became the Royal Press in Stockholm, managed by Richolff,[21] and during January and the first days of February the first evangelical book in Sweden was printed. On the fourteenth of February it issued from the press.

Our second problem concerned the relationship between *An Useful Teaching* and *The New Testament in Swedish,* which followed the former book from the press half a year later. Because it helps to throw light on the authorship of the Translation, we have deemed it important to go into this relationship as thoroughly as possible.

The points of contact are the Scriptural citations in the February work. There are in *An Useful Teaching* some forty important passages from the New Testament. The question arises, Were these made directly from the Latin, or German, or did the writer refer to a Swedish translation? If the latter can be assumed to be the case, how does it compare with the official translation printed in August? And finally, what can be deduced as to the authorship of the August work?

Here, too, there have been differences of opinion. Steffen does "not believe that they are produced by

[21] Andersson, *op. cit.,* XI, 3, pp. ii, iv.

the same person."[22] Andersson is positive that "the author (of *An Useful Teaching*) and the translator of *The New Testament* must be the same person.[23] The latter has observed the Scriptural quotations in the earlier work, and has drawn the conclusion that the writer followed the manuscript of the Translation. On the basis of the text in the section on The Magnificat from Luke i, Andersson claims that "the translation already (by 1525) proceeded at least to Luke."[24] But his statement that the quotation in The Magnificat and the passage in the Translation are entirely alike (*"alldeles ordagrant"*)[25] overlooks the wide variation in spelling and an important difference in the exposition from the Testament text.[26] Lindqvist's studies in the language of the New Testament give new importance to the question of the relationship between the two works.

First, it would seem necessary to determine the sources of the quotations found in *An Useful Teaching*. A careful study will soon show that they are *not* derived from the official Translation—the differences are too many and great. The passage in Luke i pointed out by Andersson is the exception and not the rule. And, as observed, even that exception is not identical with the later text.

Eliminating this possibility that the author of *An Useful Teaching* referred to a finished Ms. of the New Testament Translation for his Scriptural quotations,

---

[22] *Samlaren, Extra häfte,* 1893, p. 27.
[23] *Op. cit.,* XI, 3, p. lxviii.
[24] *Ibid.,* p. lxix.
[25] *Ibid.,* p. xxxv.
[26] *Useful Teaching* has: *"strax iach hördhe rösten aff thinne helssningh medh min öron"*; the Translation: *"strax rösten aff thina helsning kom j min öron."*

Ecclesiastical Transformation in Sweden 97

we have left four possible sources: He may have
quoted from (1) Vulgata, (2) Erasmus, (3) Luther,
(4) some translation of his own different from that
later printed. Under (3) may be included such
passages as are quoted more or less exactly from
Betbuchlein.

A critical study of the principal Scripture passages
in *An Useful Teaching* yields the following results:
UT signifies the work in question; V = Vulgata;
E = Erasmus; L = Luther; LB = Luther's *Betbuchlein*. The page numbers refer to Volume I of Olavus
Petri's *Collected Works*, where *An Useful Teaching*
is printed. < signifies derivation.

p. 51, Matt.	vi	UT<E	
54, Matt.	vi	UT<LB	
83, Matt.	ix	UT<V or E	
83, Matt.	v	UT<L	
70, Mark	ix	UT	resembles LB (UT *gråtande tårar*, LB *waynenden augen*).
105, Mark	vii	UT<L	
73-74, Luke	i[a]	UT<LE	and reminiscences of *Tideboken's* Magnificat.
74, Luke	i[b]	UT<EL	
53, Luke	xviii	UT<EL	
86, Luke	xxiii	UT<L	(a quotation from *Betbuchlein*, but the translation follows Luther's new Testament rather than LB).
93, Luke	xxii	UT<E	
90, John	iii	UT<LB	
83-84, Romans	iii	UT<L	
89, Romans	iv	UT<LB	
31, Romans	viii	UT<L	
26, Romans	xi	UT<E or L	

80, I Cor.	i	UT<E
80, I Cor.	iv	UT<L
29, I Cor.	iii	UT<E
29, I Cor.	xv	UT<E
28, II Cor.	v	UT<E or V
89, II Cor.	v	UT<L or V (a quotation from LB, but translation follows Luther or Vulgata rather than *Betbuchlein*).
30, Gal	v	UT<L
31, Gal.	ii	UT<E or V
91, Gal.	v	UT<V (a quotation from LB, but translation not as LB).
106, Gal.	vi	UT<EL
46, Eph.	iv	UT<E
47, Phil.	ii	UT<L
50, Phil.	i	UT resembles E or V.
88, I Pet.	ii	UT<LB
91, I Pet.	iv	UT<LB
91, Heb.	xii	UT<V (rather than LB, of which it is a quotation).

One conclusion from this study is evident—the author has not slavishly followed one translation then in print. Sometimes even in the matter of translating a verse or more from *Betbuchlein* he has independently followed some other source. In only a few cases does Vulgata appear to be his guide. In most instances he follows Luther or Erasmus.

Did the author choose his passages and sources as he wrote, or did he have his own translation before him, a translation based upon these various sources? When we consider how skillfully the writer uses these references, and how closely knit they are into the fabric of the book, it is difficult to believe that he had not long had them in his mind and used them in other connections. For these quotations are not added to the text as references, they are the very essence of the text, from which the exposition easily follows. The impression is left upon the reader that the writer moved in a Scriptural sphere and that his thought was formed by Scriptural truths that he had translated mentally as well as verbally. In some instances it almost seems that he quoted from memory, in the Swedish.

From a study of this problem I would venture the opinion that at least in large part the New Testament had been translated by this author, and that his Scripture quotations are not directly from other works but from his own, based on Erasmus and Luther.

And here we are reminded of a statement by the chronicler P. Swart, that Olavus Petri, in his Strengnäs years, c. 1523, used passages of the Old and New Testament, as the basis of his instruction.[27]. Is it not likely that he continued this using of Scriptural passages, translating them into the Swedish, and that by the end of 1525 he could have a considerable part of the New Testament in Swedish in his possession? That such was the case is the impression received from a study both of *what* he uses for his references, and, not less, *how* he uses them.

But when we turn to a comparison of these passages with the official translation, we cannot agree with Andersson that this was completed as far as Luke in 1525. For if we may use the term, "Olavus Petri's translation," we must say that it did not become the official translation in the form it existed in November,

[27] Swart, *Krönika*, p. 84.

1525. Judging by the passages before us in *An Useful Teaching*, we would make two propositions:

1. The translation of Olavus Petri is the basis of the official work.
2. The official translation is the result of a revision, by some other hand, of the basic material of Olavus Petri.

Further, judging the manner in which the translation of Olavus Petri has been changed, we can assume the norm of the reviser.

Returning to our list, p. 93, we would complement it by showing the nature of the revision. T = Translation. The smaller capitals E and V and L signify the text according to which P (Olavus Petri's) translation has been modified.

Matt.	vi	$T<P^{VL}$
Matt.	v	$T<P^{E}$
Matt.	ix	$T<P^{EL}$
Mark	ix	$T=P$
Mark	xiv	$T<P^{E}$
Luke	i^a	$T<P^{V}$ (almost identical, except for spelling and one change, which most closely follows V).
Luke	i^b	$T<P^{E}$or^{V}
Luke	xviii	$T<P^{EL}$
Luke	xxiii	$T<P^{E}$
Luke	xxii	$T<P^{E}$
John	iii	$T<P^{LE}$
John	xii[28]	$T=P$
Rom.	iii	$T<P$
Rom.	iv	$T<P^{L}$
Rom.	viii	$T<P^{E}$
Rom.	xi	$T<P^{V}$

[28] *Works*, I, 10.

I Cor.	i	$T<P$
I Cor.	iii	$T<P^L$
I Cor.	iv	$T<P^L$
I Cor.	xv	$T<P^L$
II Cor.	v	$T<P^{LE}$
Gal.	v	$T<E$
Gal.	ii	$T<L$
Gal.	v	$T<L$
Gal.	vi	$T<P^E$
Eph.	iv	$T<L$
Phil.	ii	$T<L^E$
Phil.	i	$T<L$
I Pet.	ii	$T<E$
I Pet.	iv	$T<L$
Heb.	xii	$T<V$

To these passages might be added Matt. vii (pp. 24, 49) and Matt. xxvii (p. 93), which have instances of $T = P$.

Returning now to the first proposition, that the translation of Olavus Petri was the basis of the official work, we would adduce as proof the striking similarity, in some cases even identity, between the two productions. The passages are too many, and the resemblances too great, to be only accidental. At the same time, a qualification of the proposition is necessary, for we have no evidence after the Epistle to the Galatians of an influence from Olavus Petri on the Translation (that is, evidence from *An Useful Teaching*). From Galatians, through Ephesians, Philippians, I Peter, and Hebrews the Translation has little in comman with the passages quoted in Olavus Petri's work.

But in the Gospels, and in Romans, I and II Corinthians, and in the last chapter of Galatians, there is abundant material to justify the statement that the final editor of the Translation had these books before him. But they have not entered into the official work unaltered. In most cases they have been revised so as to conform more strictly with Erasmus, in some instances with Vulgata. And even when the Translation follows Luther, it does so when it does not contradict Erasmus. In Mark and John we have passages that are identical. In I Corinthians the translation of *An Useful Teaching* has been corrected more nearly to Luther's.

In summary, our conclusion is that Olavus Petri had translated, by the end of the year 1525, at least the Gospels, Romans, I and II Corinthians, and Galatians. This translation was based upon Erasmus and Luther, principally. When the official translation of the New Testament was undertaken, the books already translated by our author were in large part adopted, but revised according to Erasmus. The language of the Translation differs from that of Olavus Petri, in the passages studied above. Consequently in many places in the Translation the language of Olavus Petri would yield to that of the reviser and editor, but the basic material of Matthew-John, Romans-Galatians still remains the work of Olavus Petri.

Our final question, then, is this, Does such a theory harmonize with known facts and statements in regard to the translation of the New Testament in 1526?

June 11, 1525, the archbishop-elect of Uppsala sent a letter to the prelates of the kingdom informing them that the king desired the publication of a New Testament translation into Swedish. Not only did His Majesty wish in this respect to follow the example of other nations (*"quod fere omnes nationes per totum orbem cristianum nedum ipsum novum testamentum ymo totam forsan bibliam in propria lingua haberent"*), but in the present state of religious controversy the

Ecclesiastical Transformation in Sweden 103

people should have the Testament in their language, in order to realize what was in dispute, and in order that the question might rightly be settled. Furthermore it was essential that the pastors who were to teach the people should be learned in the Scriptures, contrary to the present condition when few understand the Latin sufficiently well. Therefore the king had decided to divide the work of translation between the prelates and monastic orders, and by September the work of each should be sent to Uppsala.[29] But nothing seems to have come of this Catholic translation during 1525. In a letter of Bishop Brask to the archbishop-elect, dated January 23, 1526, we learn that the matter had been discussed again at the Council meeting at Vadstena (New Year, 1526) and in accordance with that discussion he now sent Magister Eric to Uppsala with the work allotted to his diocese (originally, Mark, I and II Corinthians).[30] This is the last we hear of the Catholic undertaking, which, judging by Brask's letters, was not enthusiastically pursued. From Peter Swart we hear that the prelates "never got anywhere, because they had but one text, namely, Jerome's."[31] In August the Protestant translation was ready. Neither from itself or from contemporary sources can we learn definitely who the translators were. H. Schück traces for us the statements of the following centuries.[32]

Messenius, in *Scondia Illustrata*, written during 1620-30, but not published before 1701, after mentioning the marriage of Olavus Petri (spring, 1525)

[29] *Handlingar till Skandinaviens Historia*, XVIII, 297-300.
[30] *Ibid.*, pp. 315-316. See *ante*, pp. 18-19.
[31] Swart, *Krönika*, p. 92.
[32] *Historisk Tidskrift*, 1894, "Våra äldsta reformationsskrifter och deras författare," pp. 97ff.

says: *"Fuit autem M. Olavus cum collegis versioni nunc intentus Novi Testamenti, translationem sequens D. Lutheri verbotim."* But as Messenius' work was not printed at the time, the statement of Baazius, in *Inventarium Ecclesiae Sveo Gothorum,* of 1642, became the authority for his and following generations. Baazius wrote: *"Translationem horum, exemplo et imitatione B. Lutheri, incepit M. Laurentius Andreae."* His basis was Johannes Magnus' *Historia Metropolitana,* in which the former archbishop-elect, who left Sweden when the Catholic cause was lost, vented his feelings against the king's chancellor in the declaration that Laurentius Andreae, following the example of Ulfilas, the Gothic translator, had corrupted the gospel of Christ. The conclusion of Baazius was followed by Schefferus, in *Svecia Literata,* 1680, and by Benzelius (through Schefferus), in the Introduction to the 1703 edition of the Bible.

In 1719 Peringsköld's *Monumenta Ullerakerensia* combined the previous authorities and described Laurentius Andreae and Olavus Petri as cooperating in the completion of a Swedish translation. Celsius, 1746, in *Gustaf den Förstes Historia,* followed Baazius, and Dalin, 1761, in *Svea Rikes Historia,* followed Celsius. Bergius, 1753, in *Nytt Förråd,* took Baazius and Peringsköld as authorities.

In the nineteenth century Anjou, the church historian, pointed out the doubtful aspects of the problem. So also did Reuterdahl, who found new grounds to the advantage of Laurentius Andreae, in his letter to Archbishop Olof of Norway, in August, 1526. But Schück has, ever since 1891, favored Olavus Petri, as against Steffen who claims Laurentius Andreae as the chief editor. We have already noticed the position of Andersson, that the translator was the author of *An Useful Teaching,* namely, Olavus Petri.

The latest investigation is that of Nathan Lindqvist, 1918, who has studied the problem from the point of view of language. Finding the usages of the two Reformers in their written work prior to 1526, Lindqvist has compared their language with that of the Translation. His conclusions are that there is a dominant language, which prevails especially from Galatians to the end, and in the Introduction. John is most variant from the dominant, or "normal" language; Mark and I and II Corinthians only somewhat less so. Matthew, Luke, Acts, and Romans compromise. The dominant language is that of Laurentius Andreae, who, in Lindqvist's opinion, was the chief editor of the Translation.

One source mentioned above is deserving of fuller attention. It is the letter of Laurentius Andreae, August 10, 1526, to Archbishop Olof, in Trondhjem. In regard to the New Testament translation, he writes: *"Circa finem laboris, quando iam opus per calcographum in proximo absoluendum fuit, venit michi in manus liber unus novi Testamenti in Danicam linguam translati. Spero tamen nostram translationem, castigationem esse.—Verum continere videtur in prologis et glosselis nonnichil scandali, a quo temperavimus nos in translatione nostra neminem libenter offendentes."* [33] In this letter Laurentius defended his Protestant sympathies to a former schoolmate, now a Catholic archbishop. He compared the new Swedish translation with the Danish, which had slavishly followed Luther. The Swedish work aimed not to give

[33] Quoted by E. Stave, *"1526 Års Öfversättning av N. T.,"* *Humanistiska Vetenskaps Skrifter* 3, p. 220.

offense, and the prologue and glosses were especially mentioned. Furthermore Laurentius spoke of *"nostram translationem"* and of the coming of the Danish book *"michi in manus,"* when the Swedish work had progressed almost *"per calcographum."*

Comparing this letter with the Translation we do indeed find proof of an aim *"neminem libenter offendentes."* In the summary of chapter xiv of Romans, Luther's attack on Roman Canones and Decretals was omitted. The books of the New Testament in the Preface were not numbered, thus avoiding a classification according to value. Some of Luther's glosses were entirely omitted.[34] Most important of all was the respect paid to the authority of Erasmus, who was normative for the whole work.[35]

Yet one more incidental reference that seems so far to have escaped the notice of investigators. In the Introduction (*Almennelighit förspråk*) to the Translation the writer anticipated criticism, especially from those who had seen only one book (Bible translation). Such were reminded that the translator (*tolk*) had seen several books and the work of several teachers (*flere lärares lecturer*). Accepting the conclusion of Lindqvist that the author of the Introduction was Laurentius Andreae, we can now arrive at some interpretation of this last phrase, as well as of the statements in the letter to Archbishop Olof.

The "work of several teachers" must have been primarily the work of Olavus Petri. Stave,[36] in a scholarly study of the sources of the 1526 Translation, found that it rests not on any "one book," but on

[34] *Ibid.*, pp. 192ff.
[35] *1526 Ars Ofversättning av N. T.*, p. 211.
[36] *Op. cit.*

Ecclesiastical Transformation in Sweden 107

Luther's Bible of 1522, on Erasmus' Latin Translation of 1522, on the Vulgate, and even shows traces of influence from the Greek edition of Erasmus.[37] The weighing of sources and final selection are to Stave certain proofs of scholarship on the part of the translator, who did not allow sympathies with Luther to outweigh respect for Erasmus. And for such work, practically all scholars agree that in Sweden during these years no one was better prepared or fitted than Olavus Petri. We come again to the conclusion, reached from our study of *An Useful Teaching,* that by the end of 1525 Olavus Petri had in his possession a translation of large parts of the New Testament.

Also, we would assert again the proposition that the material of Olavus Petri formed the basis of the official translation. And to how large an extent it entered into the printed work the studies of Lindqvist help us to discern. For we would here use his studies to another conclusion. Lindqvist has shown that Laurentius Andreae must be the editor of the Translation because his language is the same used in Matthew to Galatians, the similarity in Galatians being absolutely beyond doubt. But the very fact that another writer's language disputes, and disputes successfully, the field in Matthew to Galatians, is proof positive of the presence of another contributor in this, the largest and most important part of the New Testament. The only part that can be placed to the credit of Laurentius Andreae is that wherein he absolutely dominates in language, and that is from Galatians to Revelation, and in the Introduction. And even in this part,

---

[37] In the Introduction, the writer complains that it has occasionally been difficult to find Swedish words fully corresponding in meaning to the words in the Latin *or Greek*.

wherever a form not his own appears, there is evidence of another's influence.

It would seem fair to conclude, then, that the only part of the Testament actually translated by Laurentius Andreae is this latter part, from Galatians. Even here the previous work of Olavus Petri may have guided him. The Introduction is evidently Andreae's work.[38]

In the Gospels, Romans, I and II Corinthians, the evidence from the language agrees with our findings in *An Useful Teaching*. Here the work of Olavus Petri was determinative, and the role of Laurentius Andreae was that of reviser. The aim of his revision, further, was to bring, if necessary, the work of his colleague into closer conformity with Erasmus, thus minimizing the offense that the Swedish translation might cause. Much of the revision of Laurentius may have come in the "calcographum," of which he writes to Archbishop Olof. While engaged in this, *"venit in michi manus"* the Danish work. Psychologically the two thoughts seem to be connected, as they are parts of the same sentence. As chancellor to the king, to whom he would also be responsible for this Protestant work in a year not altogether favorable for the cause, Laurentius Andreae realized the necessity, as well as did the king, for a policy *"neminem libenter offendentes."* To safeguard the project, Laurentius felt called upon, if necessary, to "censor" the Translation. This too would prompt him to write the Introduction.

---

[38] In the Register, with which the Introduction concludes, are found expressions strongly reminiscent, even identical, with passages in *An Useful Teaching*. The Register may originally have been the work of Olavus Petri.

Our view then of the situation is that Olavus Petri is the actual translator of most of the 1526 Translation, whereas the work of Laurentius Andreae, apart from the revision of the whole, is limited to the Epistles (except Romans, I and II Corinthians) and Revelation. A book of which we found little trace in *An Useful Teaching,* but which Lindqvist classifies as variant from the language of Laurentius Andreae, is the Book of Acts. It is entirely probable that, in the spring of 1526, Olavus Petri translated this large section and collaborated in the production of the whole work as well. The importance of the *language* of Laurentius Andreae need not at all be minimized, but it ought not to be emphasized at the expense of the scholarship and literary qualities of Olavus Petri.

This theory, besides explaining the references to the Translation in the letter to Archbishop Olof, and in the Introduction, agrees with the statement in the closing passages of *An Useful Teaching,* that the Bible would soon be available, especially the New Testament, in Swedish. The author of the earlier work was posted on the progress of the latter, and, we believe, was himself engaged in its completion. Indications are not wanting that Olavus Petri was also at work on the Old Testament—the passage in *An Useful Teaching* suggests this, the translation of the Seven Psalms in this book affirms it.

From this viewpoint too can be understood both of the statements on which all later tradition has credited the work either to the one or the other Reformer. Messenius' statement that in the spring of 1525 *"fuit M. Olavus cum collegis versioni nunc intentus Novi Testamenti"* would be in accordance with facts, not the least interesting of which is the first change in Olavus' language, in April-June of that year. Messenius' further phrase, *"sequens Lutheri verbotim,"* would be only partly true, and explicable from his Catholic position. Also the assertion of Johannes Magnus, the basis of Baazius, that *"translationem— incepit M. Laurentius Andreae,"* would be true in the sense that he was the responsible editor before the king. We need not doubt that the chancellor was the force impelling a Swedish translation, and that its appearance at this time was due to him. But neither can we doubt that Olavus Petri was responsible for the *nature* of the translation that appeared, and that the completed work was to a very large extent the result of labors in which he had been engaged for some time. The dress was the work of Andreae; the body was that of Olavus Petri.

What we can discern of the work of Olavus in the New Testament in Swedish of 1526 leads us to see in him an independent, competent scholar, patient and resourceful, judicial and humble, who examined Erasmus, Luther, Vulgata, even *Tideboken,* and arrived at his own text. Even this he willingly permitted to be revised and used, anonymously, for the spiritual enlightenment of his people.

NOTE.—The relationship of *An Useful Teaching* to Luther's *Betbuchlein* can hardly be considered determined by Bang's conclusion, and is a problem which warrants greater study than has been accorded it by Swedish scholars. It might even be questioned if the Swedish work rested on *Betbuchlein* at all. In fact, the *Useful Teaching* seems to have been based on works of Luther that preceded the *Betbuchlein,* in which he gathered several previous productions. The section on the Creed in Olavus' work may have followed Luther's *Ein kurze Form* of 1519 as well as the *Betbuchlein,* and the section *"En gudeligh ååtanke"* in *An Useful Teaching* is more akin to *Auslegung deutsch des Vaterunsers,* 1519, than the *Betbuchlein.* The connection of the Swedish work to Paul Eliae's Danish translation of the *Betbuchlein* is also still in obscurity.

CHAPTER IV

THE POLEMICAL WRITINGS

IN 1524 the Imperial Reichstag met in Nürnberg. Its decisions in regard to the difficult situation created by Luther's teachings did not go far toward remedying it. "As far as possible" the Edict of Worms should be enforced, a General Council should be called to consider grievances ecclesiastical and civil, a German Assembly in preparation for this Council was to convene in Spires in November, at the Assembly the princes and estates should present the judgments of their universities and learned men on the disputed questions—such were the resolutions of the Nürnberg Reichstag. They were rendered invalid by the veto of the emperor in regard to the Council. The one decision that Charles V did accept, and proposed to execute, was that relating to the Edict of Worms, 1521, and this was the most reluctant and ambiguous of the Nürnberg decisions. The estates knew that the Edict of Worms could not satisfactorily settle the problem, but they had no other remedy to propose than a Council. The emperor would not consider the Council, and had recourse to the Worms decision. The result was the Catholic Convent of Regensburg and the Lutheran agreement at Spires.

A group of the Lutheran princes, however, did not consent to the elimination of the conciliar proposition. In August, 1524, Markgraf Casimir of Brandenburg,

Graf Wilhelm von Henneberg, and the Rath of Nürnberg met in Windesheim, and agreed upon twenty-three articles on which the controversy hinged, and to which the religious leaders should give their replies. In September, Casimir convened a Landtag in Brandenburg, and secured Roman and Protestant replies. From Graf Wilhelm, Graf George von Wertheim, as well as from Windesheim and Rothenberg, replies also came. In Nürnberg the Protestant reply, or Ratschlag, was written by Osiander, in consultation with Schleupner and Venatorius, preachers in the St. Sebald Church and in Neuen Spital, respectively. A Roman answer was also secured. The Ratschlag of Osiander, however, was not forwarded to the princes. Instead, the Rath commissioned three of the other clergy—Volprecht, prior of the Augustiner cloister; Stöckel, prior of the Carthusian cloister; and Furnschilt, preacher at St. Aegedien cloister—to formulate a Ratschlag. Osiander's work was a book of three parts, only the latter part of which dealt with the twenty-three articles; the Rath probably felt that a more concrete reply was necessary.

Neither the Volprecht Ratschlag nor the third part of Osiander's work appeared in print. But in 1525 there was printed in Nürnberg the Ratschlag of the Markgraf of Brandenburg's commission, consisting of six members, "preachers and others." It is this document that has a hitherto unnoticed bearing on the history of the Reformation in Sweden, and thus deserves further attention.[1]

[1] The foregoing is based on: Joh. Barth Riederer's *Abhandlung von Einführung des teutschen Gesangs in die evangelischlutherische Kirche uberhaupts und in die Nürnbergische besonders;* W. Möller's Andreas Osiander—*Leben und ausgewahlte Schriften;* the Preface to the Ratschlag.

The title of the book—a volume of over one hundred pages—reads: *Eyn Ratschlag/Den etliche Christenliche Pfarherrn/Prediger/uund andere/Gotlicher schrifft verstendige/Einem Fürsten/welcher yetzigen stritigen leer halb/auff den abschied/jüngst gehaltens Reichstags zü Nürnberg/Christlicher warhait underricht begert/ gemacht haben/die auch solchs Ratschlags zur notturft bekendtlich sein/Uund durch gotliche schrifft verthedigen wollenn.—Cum Gratia Privilegio Senatus 1525.*[2]

The twenty-three articles—the basis of this as well as of the other replies—are in content as follows:

1. The relationship of the Roman Church to the Holy Christian Church.
2. The binding power of the statutes of Pope, Bishop, and Council.
3. The interpretation of the Holy Scriptures.
4. The seven so-called Sacraments.
5. Penance.
6. Withholding of Absolution in certain cases.
7. Indulgences.
8. Withholding of wine in Communion.
9. The Sacrament in Monstrance and Procession.
10. Foundations, Masses, Vigilia.
11. The Mass in German.
12. Baptism in German.
13. Clerical marriage.
14. Denial of marriage in certain degrees of relationship.
15. The Monastic Orders.
16. Priests, other than those of Word and Sacrament.
17. If faith alone can save.

---

[2] A copy of this 1525 book is in the Royal Library at Berlin. A reprint is given in M. J. H. Schulin's *Frankische Reformationsgeschichte*, Nürnberg, 1731. The writer has had access to both.

18. The freedom of man's will.
19. Prayer to the Virgin and the Saints.
20. Images.
21. Ceremonies.
22. Fastings and holidays.
23. Prohibition of certain foods.

In December, 1526, Dr. Peder Galle in Uppsala received a circular letter from King Gustavus. "As you well know," it ran, " a great division has arisen in regard to the doctrines. We have written to learned men throughout the kingdom, giving them certain questions concerning those points on which the controversy most hinges, and requested to know their opinions as to what is most in accordance with the Scriptures." A reply was asked before Christmas Eve. The articles were ten in number.[3]

1. If one may disregard the usages and customs of the Church as taught by pious men, but without foundation in the Word of God.
2. If it can be proven that Our Lord Jesus Christ has given priests, Pope, Bishops, etc., any authority or power over men, other than that of preaching the Word and will of God to them; and, if there ought to be any other priests than such that do so.
3. If their laws, commandments, or statutes can bind men, so that it were sin to disobey them.
4. If they have any power to separate, by ban, any man from God, cutting him off as a member of the congregation of God and making him a member of the devil.
5. If that power and lordship which the Pope

[3] *GR* III, 331-333 (Dec. 4).

and his crowd *("hoop")* now have acquired, be in accordance with or contrary to Christ.
6. If there be any other service to God than that which consists in keeping His commandments.
7. If man can be saved through his merits, or solely through the grace and mercy of God.
8. If one shall venerate, adore, or worship the saints, and if the saints be our defenders, patrons, mediators or advocates before God.
9. If one shall be guided by any revelation other than has been given in the Holy Scriptures.
10. Concerning the Scriptural teaching of purgatory.

Olavus Petri also received a similar letter from the king.[4] He not only replied, but wished to debate the issues with Galle. Galle refused, whereupon Olavus alone defended his answers before the king, some of the Royal Council, Galle and others, in Uppsala, between Christmas and Epiphany.[5] Presumably at this time, two further questions were added:

1. If monastic life has any Scriptural foundation.
2. If any man has, or has had, power otherwise to institute the Lord's Supper than Christ has ordained.

On what grounds can a relationship between the Brandenburg Ratschlag and the Swedish "Twelve Questions" be affirmed? In the first place, the questions are practically the same. This, however, would not prove the one to be the source of the other. In the second place, Olavus, in a later work (*A Minor*

---

[4] Foreword to "Reply to Twelve Questions," *Works,* I, 225.
[5] Westman, *Reformationens genombrottsår i Sverige,* pp. 65-66.

Reply to Paulus Eliae, printed 1528, defended the king's circulating of the questions with these words: "Christian princes have done likewise before him, and therein manifested themselves as Christians in their office and responsibility."[6] That Gustavus himself had not formulated the questions is quite certain. In Denmark the Carmelite monk, Paulus Eliae, set himself to answer the questions, though he was "convinced that a heretic of Luther's group caused them to be given out, under such a title, that they might seem to be more authoritative when they came from a powerful prince and mighty king."[7] But Olavus himself confessed that "the king had been advised that on especially twelve points the controversy hinged," and these the king had "let be formulated in question form" and circulated.[8] Thus it is clear that they emanated from the Lutheran party, who knew of precedents to this procedure. That the precedent was the Brandenburg course becomes certain when we find that an important Swedish publication of 1528, *A Little Book Concerning the Sacraments,* is practically a literal translation from the Brandenburg Ratschlag! The importance of this latter influence is the more noteworthy when the close relationship of the works of 1527 and 1528 is considered. Nürnberg, as well as Wittenberg, gave inspiration to the polemical writings of the Swedish Reformer.

In May, 1527, the *Reply to Twelve Questions* was printed. It appears from the Preface that Peder Galle's reply had circulated in written if not in printed

[6] *Works,* I, 337.
[7] C. E. Secher, *Povel Eliesens Danske Skrifter,* p. 170.
[8] *Works,* I, 225; Preface to *Reply to Twelve Questions.*

form.[9] As might be supposed, the answers of Galle were "diametrically opposed" to those of Olavus. The Reformer therefore took Galle's answers, one by one, placed his original answers beside them, and concluded each section with a rebuttal of Galle's arguments. We thus have in this book a combat of the two forces, the old and the new, in the Swedish Church. The positions of the combatants were similar to those of their respective parties on the Continent. Galle argued that the Scriptures were too difficult to be understood in themselves; the Church, led by the Spirit, had to interpret them. The tradition of the Church furthermore must be respected. To this Olavus replied that only insofar as the Church's teachings could be proved by the Scriptures were they binding, and the traditions were not binding, since they were based on temporal expediency and did not affect the salvation of man. The second question, regarding the function of the clergy, Galle evasively answered by referring to the power given St. Peter to absolve sins and to the passages in St. Paul describing a variety of gifts in the Church. Olavus readily replied that pope and bishops cannot be greater than their Master and predecessors, Christ and the Apostles, who had no worldly dominion, and that the sacraments and *Horae,* with which the clergy occupied themselves, were unscripturally practiced, whereas the true duty

[9] Brask's printing press had been suppressed in January. In February the king accused him of having had literature printed in Copenhagen, and circulated in the kingdom (letter to Brask, Feb. 2, 1527, *GR* IV, 42, 43). It is not impossible that Brask had had Galle's reply printed in Copenhagen, and that thus the questions came to Paulus Eliae. If the answers of Galle were in print at the time of Olavus' appearance before the king in Uppsala, before January 9, they were most likely printed at Brask's press in Söderköping.

of the clergy was to preach, as it was the duty of the smith to forge. In his answer to the third question, Galle upheld the power of the Church to legislate in spiritual matters, through the activity of the Holy Spirit in the Church. Olavus thereupon pointed out that the legislation of the Roman Church not only violated or added to the Scriptures, but even contradicted itself in its teachers. Olavus, as did Luther, held to the sufficiency of the Word for the salvation of the soul, with which alone the Church had to do— in other spheres its decisions were not binding on the soul, in this sphere only the Word could bind. As a natural and logical sequence, Galle, in the reply to the fourth question, affirmed while Olavus denied, that the ban of the Church could sever a soul from communion with God. To the Roman doctor, the ban was a weapon of the temporal power of the visible Church. To the Reformer, it was but the exclusion of an unfaithful member, whose impenitent heart had already separated him from the fellowship of Christ. In his attempt at the defense of the temporal power of the pope—the fifth question—Galle had mostly to fall back on custom and "chronicle-histories," and Olavus found openings for direct thrusts. The deeds of churchmen "should be judged according to the Word of God, and not the Word of God according to human deeds." "The important thing is not how old a thing is, but how right it is. The devil is old, but not on that account any the better." In regard to the sixth question, both agreed that it was sufficient for a Christian to serve God by obeying his commandments, but the ways parted when Galle applied this obedience to a fulfillment of the customs of the Church, whereas Olavus placed this obedience in the daily life of love. "Since the commandments of God are commandments to love, all things can be accounted service to God which each one in his place and office does, out of love, to the benefit of his neighbor, as God has commanded. Thus when a man works for his wife and children, and children work for the parents, it is to be reckoned as service to God." A remarkable agreement occurred in the answers to the seventh point—both traced the salvation of man to the free grace of God.

Olavus admitted the similarity of the replies, but claimed that Galle did not realize what logical effects his answer would have to the matters of indulgences, fraternities, masses, etc. If he was sincere in his reply, Galle could not longer defend the works by which men sought righteousness. If salvation was a gift of God, it was free, and not to be earned. On the question of the Orders, the two were far apart. Galle defended the monastic life as a "pathway to salvation," a pathway making easier the journey of the soul to life in God. Olavus knew of but one "Way," namely, Christ. Only He could take away sins, and the grace of forgiveness was apt, nay more apt, to be found outside cloister walls. And what could be adduced as the special virtues of monks and nuns were in reality virtues to which all Christians were, in baptism, pledged. Again, in the matter of the Lord's Supper, Galle took recourse to the argument of the activity of the Holy Spirit in the Church, through which customs and rites not in the Scriptures are developed. And once more Olavus defended the principle of Scriptural normativeness. The withholding of the wine and the making of the sacrament a sacrifice were not the work of the Spirit, for they contradicted the Spirit's revelation in Holy Scriptures. The tenth question involved anew the continued revelation of the Spirit in the Church. Galle went to considerable pains to defend such revelation, and himself revealed the force of this argument on the minds of Roman churchmen. As a conclusion to a description of a revelation given to St. Augustine, he declared, "by this revelation the existence of purgatory can be proven. Though it is not related in the Old or New Testaments, yet this revelation is, on account of its truth and of St. Augustine's writing and wisdom, as certain as if it were related in Holy Scriptures." Equally clear was the assertion of the Reformer. "In the Scriptures sufficiently much is revealed for the salvation of the soul," wherefore no additional spiritual revelations were necessary or promised. Revelations beyond the sphere of the Bible were more apt to come from the Deceiver—the Devil—than from God. For the doctrine of purgatory—the eleventh topic—Olavus found ground neither in Scripture nor in the teachings deduced from Scripture. Galle found support mainly in "holy men's writings" and ancient custom. His method of argument drove Olavus, in his rebuttal, to the threefold "The Word of God, the Word of God, the Word of God" as the basis for proof. Likewise for the twelfth question Olavus found no affirmative reply, and expressed the suspicion that the adoration of saints was grounded more on a desire of the Church for financial income than on a desire of the adorer to praise God in His saints. The treatise closes with a confession of Olavus that some of its contents are contrary to the opinion of a part of the prelates, but "necessity demands it."

The *Reply to Twelve Questions* has always been

considered one of the most important of the Reformation treatises in Sweden,[10] even being termed "the first symbolical book" of the Swedish Reformation.[11] And its importance is not lessened by the fact that much of the material in the replies, as well as the questions, is derived from the Brandenburg Ratschlag. Olavus did not copy the answers there. Evidently he had studied this, drawn many Scriptural quotations from it, and found references to the Fathers. But he took these as raw material, worked them into other molds, fashioned his patterns according to needs in his Church, and, above all, imbued his replies with a personal seriousness and earnestness that made his work a creation of his own. The Ratschlag was more comprehensive, more judicial in form, almost impersonal. The *Reply* of Olavus was living, vibrant, not lacking in sarcasm, irony, even ridicule. But he was conscious of the importance of his work—the first *official* attack on the Roman Church to appear in print. Prestige and tradition were on the side of the old man; virility and a conviction of truth on the side of the young man. In this work the evangelical forces of Sweden found a clear statement of the nature of the Church which should replace the old structure when it fell—as it did at Vesterås Riksdag, the month following the appearance of this book.

Two months earlier, March 28, the first polemical writing of Olavus had issued from the press. It bore the title, *Reply to an Unchristian Letter,* and was directed against a monk in Denmark, Paulus Eliae (also called Povel, or Paul, Helgeson). We have, however, treated of the *Reply to Twelve Questions*

[10] Westman, *op. cit.,* p. 346; *cf.* Anjou, *op. cit.,* I, 186-203.
[11] Holmqvist, *Svenska Reformationens Begynnelse,* p. 88.

first, since this work occupied Olavus as early as December, 1526.

Paulus Eliae was the leading Humanist in Denmark in the beginning of the third decade of the century. Born of a Swedish mother and Danish father, about 1480, in Varberg, Halland (then Danish territory), he seems to have spent his early years at Marie Cloister at Helsingör. In Scholasticism he had no great interest, but was attached to the Church Fathers, and to St. Bernard and St. Birgitta. For Erasmus he had great admiration, and, as his disciple, not only often quoted him, but translated some of his works. Like Erasmus, he deplored the ignorance and customs of the clergy, and wished for a reformation within the Church. In 1519 Paulus was named *primus regens* at the newly instituted collegium of the Carmelite cloister in Copenhagen, and along with this office held the position of the docent of the Order at the University. His main interest lay in the Scriptures. This gave him the inspiration of his own life, determined his conception of Truth, and led him to a criticism of the abuses existing in the Church. Toward Luther he was at first friendly, and kindly received Martin Reinhart, whom Luther sent to Copenhagen in 1520 on the request of King Christian for an evangelical preacher. But when, in October, Luther published the *Babylonian Captivity,* and, the following January, the pope published the ban, Paulus Eliae showed stronger sympathy for the Roman Church. With the king he came to odds. Christian II had asked for a translation of Machiavelli's *Il Principe*. Paulus presented him with a translation of Erasmus' *Institutio principis christiani,* explaining that this might serve a more righteous purpose. His further attacks on the king in his sermons led Christian to revoke the grant on which his docenture was founded, and Paulus left Copenhagen in 1522. But he continued to aid the enemies of the king, who finally was forced from the kingdom (1523). Frederick, his successor, did not long meet the hopes of the monk, and in his *Chronicle* of 1524 the latter characterized the confiscatory policy of the king as the acts of a "Church-robber." Toward the nobles he was as critical as toward the ignorant clergy, criticizing their pride and abuse of worldly power. In 1524 he became provincial superintendent of the Carmelite Order. His doctrinal position, however, was as unsatisfying to the Lutherans as to the Roman adherents, and his vacillation in time earned him the name of "turncoat." When Luther's *Betbuchlein* appeared in Denmark in 1524, he translated it in an orthodox spirit, but when, that summer, the Roman bishops prevailed upon the nobility to oppose the Lutherans, and to forbid Luther's books in the country, Paulus concealed his translation. The Lutherans, however, counted him as one of their party. In 1526 he let his *Bedebog* (*Betbuchlein*) be printed, declaring, however, in the Preface, that he was no Luther disciple—he merely made use of material that Luther had taken from others. On June 24 he preached a sermon before the king, at the castle, in which he openly attacked Luther. The response was ridicule on the part of soldiers and people. His spokesman before the king was the marshal of the kingdom, Sir Tyge Krabbe, one of the most powerful men in Denmark. In 1527 Paulus was again Lektor at the University on behalf of his Order—in 1525 he had been named professor of theology as a member of the faculty. His position was now definitely Roman. In

1530 he left Copenhagen, to appear there again in 1533 as the accuser of Hans Tausen, the Lutheran leader. Retiring to Roskilde, Paulus after 1534 is lost to history.[12]

Between the Catholic party in Sweden and in Denmark a relationship may not only be assumed but can also be proved. In December, 1526, Bishop Brask wrote to Ture Jönsson, a leader of the Roman party, to inquire concerning a letter that Sir Ture had written to Sir Tyge (Krabbe) in Denmark.[13] From some one of the old order in Sweden Paulus Eliae had received the questions the king had submitted to his prelates in the same month.[14] The following February Bishop Brask was accused by Gustavus of having propaganda printed in Copenhagen.[15] When, later in the year, Brask deserted his diocese and country, it was to Denmark that he turned. Two years later the fugitives, Sir Ture and the Bishop of Skara, followed, and received the protection of the Danish Council. In May, 1529, Sir Tyge advised Gustavus that the Lutheran case had no prospects.[16]

To Olavus the meddling of Paulus Eliae in the Swedish situation was unwelcome. Sometime during the latter half of 1526 Paulus had written a letter to Sir Tyge, his protector, in which he undertook to overturn the whole Lutheran structure of teachings.

[12] C. J. Engelstoft, *"Paulus Eliae,"* in *Nyt historisk Tidskrift,* II; A. Heise, *"Paulus Eliae og Martin Reinhard,"* Ny Kirkehistoriske Samlingar, V; *Povel Eliesens Danske Skrifter,* utg. E. C. Secher; Ehrencron-Müller, *Författar Lexicon III,* p. 500; Schück, *Striden mellan Ol. P. samt P. Galle samt Paulus Heliae,* Samlaren, 1886, pp. 65ff.
[13] *GR* III, 424.
[14] *Works,* I, 343.
[15] *GR* IV, 42, 43 (Feb. 2, 1527).
[16] *GR* VI, 383 (May 22, 1527).

Copies of this letter circulated in Sweden, and Olavus paid it the tribute of being, on first thought, "quite true."[17] It was, indeed, so persuasive that many might be misled, and therefore Olavus thought it necessary to refute it, item by item. Paulus' letter is not preserved, and its contents can be judged only by the excerpts or points that Olavus first presents from it, before his own rebuttal. The work was printed March 28, 1527, under the title *Reply to an Unchristian Letter*.

In the main, the *Reply* is a defense of Luther. Olavus did not think that Luther needed a defender—"he can indeed defend himself"—but he did not wish Paulus' attack on Luther's teachings to go unchallenged. Paulus had first aimed at Luther's denial of authority in the Church, a teaching that had produced bloodshed. The reference was to the Peasants' War, and Olavus took pains to distinguish between the spiritual freedom which Luther asserted for the Christian, and the obedience to temporal authority which Luther had never questioned. As to the cause of bloodshed and strife, it was to be found not in the Reformer, but in the long history of Roman abuses which made a Reformation necessary. The point was the more important on account of the political situation in Sweden, wherefore Olavus stressed the political intrigues of the pope, which had been to the detriment of kings and nations.

Luther's doctrines in regard to faith versus good works as the means of salvation was Paulus Eliae's second target. Olavus did not enter into a theological dispute, but instead gave a presentation of Luther's teaching in regard to faith. This calm, clear exposi-

[17] *Works*, I, 154.

tion is among the best passages in the work. "The great mercy of God is proclaimed to us in the Gospel. When we put our confidence therein, having full faith and trust in God, not doubting but that what he has promised us in Christ shall be given us, then God considers us, through this faith, righteous and upright, so that we can stand in His presence. Along with this faith—itself a gift of God—there is diffused in the heart of man the Holy Spirit which is a gift secured to man through Christ. The Spirit so transforms the heart which previously was evil that it begins to be good and to incline to that which is good. When thus the heart has become good through the Holy Spirit working in faith, then first man does deeds which are favorable to God, but not before."[18] "It is not strange that Luther speaks so much good about faith, for it is never without good deeds."[19]

A third section concerned the sacraments. Here Paulus had assailed Luther's defiance of the teachings of the Fathers, of the Church, and even of some of the books of the Bible. The reply of Olavus went to show that Luther did indeed question the authority of the Church teachers wherever they contradicted or went beyond the Scriptures. Paulus Eliae's reference to Luther's doubts concerning books of the Bible, Olavus characterized as a "manifest lie." The only exception he allowed was the Letter of James, and here Luther had Eusebius and Jerome and Erasmus of Rotterdam in his company. Olavus emphatically claimed that even Luther himself should be judged by the Scriptures. "He is a fallible man like others of us, and can go astray as well as we. But he advises us to hold to the Scriptures. If we see that his words

[18] *Works*, I, 162.   [19] *Ibid.*, p. 164.

agree with Scripture then we should follow him, otherwise not." [20] The discussion of the Sacraments naturally led to that of the mass, and here Olavus in detail expounded Luther's doctrine of the mass, not as an offer, but as a proclamation of the death of Christ and of the grace therein offered man.

In the fourth place, the Danish critic had assailed Luther's stand toward the temporal power of the Church. Luther's Swedish disciple was as clear as his master on the duties of the clergy. "The clergy are commissioned to proclaim and spread the Word and Sacraments and Mysteries of God—but therein they are servants and not masters." [21] For precedents Olavus sought only in the Bible, and he found there no justification for the temporal claims and worldly power of the papal Church. "The mission of Christ in this world was not concerned with worldly realms, so that he wanted to transform them, but He is come for the sake of the spiritual realm, which He would again establish." [22]

The following section of the *Reply* is a Paulus Eliae-Olavus Petri debate on the Erasmus-Luther dispute concerning the freedom of the will. Paulus' standpoint is that of Erasmus, and his arguments are the same. Olavus had read and studied Luther's *De Servo Arbitrio* and his refutation was based on Luther's book. The disciple could not penetrate further than the teacher, and Olavus' conclusion was that of Luther, that man cannot understand the will or way of God but must believe what He has revealed in His Word.

[20] *Ibid.*, p. 168.
[21] *Ibid.*, p. 186.
[22] *Works*, I, 183-184.

"His mysterious operations far, far surpass our understanding, so that concerning them we can give no other verdict than that we are absolutely certain that He who is Righteousness can do nothing except what is righteous." [23]

The question of the Spirit's continued revelations in the Church, by virtue of which the Church could institute new customs and build up an ecclesiastical authority, had also been a subject in Paulus Eliae's attack on Luther, who denied such an extra-Biblical revelation and authority. Olavus claimed that "in the Scriptures we seek nothing else than our salvation," and for this the Scriptures were sufficient. All practices and statutes of the Church were changing and relative. Therefore they could not be binding on the soul, and were matters subject to revision. Salvation does not depend upon them, consequently they are adiaphora, which the Church cannot enforce as essential. And in the essentials of salvation the Church is regulated by the Scriptures, not the Scriptures regulated by the Church.

Seventhly, Luther, according to Eliae, had repudiated the century-old custom of the Church in the adoration of the Virgin and the doctrine of the saints. Again, Olavus found no Scriptural authority for these teachings; in fact they were against Scripture. One should "honor God in His saints" but this is not identical with the "honoring of saints." [24] And the saints are not all dead—"a Christian is a saint," and the living saints can better appreciate our honor than can the dead saints. The Church's advocacy of so many

[23] *Ibid.*, p. 191.
[24] *Ibid.*, I, 208.

saints as "mediators" gave rise to the suspicion that it was "more for the sake of the belly than for the love to these saints." [25]

In briefer terms Olavus replied to Paulus Eliae's last criticisms of Luther, regarding fasts in the Church, the wealth and holdings of the clergy as against the nobility, and the abuses of the Mendicant Orders. He closed his book with an explanation that he had probably been more severe than some would deem necessary, but the lies and shameful statements of his opponent were to Olavus a sufficient reason for the tone of his letter. In case it should be found and could be proved that Olavus had not held himself to the truth of the Scriptures, he was willing to be corrected. His hope, however, was that he had so founded his letter on the Bible that it should stand the test.

The similarity between the *Reply* and *The Twelve Questions* is very striking. The questions discussed are practically the same in both works. In some of the items Olavus used much the same argument, e.g. in regard to true service to God, the Sacrament of the Altar, the worship of saints. It is possible that the two documents were written almost at the same time— the first months of 1527.[26] In general, however, the similarity reveals the universal nature of the factors that gave rise to the Reformation. Whether it be Luther in the *Letter to the Nobility*, in 1520, or the

---

[25] *Ibid.*, p. 215.
[26] The date of Paulus Eliae's letter to Sir Tyge Krabbe is uncertain. Schück believes "the latter part of 1526" is probable. Engelstoft (*op. cit.*) assumed a date soon before or after Paulus' sermon at the castle, which A. Heise (*op. cit.*, p. 296) corrected as being June 24, not August 29, 1526. Their circulation in Sweden could well be placed at the latter part of 1526.

leaders of the reform movement in southern Germany, the Ratschlag of 1524, or the Danish Carmelite monk in 1526, or the Swedish Reformer in 1527, all discuss practically the same questions with a fervor and tone that make manifest the pressing nature of these problems and their actual importance. They were not theoretical propositions for debate, but living issues that attracted the attention and directed the pens of the best minds from Switzerland to Sweden, from Paris to Prague. Olavus had something of Luther's vehemence and assurance in his stand as against Galle in Uppsala and Paulus Eliae in Copenhagen. There was not in his writings the originality, the power of expression, especially in respect of lucidity and terseness. But no less than Luther, he pointed to the true authority of the Church—the Scriptures—and to the true freedom of the individual directly to seek his Lord.

Meanwhile, Paulus Eliae was again preparing to enter the Swedish lists. He had received a copy of the king's *Questions* (the original ten) and the replies of Olavus and Galle.[27] He did not think Olavus had the ability nor Galle the courage rightly to answer, whereupon he decided to give the Swedish king his own answers. He took occasion to reprimand Gustavus for what had happened in Sweden at Vesterås, and described the situation in Sweden as apostate from the true religion. Furthermore, he submitted twelve questions to the king, touching mostly on the power, prestige, and property of the Church and clergy,

[27] *Works,* I, 337. Schück (p. 69) assumes that the "Ten Questions" with the replies of Galle and Olavus (without rebuttal) had been printed (though no copy is preserved) and that Paulus Eliae had received this. The Reply of Paulus had but ten questions. *Cf.* C. E. Secher, *Povel Eliesen's Danske Skrifter.*

which, in Sweden, had lost their former standing.[28] The address and questions to the king were circulated in writing during 1527; the book, with the replies to the Ten Questions, was printed April 21, 1528.[29]

In May, 1528, Olavus had come upon a copy of the Address and questions to the king. June 22, 1528, *A Minor Reply to Paulus Eliae* was printed. It was the most stinging of the polemical works of Olavus. Paulus was bidden to try his hand in stemming the reformatory movement in Denmark before offering his unwanted and unnecessary aid to Sweden. Sweden had not forsaken the true faith which Ansgarius and Sigfrid had brought to its shores, for of that faith "few have ever heard." [30] They "taught us to hold closely to the promises and Word of God, to trust in the death and passion of Christ who had reconciled us to the heavenly Father whom we had displeased, and earned for us eternal life. That we should believe and depend upon, and in that faith have a brotherly love one to another, and do good to each other." [31] From such a faith Sweden had not fallen. In fact, it was returning to it, now that its eyes had been opened to the true nature of the Church, whose leaders "had received the command of God to preach the Word of God as Christ and the apostles had done, and not ride many high horses, and rule castles and cities." [32] From the Roman Church, Olavus confessed, Sweden had departed, "but we demand always to

---

[28] Paulus Eliae had already had occasion to criticize two Danish monarchs, and his characterization of Gustavus was probably not greatly different from that of Frederick.

[29] Schück, *op. cit.*

[30] *Works*, I, 340.

[31] *Ibid.*, p. 339.

[32] *Works*, I, 335.

remain in that Christian communion, which is assembled not only in the Roman Empire, but throughout all the world." [33] To the questions of Paulus, Olavus gave very brief answers, as he did not consider it necessary further to defend the course of the king.

In the *Twelve Questions* and the *Reply to Paulus Eliae,* Olavus had given promises of a more extensive work, in which the subject of the mass would be fully discussed.[34] In August, 1528, *A Little Book Concerning the Sacraments* was issued, as the fulfillment of these promises. It does not bear the name of Olavus, and is described as being presented in Swedish (*"uthsatt på Swensko"*). Hitherto the authorship has been questioned, as well as its originality.[35] That it is a translation is no longer in doubt. Olavus Petri as the translator, however, is still the most probable explanation.

A Little Book Concerning the Sacraments is a translation from the Brandenburg Ratschlag, printed in 1525, items 4-12 inclusive. The main, and almost sole, difference is in a slight rearrangement of the topics. The order of the Swedish translation is as follows:

1. The Nature of a Sacrament.
2. Baptism.
3. Penitence.
4. Confession.
5. Distinction between Public and Secret Confession.
6. Absolution.

[33] *Ibid.,* p. 342.
[34] *Ibid.,* pp. 176, 288.
[35] Westman, in *Works* I, xxviii, attributes it to Olavus Petri. Holmquist, *Sv. Ref. Begyn.,* pp. 116-117, thinks it might partly be a translation.

7. Penance.
8. Indulgences.
9. Consecration and Election of Priests. Apostolic Practice.
10. Confirmation.
11. Extreme Unction.
12. Marriage. Forbidden Degrees.
13. The Lord's Supper (a group of items).
14. Foundations, Masses, Vigils.
15. Mass as a Sacrifice.
16. Spiritual Priesthood.
17. Mass and Prayers for the Dead. True Prayer.
18. Purgatory.
19. The Mass in the Vernacular.
20. Baptism in the Vernacular.

Among the few, minor additions, the most noteworthy are the paragraphs on the baptism, in which water is held to be the only necessary earthly element, and on the meaning of baptism as the beginning of the Christian life. The section on the distinction between public and secret confession, and a part of that on absolution, is not in the Ratschlag. Likewise the first part of the section on Penance is independent. In that on Indulgences, a short paragraph concerning the effect of indulgences on souls in purgatory is added. Some new material is introduced in the section on Marriage. The material regarding Purgatory is somewhat differently arranged in the translation, but the contents are the same. Otherwise the book (sixty-eight pages in the *Works*) closely follows the German. In it Olavus gave to his Church probably the best exposition then available of the teaching of the Lutheran as against the Roman Church. The Ratschlag was systematic, clear, decisive. In Sweden as in Germany there could no longer be any doubt as to the implications of the new doctrines. Events in Sweden soon revealed that the Book was understood. Eight months later, the manifesto of the uprising in Småland counted as one complaint, that the "king had degraded the sacraments, as is sufficiently evident in the books that he has allowed to be published this past winter, in regard to the sacraments." [36]

In the treatment of the subject of marriage in the *Book of the Sacraments* the translator promised a fuller discussion of the matter in a succeeding work.[37] August 27, 1528, the book was ready. Its title suggests its contents—*A Short Instruction Concerning Marriage/to whom it is permitted/wherein it is thoroughly proved that the clergy may live in matrimony/and thereafter a brief admonition follows to the bishops and prelates and their clergy here in Sweden.*[38] Its opening passages are reminiscent of Luther's *Vom Ehelichen Leben,* 1522, and the Swedish, as did the German Reformer, divided his book into three parts. In the first part the two developed the same thoughts. Marriage depends on the created nature of man and woman, which cannot be changed by human statutes. Its purpose is given by the Creator Himself; therefore man may be assured that the married state is well pleasing to Him. Faith in God's wisdom and support overcomes all the difficulties and cares involved in the rearing of the family. The similarity of the material of the two authors furnishes an occasion to compare their treatment, and reveals their distinguishing char-

[36] *GR* VI, 356-358 (April 4, 1529). The book printed August 24, 1528, could well be described as appearing in the "winter," as its spread would hardly have been great before September or October.
[37] *Works,* I, 400.
[38] *Ibid.,* p. 443.

acteristics. Luther handles the difficulties of the problem boldly, candidly, even humorously. His description of the father occupied with details of the nursery while amused neighbors look scoffingly on is entirely in keeping with his humanity. His discussion of the power and nature of sexual instincts is not inferior to that of modern psychologists who approach the problem from the purely scientific side. Olavus Petri, however, ostensibly drew back from the frankness and detail of his master. Instead of references to the household life (which Olavus in 1528 knew better than Luther in 1522!), the Swedish writer described man's defense of family and home in time of war. But he was equally clear with Luther in the conviction that man and woman in their everyday tasks fulfill the supreme law of God, the law of love expressed in terms of service. Olavus has been considered as revealing in this work his own melancholy view of marriage,[39] but the book is entirely objective and, like Luther's, is an attack on the celibate life as a purer or holier life. Of its joys, or of love as its deepest basis, Luther said as little as Olavus.[40] Nor can either justly be judged by a norm that belongs rather to our own than to the sixteenth century. As far as the Reformers were concerned, their aim was to show that the monastery was not holier than the home. Both were persuaded that family life, even as it was, came closer to the ideal than cloister life, even as it might be. No higher praise of marriage could come from these men than in their placing the hearth above what had hitherto been held as the highest state of man.

[39] R. Holm, *Olavus Petri*, p. 52.
[40] Elsewhere Luther has dwelt more on love as the ideal basis of matrimony.

Ecclesiastical Transformation in Sweden

Whereas Luther in his book continued in the second and third parts to speak of the grounds of divorce and the right manner of married life, Olavus treated, in the second part, of those to whom marriage was not permitted, and, in the third, of the arguments which the Roman Church had used in restricting marriage. As in the Ratschlag, denial of marriage to the clergy was attacked as being against the Will and Word of God, the nature of man, and the conciliar decrees of the early Church.[41] Then the objections of the Church to the marriage of its clergy were investigated and refuted. Olavus pointed out to his fellow countrymen that married clergy were the rule in Sweden until three hundred years ago, and that the practice still prevailed in the Greek Church. As Luther, Olavus closed his treatise with an admonition to the clergy to forsake the celibate state, if they did not find themselves in the category to which God, not the pope, had denied marriage. Olavus could even assure his followers that they stood in no danger of losing their positions, if they decided to establish a home—a suggestion of the official nature of this polemical work of 1528.

More bitter in tone than the attack on celibacy was the next production of Olavus—*A little book in which the monastic life is described/wherein something is also said of the injury and ruin this life has occasioned in Christendom/Then follows a short admonition to the monks and their friends.*[42] The title page bore the motto, "They shall have no further progress/for their folly is apparent to all." (II Tim. iii.) The work had been for some time in the mind of its author.

[41] *Works*, I, 454-457; *cf. Ratschlag*, p. 77.
[42] *Ibid.*, pp. 473ff. (printed Nov. 30, 1528).

Both in his controversy with Paulus Eliae and Peder Galle the monastic life had entered into the discussion; to both he had promised a fuller treatment later.[43] He undertook the task hesitantly—"I confess I am altogether too incompetent to express adequately (as one ought) that deception and falsehood which has been practiced in monastic life for many centuries.— The ungodly movement is greater than any one man can fully describe."[44] But once begun, Olavus worked out a comprehensive polemic against the whole system. He began with a history of the origin and growth of the monastic movement, enumerating the long list of Orders into which monasticism spread and divided itself. He went to the trouble of even describing the distinguishing garb of these Orders. Next examining the three vows of the Orders, he found nothing in them that was not included in the vow that all Christians were subject to, by virtue of baptism. "God's Word teaches that he who would be a member of His Kingdom must be chaste and pure, poor and obedient—but as this Kingdom is spiritual, so also are chastity, poverty, and obedience spiritual qualities, and he is most perfect who best exemplifies them in his spirit, even though he be married, rich, and of high position in the world."[45] Developing this argument, Olavus showed that the virtues of chastity, poverty, and obedience not only were compatible with the life in the home and the community, but were more sincerely and fully practiced there than in the cloistered cell. The fundamental error of monasticism was its selfish-

[43] *Works*, I, 167, 280. The book of 1528 is to a great extent an elaboration of the answer of Olavus to the eighth question in *The Twelve Questions*, pp. 278-280.

[44] *Ibid.*, p. 475.

[45] *Ibid.*, p. 486.

Ecclesiastical Transformation in Sweden 139

ness, the desire for reward which men believed could be earned in solitude better than in social life. Taking especially the vow of chastity, Olavus endeavored to prove that not the outward state but the inner nature determined man's position before God, and that the inner character had little to do with monastic rules and purposes. Far from improving the condition of Christendom, the Orders had done irreparable harm to the Church by their divisions, their perversion of the Christian ideal of life, their forfeiting of chastity for immorality, poverty for untold properties, obedience for social immunity. Their distinct garb had been to the offense of Christian life, no less than their sale of good deeds by letters of indulgence and fraternities. The whole movement was but a market—"Vigilia mart, mass-reading mart, singing mart, fasting and wake mart."[46] Worst of all were the Mendicants. Of the previous Orders it could at least be said that they did some work, but these substituted begging for work, and deceit for need. "There can be no doubt that when the Devil was loosed after the lapse of one thousand years, as the Revelation of John relates, he instituted the Begging Orders."[47] The constitution of these four Orders is then described. Of them all Olavus could say, "No true monk who wishes to adhere strictly to the monastic life can be a true Christian, in like manner as no upright Christian can be a good monk."[48] As in the treatise on "Marriage," so here, an admonition concludes the work. Here Olavus called upon the cloister members to forsake the ungodly life, and urged parents and friends to aid the

[46] *Works*, I, 503.
[47] *Ibid.*, p. 504.
[48] *Ibid.*, p. 511.

monks to a more normal form of life in the Christian community.

In both Luther and the Ratschlag Olavus had precedents for his polemics against the monastic life, and undoubtedly much other anti-monastic literature had found its way into Sweden. But in this treatise the author has followed no known models, but built up his own attack. From the earliest years of his preaching, beginning at Strengnäs, Olavus had preached against the Orders. Never himself a monk, he seems to have had deep prejudices against the vow. To him it constituted a repudiation of the Christian doctrines of the free grace of God and the liberty of a Christian. But he saw also the political and social implications of the system, and was one with his king to rid his country of the "plague." To the realization of that purpose, his book undoubtedly contributed much.

The last of the long list of anti-Roman writings of the year 1528 came from Olavus in December, under the title *Concerning the Word of God and the commandments and statutes of men in things spiritual/which is/the realm of the soul.*[49] The title indicates the two large divisions of the book: The Word of God; The Statutes of Men. In the first part the author entered into a consideration of the metaphysical nature of the "Word," which is discussed in a manner unlike Olavus' usual style. This has led Schück to call this work the noblest and deepest of all Olavus' writings. This treatment of the "Word," however, is not original with Olavus. Its source, like that of the *Book of the Sacraments,* was in a book from Nürnberg.

We have already noticed that the Nürnberg Rath

[49] *Ibid.,* I, 525ff.

turned to Andreas Osiander for a "Reply" to the questions formulated at Windesheim, and that his work was evidently not suitable for the requirement, for the Rath submitted not his, but the formulations of another commission. The Reply or Ratschlag of Osiander did not, however, die unborn, for in 1525 two of its three parts were printed in Nürnberg[50]— the third part was omitted since the questions it dealt with had already been sufficiently treated in the Ratschlag accepted by the Rath. Part I treated of the Word of God, Part II of *"Menschen wort und leren."* It is in Part I that we find the metaphysical discussion of the Word that again meets us in the work of Olavus Petri. The subject merits some detail as illustrating a relationship between Olavus and Osiander not previously observed.

All that God is, according to Osiander, is expressed in Scripture by the terms *"Gottes hertz/Sinn/ Gedancken/Wort/Weisheit/Ratschlag/Kreftiger arm/ Gerechte hand/und eingeborner Son."* God's Word is not *"ein stim/Sonder viel mehr ein Inwendig Geistlich Wort/welches durch das mundlich/als durch sein zeichen/herfur gebracht und angezeigt wirt/und doch nichts deste minder innen bleibt. Und ist nur ein Einiges Wort/wie auch das nur ein Einig Gottlich Wesen Ist/das im Wort abgebildet wird/unangesehen/ das man viel tausent wort darzu bedarff/wenn mans in auswendiger stim/und menschliger sprach wil anzei-*

---

[50] *"Ein gut unterricht uñ getreuer Ratschlag/aus/heiliger göttlicher schrifft/wes man sich in diesen zwitrachten/unsern heiligen glauben und Christliche lere betreffend/halten sol/darin was Gottes wort und menschen lere: Was Christus und der Antichrist sey/fürnemlich gehandelt wird. Geschriben an ein Erbarn Weisen Rath der löblichen Stadt Nörnberg durch jre prediger MDXXV."* (Reprinted in Königsberg, 1553.)

gen/und aussprechen." When God reveals Himself in His word, "*fleust sein gantz Gottlich wesen in das bild/und das bilde/ist das recht inwendig Ewig Wort Gottes/Gott selbs.*" This Inner, Spiritual Word is comprehended by man in the audible "outer" words. "*Den wer verstehet nicht/das aller menschen sprach allein darumb erfunden sein/das einer dem andern sein gedancken/und sein inwendig wort und meinung mog anzeigen?*" God thus being Himself in His Word, the believing "hearer" receives God with the "Word." Adam and Eve's sin consisted in their reliance on their own *vernunfft,* in which Truth does not lie. Salvation is offered to man in the incarnation of the Word in Christ. "*So nu durch den Glauben das Wort Gottes/Christus unser Herr in uns wonet/und Wir mit Im eins sein worden/mögē wir mit Paulo wol sprechen. Ich lebe/lebe aber nich ich/sonder Christus lebet in mir. Und da sein wir deñ durch den Glauben gerechtfertigt.*" With Christ comes the Holy Spirit, "*der die Liebe in das hertz geust/und wirt durch den Glauben der Tod/durch die Liebe aber die Sünd vertriben.*"

In his own words Olavus sought to express this mystical conception of the revelation and nature of God.[51] "God's eternal and incomprehensible wisdom and council, in which his incomprehensible Being is known to Himself, is called His Word, in which all His wisdom and purpose is contained, through which also He has created all things." To know God in any real sense we must know Him through Christ, "the innermost thought of God." As human words express human thoughts, so the Word reveals the mind and heart of God. When man receives the Word, he

[51] *Works,* I, 527-534.

Ecclesiastical Transformation in Sweden

receives its contents, "God Himself"—"so we are united with God, not otherwise." And "where the Father and Son are, there the Holy Spirit also is." To overcome the sin of Adam and Eve, the Word has come into the world "to be planted in the heart" of man, so that "The word of the Devil might be driven out." Man's reception of the Word when it is preached is itself an accomplishment of the Spirit of God.[52]

The mystical strain was more native to Osiander than to Olavus Petri, who nowhere else in his writings entered deeply into the metaphysical basis of his faith.[53] Even here the treatment had a practical purpose. As in Osiander, so in Olavus, it became a foundation for an attack on what was foreign to the Word of God—man's words and statutes. Here the Swedish writer left the Nürnberg preacher. The latter proceeded, in Part II of his work, to an exposition of the works of Antichrist. The former, in calmer mood, sought to undermine the positions of his opponents. God's Word sufficiently taught all that was necessary for the life of the soul, so that a sincere study of the Scriptures made human glosses unnecessary. When the assertion was made that they were sainted men who had expounded the Scriptures, it should be replied that if their teaching was true it would accord with the Word, wherefore the Word, not the teachers, was the authority. If their teachings differed from, or added to, the Word, man was not bound to accept their decrees. To the argument that Paul urged order in

---

[52] A modern Swedish theologian, Aulen, in *Allmäneliga Kristna Tron*, has laid much stress on this point.

[53] See Chap. V, pp. 165-166, for the influence of this Osiander mysticism on one of the hymns of Olavus.

the Church, Olavus maintained that insofar as the rules of the authorities were truly based on Scripture, such rules derived their force from their source, not from their expounders. Rules of ceremony, moreover, were not Scriptural laws, and could be changed by men as circumstances demanded, because they were originally formulated by men under the stress of circumstances. Least of all was it in the power of men to establish forms whose observance would bring special rewards. Then followed a refutation of a series of Scriptural passages on which the Roman Church built its practices—the commission to St. Peter, the promise of Christ to send the Holy Spirit who would continue to teach, the representative function of the disciples—to all of which Olavus opposed the doctrine that the Word should determine the interpreters, not the interpreters the Word. To this argument even the argument of history should be subordinated, for sainted men, learned doctors, conciliar decrees, and the customs of generations, were not to be placed above the eternal, unchanging Word of God. After enumerating some of these human statutes, as opposed to God's commandments, Olavus concluded by explaining that all these human customs and regulations could not immediately be abandoned, but it was necessary to point out the distinction, so that souls might not falsely place their trust in the human rather than the divine. For the present the weak should be instructed, in the hope that in time the Truth might rule, unshackled by man's inventions in the spiritual realm.

The second part of this work was more naturally Olavus' thoughts than the first part, and in it we find lines of reasoning that had been expressed in his earlier

Ecclesiastical Transformation in Sweden 145

works, especially in the *Reply to the Twelve Questions,* where the third question had referred just to this matter of obedience to human ordinances.[54] In one section the argument resembles that of Luther's *Von Menschenlehre zu meiden und Antwort auf Sprüche* (1522),[55] and in passages we are reminded of the Ratschlag (Brandenburger), but in the main the development is Olavus' own, characteristic of him especially in the conclusion that reforms in the matter of the cult must be slow. Just this principle prevailed a couple of months later in the Örebro Council.[56]

The years 1527-1528 witnessed the production of practically all the polemical work of Olavus Petri. After the devotional writings of 1526 (including the Testament translation) Olavus had been drawn into controversy with Paulus Eliae and Peter Galle, and the religious situation in Sweden prompted his attacks on monasticism, clerical celibacy, the Roman conception of sacraments and Roman customs in general. After this period, polemics tended to disappear from his writings, and he turned to the task of reconstruction, whereof the homiletical, liturgical, and historical works were fruits. Thus these years form a distinct period in his activity, which may be termed the polemical period. All of its productions, furthermore, were akin in their material, and there can be no doubt that the Brandenburg Ratschlag as well as Luther's writings furnished a source for the ammunition of Olavus. His further relationship to Nürnberg, as evidenced in his use of Osiander's work, gives rise to the query, Through what channels did the influence from

---

[54] *Works,* I, 550, *cf.* p. 43; pp. 538-555, *cf.* pp. 254-260.
[55] *WA* VI, 87-89; *cf. Works,* I, 543-545.
[56] See Chap. I, pp. 45-48.

southern Germany reach Sweden?[57] Though this question lacks an answer, it is certain that from Nürnberg, as well as from Wittenberg, forces emanated to play a part in the Swedish Reformation. Yet the independence of Olavus should not be lost sight of. No German works were translated as such. Only so much was used as could affect the situation in his land. And always a distinct purpose was reflected in the writings, either to defend charges against opponents, or to prepare the way for needed reforms or political measures. Polemics in Olavus Petri were not for their own sake, but for the progress of the Reformation in Sweden.

[57] *Cf.* reference to Nürnberg, in *Commentary to Municipal Law, Works,* IV, 320.

CHAPTER V

THE LITURGICAL WORKS

AMONG the most important of the labors of Olavus Petri were his undertakings in the field of liturgics. In regard to the form and material of the service in the Swedish Church no one has had so directive an influence as he. The form of service suggested by him is in use to-day, with few modifications, in the Established Church of Sweden. His collections of songs laid the foundation of the Swedish Hymn-Book. His Manual of Service, or "Handbook," has the distinction of being the first of its kind to appear in any Protestant Church. His Postils went far to create the body and soul of the preaching of the Church of his own country. To the determination of the form of worship and of the character of religious instruction Olavus Petri meant to the Swedish Church what Luther meant to the Evangelical Church in Germany.

The genius of the Swedish Reformer, here as elsewhere, manifests itself not in creation of new forms and doctrines, but in selection of material produced by the German Reformation and emphasis on what he considered essential and best. No genius can be more worthy than that which fits measures conducive to a noble goal. To Olavus Petri the need was above all else for constructive measures whereby the Church could come into the inheritance that Luther had discovered. He set himself to the task of making that inheritance available. His judgment was justified by the endurance of his work throughout centuries.

The Mass

The Swedish Mass (*Then Swenska Messan*) first appeared in print in Stockholm 1531. As subtitle the work has these words: "as it is now held in Stockholm, with reasons why it is so held." Thus it was already in use. A pamphlet by Olavus Petri entitled *Why the Mass ought to be held in Swedish* came from the press May 10, 1531. It is a spirited defense of the vernacular language in the Mass. "We Swedes, as well as other nations, also belong to God, and the language we have, He has given us, in the same manner as He has given to the Hebrews, the Greeks, and the Latins their speech."[1] Therefore the Swedish is as holy a language as any other, and for the Swedes the most useful language in their Church. This pamphlet makes clear that the Mass had been held for some time in Stockholm and some "other places in the kingdom," and was an answer to attacks made by opponents of the Swedish service. How long had it already been a practice? The question is unsettled. Messenius, indeed, states that Olavus Petri had witnessed a German Mass at the wedding of Carlstadt, and that Swedish Mass was held in Stockholm at Olavus' nuptial ceremony. The statement as a basis for the assertion that Swedish Mass began in Stockholm in 1525 (Olavus was married February 11) is clearly untrustworthy, for Carlstadt's wedding occurred January 19, 1522—three years after Olavus had left Germany— and the Order of Service followed at the German event

[1] *Works,* II, 394.

bears no resemblance to the Swedish Mass.[2] A more reliable source is the decision of the Stockholm Council, May 10, 1529, that the Swedish Mass should be continued.[3] Thus by that date it had been tried and had won approval. Evidence for an earlier date than 1528 [4] is lacking.[5]

More important than the date is the character of this Mass. In the Preface,[6] Olavus informed the reader that it was not in every respect a translation of *Canon Missae*. He entered into a description of the rise and growth of the Latin Mass, which was not a universally accepted form, nor even so intended to be. The only unalterable part of the Mass he believed to be the words of consecration. Moreover, a proclamation of the Gospel must accompany every celebration. Otherwise the method of the Sacrament of the Altar was liable to variation. The fact that the Canon was old in authority was not binding. "We must look to what is right, not what is customary." Nor did the descendants always need be bound by the usages of their ancestors. "Our ancestors are not

---

[2] *"Die Messe von der Hochzeyt B. Andre Carolstadt uund der Priestern so sich Eelich verheyratten"* (in Berlin *Kön. Bibl.*).

[3] *"Stockholms Stads Tenkiebook,"* in *St. Erik's Årsbok*, 1914, p. 230. The raising of the question in the Council at this time was probably connected with the uprising in Småland. It is significant that the king had asked the Council to consider the matter.

[4] A passage in *"Om Guds Ordh och Menniskios Bodh och Stadhgar"* (December, 1528), in which it is stated that a change in ancient ceremonies is of necessity, may refer to such an innovation as a Swedish Mass (*Works*, I, 541: "changes occur according as time and conditions demand"). *Cf. Svenska Messan*, I, 410: "What men have instituted, that men also may change according to conditions."

[5] The first appearance of the Mass in the political situation is noted in the complaint of the rebellious Småland, April 8, 1529: "the Mass has been transformed into Swedish" (*GR* VI, 358-359).

[6] *Works*, II, 391ff.

accountable for us, nor we for them." To the argument of some that a Council (Ecumenical) should decide on such a reform, Olavus replied that those at present in authority gave no promise of reform, and, moreover, "we do not need their Councils. We have the Word of God before us, according to that we can regulate ourselves."

Olavus Petri had no doubt of the freedom that was his to create a Swedish liturgy. His use of that freedom distinguishes him as one with whom liberty was safe. For the Order that he produced was not radically different from *Canon Missae*. He had, in fact, followed it so closely that it has been believed that the Mass of 1531 was but a reworking of it. Thus Quensel held that "this form of mass is, in general, but a critical reworking of the medieval Roman Mass, with some innovations derived, partly from *Formula Missae* (1523), partly from *Deudsche Messe* (1526)." [7] A careful comparison of the momenta of the two forms will show that the two are intimately related. In some details Olavus prefers the Canon form to one suggested by Luther; in some he follows neither. In outline, the variations are these:

    1. Olavus transformed the Confiteor of the Canon from a priestly to a congregational confession, with absolution. Luther had discarded this moment.

    2. Introitus, Kurie, Gloria, Laudamus were retained from the Canon. As Luther in the 1523 *Formula Missae*, so the Swedish Mass prescribed a psalm or other song from the Scriptures as Introitus.

    3. The place of the Lectiones remained the

[7] Oscar Quensel, *Bidrag till Svenska Liturgiens Historia*, II, 47-48.

same. Olavus and Luther (1526) suggested Lectio Continua in place of the pericope texts. Both had, for Gradual, the song of the "Ten Commandments."

4. The Credo retained its place, though Olavus prescribed that it should be read.

5. The Offertorium of the Canon was rejected by Luther and Olavus, and both (Luther in 1523, but not in 1526) combined Praefatio and Verba Consecrationis, though Olavus' form is not the same as Luther's. The Elevation was retained, followed, in Luther (1526) and Olavus, by Sanctus, and Pater Noster. Pax and Agnus Dei remained the same.

6. The Exhortation here inserted by Olavus was not according to Canon. Luther had one (1526) in another place.

7. The Words of Distribution were, in Luther, an alteration of the Canon; a Communion Hymn was common to both the Protestant forms.

It might seem, therefore, that Olavus had but changed the Canon so as to make of the Mass a Communion rather than a Sacrifice, and that in his changes he had observed the suggestions of Luther, in some cases following the 1523, in others, the 1526, Order.[8] But another possibility needs consideration. In 1525 Andr. Döber's *Evangelische Messe,* as celebrated in Neuen Spital in Nürnberg, appeared—a German translation of a Latin service introduced in Nürnberg, June 5, 1524.[9] This Nürnberg *Messe* was printed not only separate, but found its way also into the earlier collections of evangelical song books. Thus, we find it

[8] Quensel, *op. cit.,* II, 47-48.
[9] Art. *"Abendmahlsfeier,"* in *Real Encycklopedie,* I, 69.

152 *Olavus Petri*

in the Nürnberg Enchiridion of 1527 [10] and in Sluter's Low-German Song Book of 1531. A noteworthy fact is that these forms do not agree, though all bear the common title of the Mass, *"wie sie zu Nürnberg, in Newen Spital gehalten würdt."* Thus, neither of the two mentioned forms agrees entirely with the other or with the original form.[11]

With one of these forms the Mass of Olavus Petri strikingly agrees, namely, that of Sluter's *Gesangbuch* (Rostock, 1531). A survey of this Order will reveal how close the agreement is.

The Rostock Order opens with the Confiteor. The contents thereof are not given, but we find them in both the Enchiridion and in the original. After an Exhortation to confession, follows a Confession of sins. The thoughts in the Swedish are practically the same as in the German, and in many cases the same modes of expression are used. The Absolution is also common to both, though the Swedish is shorter and more decisive than the German.

The Introitus is, in the Rostock book, sung by the choir, and Luther's hymn based on Ps. cxxix, *"De Profundis,"* is prescribed. The Swedish suggests "some psalm or hymn from the Scriptures."[12]

---

[10] The title page in the book in the Royal Library, Berlin, where I have studied it, is lacking—*"Das Confiteor"* of the Mass is the first line of the preserved book. The last lines of the book are: *"Gedruckt zu Nürmberg durch Hans Herrgott. M.D. xxvii."* A description of it may be found in Wackernagel, *Das Deutsche Kirchenlied von Martin Luther bis auf Nicholaus Herman und Ambrosius Blaurer*, LXV, pp. 735-736.

[11] The original form is given in Riederer, *Abhandlung von Einführung des Deutschen Gesangs in die evangelisch-lutherische Kirche überhaupts und in die nürnbergische besonders*, p. 313; also in Löhe, *Sammlung Liturgisches Formulare*, III, 42ff.

[12] The original form here has Ps. ciii.

The threefold Kyrie Eleyson, the Gloria in Excelsis and Laudamus, are the same in the Swedish and the Rostock forms. So, also, the Salutation and Response and the Collect, except that in the Rostock Order the minister sings the Salutation, while in the Swedish he reads.[13]

As Epistle, the Rostock form has "a chapter from the Epistles of St. Paul." The Swedish prescribes a whole or a half chapter, from Paul or some other Apostle.[14] In both the gradual is the hymn of Luther, "The Ten Commandments," though the Swedish allows "some other" hymn.[15]

Again, in the Gospel, the Rostock book suggests a "whole chapter," while the Swedish has "a whole or a half." [16]

The Creed may, in the Rostock edition, be sung, in which case Luther's *Glauben* is used, or it may be read by the minister—in which case the Apostolic form is given. The Swedish Creed is read, and may be either the Apostolic or the Nicene.[17]

The Prefatio and the section on through the Words of Institution have the same order in the Rostock and the Swedish forms. A remarkable divergence occurs, however, in that the Swedish form has an introductory prayer before the Words of Institution in which thanks is said for the benefits of the life and death of Christ. The Enchiridion and the original form of the Nürn-

---

[13] Enchiridion in this respect agrees with Rostock; the original form, with the Swedish.

[14] Original, Romans v is prescribed; Enchiridion as Rostock.

[15] Enchiridion, "The Ten Commandments, or a Psalm."

[16] Enchiridion, as Rostock; original, John vi.

[17] Enchiridion prescribes that the minister shall be silent, while the choir sings the Creed; original, the minister reads either of the two Creeds.

berg *Messa* agree with the Rostock. Elevation of the bread and wine is common to all.

The Sanctus is, in the Rostock form, sung by the choir. The Swedish Order permits either its being sung or read. Then follows the Pater Noster. The Swedish form lacks the short prayer that in the German form follows the Lord's Prayer, and the Introductory Exhortation to the Prayer is shorter.

Pax and Agnus in the Rostock book agree in place and expression with the Swedish.[18] An Exhortation now follows. The Rostock edition gives two alternate forms. The Swedish is a similar rendering of the same thoughts as are expressed in the first of these two Exhortations.[19] Between the Exhortation and the Distribution, the Rostock has a short prayer that is not found in the Swedish.

The words used in the administration of the Sacrament are practically the same in the Rostock and the Swedish forms. The only difference lies in the words said in the giving of the bread. The Rostock has: "The body of Christ, etc."; the Swedish, "The body of our Lord Jesus Christ."[20] The Rostock and the original form have also a formula for self-communion.

The Communion is followed, in the Rostock form,

[18] So in the original, except that the minister reads the Agnus Dei, while in the Swedish it may be sung or read. In the Rostock, the choir sings the Agnus. The Enchiridion here diverges, for its Exhortation follows the Pater Noster.

[19] Enchiridion mentions but does not give in full the Exhortation. The original form has the first of the two forms in the Rostock. Olavus had used this Exhortation in the Handbook two years earlier (*cf.* p. 172).

[20] The original and the Rostock wording here agree, while Enchiridion agrees with the Swedish! This fact is the more interesting since this formula seems not to have been a common one. (*Cf.* Höfling, *Liturgisches Urkundenbuch*, pp. 124-125.)

Ecclesiastical Transformation in Sweden 155

by Nunc Dimittis. This is also prescribed in the Swedish, as well as a Swedish psalm *"pro communione."* [21] A Collect is common to both, though the contents differ.

The Benedicamus and Benedictio conclude the service, and are alike in the German and Swedish, except that the latter has "us" in the formula of benediction, where the former has "thee" or "you." [22] In the Rostock (and original) form a sentence prayer is uttered by the pastor as he leaves the altar.

In the Swedish Mass, Olavus Petri appended a translation of the Seven Penitential Psalms, which he suggested might be used as Introitus Psalms, "as used to be the custom in former times." These Psalms are the same as occurred in the *Nyttig Undervisning* of 1526, and seem to be but a reworking of that translation.

The above comparison brings us to the conclusion that a uniform Nürnberg Messa cannot be assumed. The form in the Nürnberg *Enchiridion* of 1527 is not the same as in Sluter's *Gesangbuch* of 1531. True, the essential elements are the same, but individual rubrics have been changed, and in one important item, the place of the Exhortation, an important liturgical change had been made. The differences are not printer's errors or licenses; they indicate a revision by the respective editors. The original form of 1525 shows an elaborated liturgical order. The Enchiridion has an abbreviated form. The Rostock takes a middle position, not as full as the original form, not as abbre-

[21] The original has the Nunc Dimittis, not the Psalm. Enchiridion has the Psalm, or *lied,* and not the Dimittis. Rostock and the original agree in the rubric as well as in the Nunc Dimittis.

[22] An unusual form. Höfling cites it as occurring in the Erbacher KO. (1560?), *op. cit.,* p. 132.

viated as that in the Enchiridion. The Rostock form
is found again in the Hamburg *Enchiridion Geistlicher
Leder und Psalmen* of 1558,[23] and here in a practically
unaltered form. We may be justified in speaking of
it as a Low-German revision of the Nürnberg *Messa*.
The development of variations is traceable. The
Enchiridion of 1527 diverges from the form of 1525.
The Rostock form is more nearly allied to the Enchiridion, but in a few details goes back to the earlier form
(e.g. Communion rubrics). The Swedish Order in
most respects agrees with the Rostock, while in the
reading instead of singing, on the part of the minister,
it resembles the orginal form. It is not impossible that
between the Enchiridion of 1527 and Sluter's *Gesangbuch* of 1531 a slightly differing form circulated in
north Germany, which formed the basis of both Sluter's and Olavus Petri's Orders. We can agree with
Rodhe in his statement that, "if we compare the
Nürnberg *Messa* with the Swedish of 1531, we find
the resemblance so comprehensive that we must hold
that Olavus Petri has had access to it."[24] Only we
would add that it is the Low-German revision of that
Order, as it appears in Sluter's Rostock *Gesangbuch* of 1531, that the Swedish Mass most nearly
resembles.

The work of Olavus Petri is to be considered, therefore, as a selection of that form of service which to
him seemed the best for his countrymen. Even his
use of the available material shows that he was no

[23] Geffcken, *Die Hamburgischen Niedersachsichen Gesangbucher des 16 Jahrh*, pp. 137-142.

[24] E. Rodhe, *Svenskt Gudstjenstliv*, p. 31 (1926); *cf.* C. R. Martin, *Sveriges Första Svenska Messa*, p. 91; Y. Brilioth, *Nattvarden i evangelisk gudstenstliv*, pp. 397ff. Swedish scholars have not distinguished between the various forms of the Nürnberg *Messa*.

mere translator. He could have translated *Formula Missae*, or *Deutsche Messe*, of Luther. He did neither. And in his translation of the Nürnberg *Formula*, he used his judgment. Knowing the limitations of his fellow citizens in the matter of song, he prescribed that the minister should read where he did not think the congregation could sing. His Mass did not presume the existence of a choir.[25] Where all the Nürnberg forms suggested an opening hymn as Introitus, he indicated the use of a psalm, and offered a translation of seven psalms. His substitution of Lectio Continua for the ancient pericope texts was not blind, for he motivated the measure by saying that in this way the congregation could better be introduced into the Word of God, which to them now was foreign.[26] The sermon was not included in the Mass, as Olavus conceived of the sermon as preceding the Mass, as a special service.[27] As a matter of fact, Olavus considered the Sacrament of the Altar in itself a proclamation, or a sermon, and urged therefore that it be in a language understood by participants and audience. The making of the entire service a Swedish service also distinguished Olavus from some of the Continental reformers. In Nürnberg,[28] in Prussia,[29] even in Wittenberg,[30] the service was often bilingual. True,

[25] The wording of the rubrics is such, however, that a distinction may exist between "minister" and "one"—the latter might well refer to a choir, where such existed, e.g. "As Graduale one reads or sings the hymn 'The Ten Commandments.'"

[26] *Cf. Works*, II, 316: "As conditions are in our land, where the people, up to this time, have heard very little of the Word of God."

[27] The discussion of the relationship of these two services we have reserved for Chap. VI.

[28] G. Ritschel, *Liturgik*, I, 408.

[29] E. L. Richter, *Die Evang. Kirchenordnungen*, I, 29-30.

[30] Ritschel, *op. cit.*, p. 412.

in the edition of 1537 of the Mass, Olavus sanctioned the use of the Introit and Gradual in Latin,[31] but in the same document he mentioned the appearance of a Swedish translation of the Psalter, from which the Introits and Graduals were usually taken," [32] indicating thus that the Latin could no longer be defended as being necessary on the grounds of a lack of Swedish translations. Olavus Petri knew his countrymen and their condition. The cultural motives that made Luther desirous of retaining the Latin language in the Mass did not find a response in the Swedish disciple. Until the Swedish Church could intelligently follow a Mass in Swedish there could be no benefit from attempts to educate them to a Latin Mass. The same practical nature manifested itself in the reduction of the part music played in the service. Olavus knew that some of the clergy could not read a service, let alone sing one, to the profit of the congregation. He suggested therefore that all should be done plainly and intelligibly, and to his mind this could best be realized by the words of the pastor. That he was not adverse to a Mass being sung, a rubric in the 1537 Mass makes evident.[33] For the sake of the weak, the priestly robes were still retained in the service, but Olavus would not yield to these in all details, for signs of the cross were not used as much as formerly.[34] In general, the Swedish Mass was an

---

[31] *Works,* II, 443.

[32] *Works,* II, 440.

[33] "Where the Mass is sung, etc." (*Works,* II, 443); *cf.* p. 412 in reference to the 1531 Mass, "we read or sing, etc."

[34] *Ibid.,* pp. 408, 411. E. Rodhe, *Svensk Gudstjenstliv,* p. 29, well characterizes the Mass of 1531 when he says that "Olavus Petri moved the center of gravity in the Service from the visual to the auditory."

adaptation to Swedish conditions of a revised Latin service such as Olavus Petri found in the north German forms of the Nürnberg *Messa*. Those forms seemed to him to embody the essentials of Luther's recommendations, while they still followed closely the ancient ritual of the Church. Later generations returned to a use of the age-old pericope texts and incorporated the sermon in the service, and gave to congregational song a greater place in the order of worship. But it can hardly be denied that the Mass of 1531 had a determining influence upon the character of the Swedish liturgical service into the present time.

THE HYMN BOOKS

As early as 1526 the first collection of Swedish hymns made its appearance. No copy of this earliest book is extant,[35] but it is believed that it consisted of a part or all of the ten hymns found in a fragment of the Hymn Book of 1530 (*Några Gudhelige Wijsor uthdragne aff then Helga Skrift, the ther tiena till at siungas i then Christeliga Församblingen*).[36] Both the lack of evidence for a Swedish Mass as early as that

[35] The evidence for an edition of 1526 is the complaint from Dalarne the following year. In 1529 the Danish Hymn Book included four hymns of Olavus Petri "derived from the Swedish copy." They were the first four, as found in the 1530 edition (S. Ek in *Samlaren*, 1918, pp. 2-3). Ek's thesis that the 1526 book contained eight hymns is plausible. The increase of 1530 would then consist of two hymns, and the addition of two stanzas to one of the original eight. It is not impossible that Olavus in 1530 knew of the 1529 Danish Psalm Book, but its influence is small compared with the German collections. Ek also cites a statement in Hallman, indicating a 1531 edition, and believes it to have been the 1536 collection, in the main. *Cf.* G. E. Klemming, *Sveriges Bibliografi, 1481-1600*, I, 166.

[36] *Works*, II, 561ff.; Introduction, XVII; *cf.* H. Schück, "*Våra älsta psalmböcker*," *Samlaren*, 1891.

date (1526), and the original character of the Mass,[37] lead us to connect the singing of vernacular hymns with the preaching rather than the Communion service.[38] In his Introduction to the third edition of the Hymn Book (1536) Olavus defended the singing of spiritual songs, both because they were instructive and edifying and because they expressed the prayer of the heart. This latter edition (forty-four numbers) contained many new songs not in the previous collection, and were justified for use in the congregation by ancient usage and, in the case of the new songs, by Scriptural bases. Kliefoth has pointed out that even in Germany the printed hymn books were primarily used by the preacher or cantor.[39] The people could not read, and they could sing these hymns only after careful instruction by the pastor or cantor.[40] So also the Swedish hymn books must be looked upon as collections of hymns and songs partly for the use of the minister, who here found substitutes for Latin songs used in the *Horae*, which were replaced by Matins and Vespers,[41] partly for the choir, who for a century or more represented the congregation in sing-

---

[37] *Cf.* Rodhe, *op. cit.*, p. 12: "The Mass of 1531 does not provide for congregational singing."

[38] In a letter dated May 14, 1527, the king defended himself against the complaints of the men of Dalarne. In the twelfth complaint reference was made to "the preaching in Stockholm and Swedish hymns and songs" (*GR* IV, 169ff.). The combining of the two may not be without significance, and it is noteworthy that no mention was here made of any Swedish Mass.

[39] Th. Kliefoth, *Die ursprungliche Gottesdienstordnung in den deutschen Kirchen lutherischen Bekenntnisses*, pp. 126-7.

[40] The titles of some of the early hymn books indicate that they were to be used in the teaching of the youth.

[41] *Cf.* the title in the Speratus Hymn Book, *"tho dagelyker övinge."*

Ecclesiastical Transformation in Sweden 161

ing."[42] That the Swedish songs found enemies as well as friends is evident from a passage in the letter of Gustavus Vasa to his troublesome Dalkarlar. In 1527 they had made the use of these songs one of their complaints to the king. Gustavus had a ready reply: "His Majesty wonders why the singing of Swedish songs should be punished in Stockholm, when it is a custom in all parish churches all over the kingdom to sing and praise God in Swedish. And it is as well that it is done in our own language which we understand, as in Latin which one does not at all understand. Yet Latin is sung in Stockholm now as hitherto."[43] Besides indicating that the use of vernacular songs was not new in the Church of Sweden, this passage reminds us that the entry of evangelical songs did not displace immediately the old Latin hymns, just as the Latin Mass lived on alongside the Swedish. But the Swedish hymn had found root in the Swedish Reformation from its very start, and has a common date with the Swedish New Testament.

The contents of Olavus Petri's hymn books reveal, again, the community of aims and methods of the Swedish and German Reformation. Among the principal collections of hymns between 1524 and 1530 the following are noteworthy.[44] In 1524 a group of eight hymns was printed in Wittenberg. The same year brought the Erfurter Enchiridion with twenty-five hymns. Wittenberg, in 1525, produced Johan

[42] See Emil Liedgren, *Svensk Psalm och Andlig Visa*, Chap. II.

[43] Thyselius och Ekblom, *Handlingar rörande Sveriges Inre Förhållande under Gustav I*, I, 67.

[44] Described in K. C. P. Wackernagle, *Das Deutsche Kirchenlied von Martin Luther bis auf Nicolaus Herman und Ambrosius Blaurer*, pp. 723ff.

Walther's *Gesangbuch,* containing thirty-two hymns. A Nürnberg Enchiridion of 1525 and another Erfurt Enchiridion, the same year, contained practically the same hymns, the latter having thirty-nine, the former thirty-seven hymns. In 1526 the oldest now known Low-German collection was printed, though its place of printing is not known. Because it had an Introduction by Paul Speratus, it is sometimes known as Speratus' *Gesangbuch.*[45] Two Nürnberg collections are known from 1527. A Wittenberg *Gesangbuch* by Joseph Klug, from 1529, is now recognized in a reprint, forming part of Sluter's Rostock *Gesangbuch* of 1531.[46]

Comparing the hymns in the Swedish Hymn Book of 1530 with those found in these German collections, we find that some of the ten Swedish songs are translations, to a larger or lesser extent, of the German models. Four of the ten can be recognized in the Erfurt collection of 1524 (Hymns 4, 6, 8, 9); six (2, 4, 5, 6, 8, 9) in Walther's Wittenberg collection, 1525; in the Nürnberg Enchiridion, 1525; in the two Nürnberg Enchiridions, 1527; in Speratus' *Gesangbuch,* 1526; and seven (2, 4, 5, 6, 8, 9, 10) in the Klug edition, 1529. In Germany, we find, naturally, the recurrence of hymns in many collections, the numbers growing each year. Luther's hymns were primary, but were not always reprinted accurately, a fact that brought displeasure to and criticism from the

[45] *Eyn gantz schone unde seer nutte ghesangbock/tho dagelyker övinge geystlyker geseng im Psalmen/uth Christlicher und Evangelischer schryfft/bevestyghet/beweret/unde op dat nyge gemeret/ Corrigert und in sassycher sprake klarer wen to vorn verdudeschet/ und mit flyte gedruckt M. D. XXVI.* The sole surviving copy is in the Royal Library, Berlin, where the writer has studied it.

[46] *Joachim Slüters ältestes rostocker Gesangbuch vom Jahre 1531, nach dem originaldrucken wortgetreu herausgeben von C. M. Wiechmann—Kadow, Schwerin, 1858.*

Reformer.[47] Often the editions were hardly more than reprints, and many times but a reprint in different order or with additional hymns. Thus it is quite natural that the Swedish Reformer would make use of the German collections. It cannot be determined which were available to him, but the relation of the 1530 and 1536 collections to the known German books presents at least one interesting aspect: The two German collections that most nearly resemble the Swedish works are the Low-German books of Speratus (1526) and of Sluter (1531). Of the forty-four numbers in the Swedish Hymn Book of 1536, not less than twenty-four appear to be translations of numbers also appearing in the Speratus book of 1526. Even more striking is the resemblance to Sluter's *Gesangbuch* (Rostock, 1531). Among its hymns we find thirty-one that agree (entirely or, in the case of a few, in part) with the hymns of the Swedish book. One of these, a versification of Psalm xxxvii, we have found in no other collection of these years except in those of Sluter (1531), and Olavus Petri (1536). In the Rostock book, too, are versified selections from the Old Testament which may be considered as models for Olavus' *Parabolae*—selections from the New Testament. If we might add these, the number in which kinship is traceable would be thirty-five. In regard to the Speratus *Gesangbuch*, again, we find similarities in titles,[48] of which one, "*S. Ambrosij och Augustini loffsong Te deum*," occurs only in the Rostock and Swedish collections. If we might venture a supposition, we would consider the Speratus book as a source

[47] Foreword to Wittenberg *Gesangbuch*, 1533 (Wackernagel, *op. cit.*, p. 792).

[48] *Works*, II, 525:1; 526:17, 551:7, 18.

164   *Olavus Petri*

for the Swedish collection of 1530 (and the unpreserved collection of 1526), and the Sluter *Gesangbuch* as a main source for the 1536 collection.[49]

Thus it would seem that the earliest influences bearing upon Swedish hymnody came from Low-German sources. *The same book that has a form of Mass most nearly akin to the Swedish Mass of 1531 contains the largest number of hymns agreeing with the hymns of the Swedish collection of 1536.*

The literary treasures made available to the Swedish Church in these earliest years included the hymns which had already won a lasting place in the hearts of the Protestant people of Germany. Thus we find, in the 1536 edition, hymns based on psalms, such as "A Mighty Fortress" (Ps. xlvi), *"De Profundis"* (Ps. cxxx), "Blessed is the Man" (Ps. cxxviii), "Unless the Lord" (Ps. cxiv), "God Be Merciful" (Ps. xlvii), the two hymns on the Commandments, translations from the Latin—*Veni Redemptor, Christe qui lux, Jesu nostra redemptio, Veni Creator Spiritus.* A goodly part of the 1530 collection was composed of hymns of an occasional character—two entered into the Funeral Ritual (as found in the Handbook of

[49] It might, of course, be assumed that the 1530 edition could as well depend on the other collections named above, which also have similarities in the case of six hymns; or, even more, on Klug's 1529 collection, which has seven hymns corresponding to the 1530 Swedish (the additional being *"Dies est leticie"*—No. 10 in Olavus Petri). The Walther Collection, 1525, has been considered a source for the earliest Swedish Collection (Ek, following Schück, *op. cit.*, p. 7). But the Speratus book in 1526 was already a second edition, wherefore it is as likely a source as Walther's. As the Nürnberg Mass reached Sweden via North Germany, the Wittenberg songs probably came through the same intermediary. As Mass and songs often were printed together, we are inclined to believe that the Swedish Songs of 1526 and the Mass of 1528 had a common source, unknown to us.

1529), two found place in the Mass—the hymn of the Commandments and a Communion hymn (to which might be added the Credo hymn, which the Mass does not prescribe), and a Christmas song.

No direct evidence exists to show that Olavus Petri was the editor and translator whose work produced the first Swedish psalm books, but the lack of proof for any other author, equal in ability and spirit to Olavus Petri, and the known productions of Olavus, have led to an almost general concession of the honor to the Reformer.[50] The strongest argument in his favor, however, has not been stressed sufficiently, namely, that in those psalms which are known to be originals in Swedish, and not translations from the German, the text is practically parallel with passages in the writings of Olavus. Thus the first hymn in the 1530 collection is a prayer for the Holy Spirit. In stanza 1, God's Word is described as having created heaven and earth, as revealing the will of God, as man's guide out of error. Stanza 2 shows that man cannot receive this Word unless it be given him by the grace of God, and that the devil seeks to keep man from the Word. The prayer in stanza 3 is directed to Christ, who, in His manhood and sacrifice, became the brother of man, and now is implored to fulfill His promise of the Spirit which can teach all truth. The last stanza is a prayer to the Spirit to bring the Word into man's heart, whereby man is cleansed of sin and enabled to praise God. This hymn, both in subject matter and form, the most finished of Olavus' compositions, is a metrical presentation of thoughts in prose form in a book of 1528, *"Om Guds*

[50] J. W. Beckman, *Den Svenska Psalmboken;* H. Schück, *Våra älsta Psalmböcker.* See also Ek, Liedgren, Westman.

Ordh och Menniskios Bodh och Stadghar." [51] Though the hymn is earlier than the book, there can be little doubt as to the relation between the two. There too the Word was described as the Creator of all things, the Revealer of the Will of the Father. The sin of man was the acceptance of the devil's for God's Word, and man's salvation consisted in the reestablishment of the Word of God in man. But man cannot of himself receive the Word, it must come through the Holy Spirit, the Revealer of Truth. When man receives this Truth, he has life and salvation.

Also another of the hymns without German source is one in the 1536 collection under the title *"En song om Guds ord emoot menniskiors stadgar."* [52] Not only does its title betray relationship with the thoughts in the book of a similar name, but in Biblical references and in subject matter it seems to be based on the same ideas that found expression in the book. In relation to the above described hymn from the same source, the emphasis of that hymn lies on the Word of God; that of this second hymn, on the statutes of men which have obscured the true Word.

The other original of the 1530 Hymn Book is a hymn of thanksgiving and praise to Christ, whose humiliation and service to man is described as the reason for praise. The composition has some points of contact with Luther's *"Nun freut euch,"* [53] but cannot be called a translation. In the Handbook of 1529, in the service for the Communion of the Sick, we have a prose parallel to this hymn.[54] Both the hymn and

[51] *Works*, I, 525ff. (*Concerning the Word of God*), especially pp. 528-534. For the dependence of this book on Osiander, see *supra*, pp. 140ff.

[52] *Ibid.*, p. 556.

[53] Liedgren, *op. cit.*, p. 77.

[54] *Works*, II, 335-338.

the homily are characteristic of the message of Olavus. The good and merciful God has sent Christ into the world to suffer man's punishment for sin. In becoming the brother of man Christ has made men to become children of God.

> Is it not a wondrous gift?
> God's only Son now our brother!
> Who can now do us ill?

Again and again this was the theme of the preaching of Olavus, who saw in the objective, historical events the revelation of a disposition of God which should give man certainty and peace, and awaken him to obedience and praise.

A Christmas hymn in the 1530 edition was the work of Olavus in its last two stanzas; also a wedding hymn in the 1536 collection. Both follow quite closely the Biblical passages on which they were built. The same is true of the *Parabolae*—a series of versified Gospel passages—which are probably by Olavus. The later hymn book counted as one of its numbers a reworking of Paul Speratus' *"Es ist das Heil uns kommen her,"* with original stanzas by Olavus in conclusion. In these stanzas again we can notice the close connection between the prose and verse proclamation of the author. In Olavus' *Reply* to Paulus Eliae occurs a passage that is identical in contents and similar in expression to his stanzas in the hymn.[55] The Holy Spirit enters into the heart that has faith, creates there a new desire to do as the will of God commands, gives birth to a new love toward God and fellow men which does all good, not for reward, but out of an

[55] *Works*, I, 162-164, *Reply to an Unchristian Letter.*

inner instinct—so Olavus both preached and sang. The last stanza, touching on predestination, has a parallel in the same *Reply*.[56]

An half-dozen other hymns in the Hymn Book of 1536 are without known originals in German collections, and seem to be, in part at least, based on Latin hymns. Of his translations as a whole, we can say that for Olavus form played a very subordinate part to contents. In all his hymns he was everywhere the preacher who used the singer's form to inculcate his teachings. And since he did not conquer the form which he undertook to use, the form conquered him, and the contents of the verse were bound by it. Olavus had not the inner force which could break through the verse, as in Luther's hymns, and live despite the inadequacy of its body. The Swedish Reformer did not sing because it was a natural mode of expression for him, but rather because he felt there should be songs available for use in the congregation. His contributions belong thus to the realm of liturgics, and his merit consists in his having produced a hymn book with evangelic hymns. In the preface to the Songbook of 1536 the author found the raison d'être of hymns in their ability to give man, "who has a natural instinct and desire to sing," something to sing "which could be to the praise of God and to the use and benefit of himself."[57] Since songs should be in "an intelligible language," the Swedish Church needed hymns in the native language. It is to the lasting credit of Olavus that he provided such hymns, partly by translation, partly by composition, and thus laid the basis for future and better work. That his

[56] *Ibid.*, pp. 191-192; *cf.* II, 467.
[57] *Works*, II, 523.

work was final he never pretended to believe. He urged others to do better—"when they have done so, I will thank them for it." [58]

THE MANUAL

In the Introduction to the Manual (Handbook) of 1529, Olavus stated that in the "Council which was held this year at Örebro, it was considered that the Sacrament of Baptism might well be administered (*'wel motte skee'*) in Swedish, also it was thought that some instruction should be given in print for the benefit of the sick who ask to be prepared for their death, so that the untutored clergy might have some guidance in their dealing with those on their deathbed." [59] These two subjects thus became the nucleus of the Manual, the first in the Protestant world. The Introduction, too, prepared the clergy for the nature of the book. It was first of all a Swedish work. In the *Little Book on the Sacraments* of the previous year, Olavus had already given his countrymen the arguments for both Mass and Baptism in the native tongue. He now recapitulated those arguments—the people should understand what is taking place in the ceremony, for the ceremony depends for its effect on their faith, and faith requires understanding of the Word. In the second place, the Manual was a correction of the Latin ceremonies. These were not discarded, insofar as they agreed with the Word of God. But "we have many ceremonies and usages connected with the sacraments, which the sacraments themselves can well afford to be without." [60] Referring again to

[58] Conclusion, "Handbook," *Works*, II, 366.
[59] *Works*, II, 315.
[60] *Ibid.*, p. 316.

the Council of Örebro,[61] he mentioned as unnecessary accumulations to the sacraments—salt, chrism, oil, candles, and white garments, "which ceremonies are more of a decoration to the sacrament of baptism than of any special power." These "decorations" had no foundation in the Word of God, but since "people in this country have hitherto heard but little of the Word of God," Olavus did not strike out all the ceremonies that should be omitted, but, in accordance with the Örebro resolutions, sought rather to instruct the people, through the clergy, as to what was essential, and what unessential. He would have preferred to discard Extreme Unction, "but where it cannot so be done, one must consider the weak and teach them how rightly they should understand the unction, so that they give it no greater power than it possesses." Clearly, the principle followed was a cautious revision of the Roman forms.

For the ritual for Baptism, Olavus had Luther's guidance.[62] A careful study of the Swedish form leads to the conclusion that it was a reworking of the old Latin ceremony on the basis of Luther's *Taufbuchlein*, not only in its 1523, but, to a large extent, in its 1526 form. In 1523 Luther had retained the insufflation, but dropped it in 1526; Olavus does not have it. The first prayer over the child, in Olavus' form, is a translation from Luther's 1523 form (omitted in 1526).

[61] Resolutions in Hildebrand och Alin, *Svenska Riksdagsakter*, I, 118-122.

[62] For Luther's *Taufbuchlein*, 1523, *cf. WA* XII, 42-46; for the 1526 *Taufbuchlein cf. WA* XIX, 539-541. Quensel, *Bidrag till Svenska liturgiens historia*, I, 14-25, contains the best comparison between the Manual and the Latin ceremony as found in *Manuale Lincopensis*, but Quensel has not compared Olavus' form with Luther's 1526 revision, which Olavus followed as much as the 1523 form.

The second prayer is based partly on Luther (1523 and 1526) and the Latin. The third prayer is likewise from Luther. In 1523 Luther had an elaborate exorcism, which in 1526 was replaced by the simple form of exorcism. Olavus' form is an abbreviation of the first. So also the following prayer, the Gospel Lectio, and the Lord's Prayer follow Luther's forms. Again, in the prayer following the immersion, the words of Olavus are a combination of Luther's 1523 and 1526 prayers. It is, thus, in the matter of the prayers especially that we notice Olavus' dependence on Luther. In the forms, he has followed the Latin. Here the laity would have noticed the changes more than in the prayers, which they had not hitherto understood. Luther, in this respect, made noteworthy changes in 1526 which he had hesitated to make in 1523. In 1523 he retained, in 1526 he omitted, the insufflation, the touching of the child's ears and nose, chrisma, white dress and candle. Olavus followed him in regard to the first two points, but not in the last three. In general, then, we may consider the Swedish ceremony as a medium between the old and the new —in the contents, following Luther, in the forms, respecting the old usages.

The second subject that the Örebro Council had advocated in the Manual was a preparation of the dying, and Olavus promised a guidance for the clergy in the Introduction. Here he had, as far as we know, no Protestant forms to help him. His work included the items that were found in the Roman *Ordo ad visitandum infirmum,* and, as in *Manuale Lincopensis,* Olavus' form provided for Confession and Absolution, Communion, and Extreme Unction. In the large it is characterized by detailed homilies and long prayers. The sick person was first admonished to think of the vanity of life, and was then led on to a confession of sins, from which he was absolved. Communion then followed, after the minister had fully explained its Scriptural meaning and the communicant had confessed his faith. Both bread and wine were to be administered. Extreme Unction was also prescribed for such as desired it, but only after careful explanation of its real meaning. It was "no viaticum, as it has now long been taught, without reason or right. The Word of God alone is our viaticum. To it we shall hold, whether we live or die."[63] A long homily and consolation concluded the ceremony. In this, as in the baptismal form, we can discern the building of a new structure on the plans of the old; the skeleton is the same, the body and spirit are new. In its prayers and exhortations we note Olavus Petri's inclination toward elaborate phrasing of a few clear thoughts which could be grasped easily by an uneducated laity, to whom he wanted to bring the central truths of the Gospel. One of the remarkable contents of the form is in the Exhortation preceding the Communion. Its latter part[64] is an almost literal translation of the first exhortation in the Nürnberg *Messa*, which thus appeared in Swedish two years before the Swedish Mass, whose relationship to the Nürnberg form we have already noticed.[65]

"Of these two subjects which were dealt with in the (Örebro) Council, I have taken advantage and worked

[63] *Works*, II, 343.
[64] *Works*, II, 339-340.
[65] The use of the Nürnberg *Messa* in the Handbook is almost simultaneous with the first notices of the holding of a Swedish Mass in Stockholm! The complaint of the men of Småland was dated April 8, *supra*, p. 149, note 5. The Handbook was printed April 28.

out (*'utsatt'*) other subjects," Olavus wrote in the Introduction to the Manual, and in it he included consequently forms for marriage, for burial, for ministration to those who were to be executed, and a prayer for the churching of a mother.

Luther's *Traubuchlein* and Olavus Petri's Manual appeared in the same year.[66] Neither external nor internal evidence shows any relationship between the two. In both cases, the formulae are revisions of ancient Latin forms used in the communities of the Reformers—Luther's type following the Magdeburg, Olavus Petri that of the *Manuale Lincopensis* or *Åbo*.[67] In both, too, the civil character of marriage is recognized. Marriage proper took place before the doors of the church, and the ceremony at the altar was but a blessing of the Church on the man and wife. In the Swedish form, Olavus suggested first an exhortation to the couple reminding them of the meaning and duties and Scriptural purpose of marriage. Specifically Swedish are the threefold questioning of the couple if they wished each other; the bowing of their heads together; the words of the bridegroom "and as a token, I give thee this ring," and of the bride "as a token, I receive this ring"; and the use of the pallium over the pair at the altar.[68] An interesting item is also the fact that the minister does not say "I pronounce you man and wife," but merely calls "those who are present

[66] D. O. Albrecht, in *WA* XXX, 3, in Introduction to *Ein Traubuchlein für die einfältigen Pfarrherr 1529*. Hitherto a later date than 1529 has been supposed—Quensel believed it to be 1546 (*op. cit.*, I, 29, note 2).

[67] For a comparison of the Latin and Swedish forms, see Quensel, *op. cit.*, I, 26-40.

[68] Quensel wonders if it can have come into Sweden via the missionaries from England, where it was an ancient usage (*op. cit.*, I, 37, note).

to witness what here has taken place." Albrecht has pointed out that not until late in the Middle Ages did the betrothal change from the home to the church doors; even here the priest was at first an onlooker or at most a participant only in the blessing, and the Swedish form corroborates this civil aspect of marriage —the Church did not marry, it but recognized marriage as based on the nature of man, and in its blessing pointed to Him who could make of the married estate a fulfillment of His purposes in man. The special contribution of Olavus in this translation is the Allocution, or introductory exhortation, in which he tried to bring home to the nuptial parties the high origin and purpose of marriage. The minister should admonish the couple, so that they do not come to marriage "through some evening flirtation or hasty decision." This, indeed, was the purpose of the translation itself, that thereby the ceremony might be understood and be of instruction and guidance to the couple. Olavus himself stated as *"summa summarum"* of this Allocution that "man and woman shall mutually so love one another, that they have no other human being dearer than each the other."[69]

The ceremony for the churching of women and the form for dealing with those to be executed cannot be traced to any known Latin or German models. The former, however, was an ancient custom in the Church, and Olavus has given it the form of a thanksgiving collect, without any reference to the Old Testament idea of a purification, which made this prayer repugnant to the German reformers. The suggestions for ministering to those under the death penalty are to a large extent drawn from the form for dealing with the

[69] *Works,* II, p. 324.

sick. A glimpse into the nature of the times is presented in the final rubric of this form, where special consolation is to be given "in those cases, which are frequent (!), where he who is to be executed is in nowise guilty in that whereof he is accused." [70] Life as a whole, in both this and the longer form for the sick, is not pictured in bright colors. "This temporal life is full of sin, sorrow, and distress, therefore we may be happy soon to depart from it" [71] are words that not only are intended as consolation for the dying or death-bound, but are also an incidental revelation of the mood of him who wrote the words.

In the Vesterås decisions of 1527, the ceremony at the house of the dead was discountenanced,[72] but in line with the Örebro policy of 1529, Olavus included in his Manual a form for this ceremony. In its evangelical shape it consisted, however, of an exhortation to the friends and relatives, a reference to the Scripture promise of resurrection, and a prayer for the deceased. The last named was composed by Olavus, and was destined three hundred years later, in a slightly altered form, to be included in the Prussian *Hofagenda* of 1822! [73] In the Church of Sweden and in one branch of the Lutheran Church in America it finds a place in the service at every open grave, even to this day, transformed, however, from its original nature.

The service at the grave, according to the Manual, included the Roman act of casting earth (though in Olavus' form, three times, not as in the Roman, once); a prayer, which is an elaboration of the prayer sug-

[70] *Works,* II, p. 365.
[71] *Ibid.,* p. 361; *cf.* pp. 331, 358, 367.
[72] *Quensel, op. cit.,* I, 71, note.
[73] *Ibid.,* p. 74.

gested for the house service; two hymns translated from the German (originally Latin), a Scripture passage concerning the promise of resurrection, and an exhortation to those assembled. The order follows closely that observed in German agenda, but there is no evidence that Olavus by 1529 had any printed forms to be guided by.[74] The reading of Scripture at the grave and the exhortation were evangelical innovations. The hymn singing was not new, but hymns in the native language came only after the Reformation. On the other hand, Olavus' prayer for the deceased, even if phrased conditionally ("if our departed brother is in such an estate that our prayers can be to his benefit"), had no sanction in Germany. Once more we find the Swedish Reformer treading a middle path between the old and the new.

Such might also be the characterization of the entire Manual of 1529. In every formula the new was built upon the foundations of the old. Olavus understood the power of ceremony, and knew the conservative nature of his countrymen. Ideally, he might prefer to build anew; practically, he chose to educate the people from the old into the new. Rather than offend the weak, he would suffer the old, only that it might be given a new meaning. In baptism, in marriage, in the preparation for death, in the burial service—everywhere we notice his caution in regard to the externals. But he considered them "minor matters" (as he says in the Conclusion to the Manual), and would not argue even with those who would not go as far as he had gone in changing them. The greater matters were the Gospel and the Word of God. According to these the contents of each service must be measured. And

[74] Quensel, *op. cit.*, I, 75ff.

herein we find the sincerity and consistency of the Reformer. The prayers, the frequent exhortations, the many Scriptural passages—all witness to the eagerness of the man to bring to light the basic truths of the Christian faith which every ceremony should make clearer. The political transformation had proceeded rapidly, so rapidly in fact that the Church could not at once find itself in the new order of things. The Manual was Olavus' contribution to the Church, whereby its clergy could bring the ceremonies of the Church into accord with the doctrine that it was now pledged to preach.

The political events of the third decade of the sixteenth century had transformed the organization of the Church of Sweden. The liturgical works of Olavus Petri—the hymns, the Manual, the Mass—marked the beginnings of the transformation in the forms and ceremonies of the Church. The worth of his work is best revealed in the extent to which his suggestions were realized and still live in that Church today.

CHAPTER VI

THE HOMILETICAL WORKS. THE THEOLOGICAL THOUGHT OF OLAVUS PETRI

"It is no great art to criticize and destroy, for that even a Turk or a heathen can do. But it is an art judiciously and decently to bring to nought what is false, and in its place establish that which is right and true," Olavus once counseled his fellow reformers.[1] The years 1528-1539 saw the production of real constructive work from the pen of Olavus, by which he hoped to establish truth and righteousness in the Church. In his homiletical tasks, he turned directly to the clergy of the land. Olavus Petri was the preacher to the preachers, more than to the people, in his printed sermon literature. No one equaled him in his evangelical clearness and positiveness. Without much doubt he can be called the father of evangelical preaching in Sweden. His method and his message determined for generations the nature of the sermons in the Swedish Church. In treating of his homiletical productions we may distinguish three groups of works: the Postils (including Catechetical works), sermons occasioned by special events or conditions, general homiletical treatises.

The Postils were two in number, dating from 1528

[1] *Works,* III, 492.

and 1530. They were avowedly for the clergy who, at the Parliament of Vesterås and the Council of Örebro, had been commissioned to preach. But as it had long been a practice in the Church, "that as soon as one could read or sing a Mass, he has fulfilled the requirements of a priest,"[2] it was not at all strange that the clergy began to murmur that they could not preach: "It is difficult," they complained, "to use what one never has learned," namely, the Scriptures. For the "simple clerks and parish priests" Olavus went to "much trouble and work and expense" to enable them to perform their rightful task—preaching, "for the office of the priest is a preaching office."

Just when the preaching was to take place is a disputed question. Until recently, it has been held that Olavus had in mind a preaching service, preceding the Mass. Brilioth has objected to this theory, and argued that in the country at large Swedish Mass was not held, and that the preaching, in line with tradition, followed the reading of the Gospel in the Latin Mass. Where Swedish Mass was held, it had no sermon, but the Communion admonition served the purpose of a sermon.[3] The condition of the majority of Swedish churches surely speaks in favor of this theory. For even by 1530 Swedish Mass was the exception, not the rule. It is significant that the Örebro decisions, which say much about preaching, say nothing of the Mass. Outside of Stockholm and probably a few other places,[4] the Latin Mass was the only one used, and it may be assumed that the preaching in Swedish was

[2] Introduction to Postil of 1530 (*Works*, III, 4).
[3] Y. Brilioth, *Nattvarden*, pp. 393ff.
[4] *Works*, II, 404. "Stockholm and some other cities" is the phrase used in reference to the use of the Swedish Mass.

incorporated into the Mass.[5] But the theory can hardly be extended to apply either to Stockholm or to the services for which the Postils were intended.

In Stockholm the Swedish Mass had been introduced. The best commentary on its nature and intended use is found in the Foreword to the Swedish Mass, together with the earlier defense of Olavus, *Why the Mass Should Be in Swedish*. Here we learn that Olavus considered the Latin Mass a mosaic of the original institution and the customs of succeeding generations. Consequently, he argued, the true ought to be separated from the false, the human from the divine. The Lord's Supper, that is, the words of institution and the eating and drinking, was the central and principal part of the Mass. All else—collects, prayers, hymns, special garments—were human additions. The selections from the Scriptures had their foundation in the admonition of St. Paul "that when Christians were assembled together, then the Word should be preached, and especially ought the Word be proclaimed at the Lord's Supper."[6] In these "Epistles and Gospels some special instruction would of course be given the audience."[7] In the analysis of the Mass the sermon was not mentioned. It seems that Olavus conceived of the Mass, most of all the Evangelical Mass, as simply a Communion rite. He wanted to restore the Mass to its primitive function—the celebration of the Lord's Supper. Insofar as the momenta of the

---

[5] If this were the practice, it was contrary to the ideals of the Reformer, who charged that "Those who say that we should preach the Word of God, and still celebrate the Mass in Latin, clearly admit that they are ignorant of the purpose and nature of the Mass" (*Works*, II, 402).

[6] *Works*, II, 409.

[7] *Ibid.*, p. 396.

Ecclesiastical Transformation in Sweden 181

Latin Mass contributed to this purpose, they were retained, especially for the sake of "the weak," but the Mass itself was no longer the climax and fulfillment of the services of the Church. It was but the rite of Communion for those who partook of the Lord's Supper.

Simultaneously the preaching service came into greater prominence—in Stockholm, evidently preceding the Communion service—for Olavus was of the opinion that "Mass shall not be held unless preaching has preceded." [8] For this service the Council at Örebro had made provisions, including one that Pater Noster, Credo, Ave Maria, and the Commandments should be incorporated in the preaching, and that prayer should precede and conclude the sermon.[9] To help the preachers for this service Olavus issued the Postil of 1530, which along with the sermons contained forms for the introductory and concluding prayers, and the Commandments, Credo, Pater Noster, and Ave Maria. It provided also an admonition to be used in addressing those who wished to go to Communion, as well as an admonition "before he begins the Mass." Another admonition, introducing the sermon, is so worded that one cannot escape the conclusion that two distinct services were provided for—a preaching service and a Communion service.[10] For the preaching service the Gospel for the day was advocated as the preaching text and on these texts the Postils were constructed.

---

[8] *Ibid.*, p. 403. The context forbids us to interpret the word "preaching" in any other sense than the literal. It cannot refer here to the reading of the Epistles and Gospels, but to a sermon *preceding* the Mass.

[9] Hildebrand och Alin, *Svenska Riksdagsakter*, I, 118-122.

[10] *Works,* III, 9; *cf.* p. 13. In the one case the assembly is for the purpose of hearing the Word; in the other for the Lord's Supper.

To aid the "simple" clergy in the explanation of the Credo, etc., which they had been enjoined to teach their people by the meeting at Örebro in 1529, the Postil of 1530 presented a Catechism, based on Luther's Large Catechism, with expositions of the Commandments, the Creed, the Lord's Prayer, and the Sacraments of Baptism and of the Altar. It was probably at the preaching service that the congregational singing found place. Altogether the substance of this service was not small, and its importance corresponded to the stress that Olavus placed on the education of the congregation. Just as he held that the clergy's function was to preach rather than to celebrate Mass, so he hoped that the preaching service rather than the Swedish Mass would be the means of transforming the inner life and cult of the Church.

To the Postil of 1530 more than to that of 1528 the name of Olavus Petri is attached. The earlier Postil was a translation, which it is assumed was the work of our Reformer. With few exceptions it was a literal reproduction in Swedish of the German Postil of Luther.[11] The latter had been issued by Stephan Roth in Wittenberg, 1526, and was referred to in the Swedish as the "German postil which has recently been produced." Not without some dubiousness had it been translated for the Swedish clergy, "for in it there is treated occasionally of many abuses that have arisen in Christendom, in such a way as might be beneficial not at all for those who are yet weak, but alone for those who have some experience in the Scriptures."[12] Therefore the work had not been completed; only about one-half of the German work was translated, or

[11] *Weimar Ausgabe*, Vol. XII, and Vol. X, 1, 2.
[12] *Works*, II, 3.

twenty-seven sermons in all. These, it was hoped, could at least help the Swedish clergy to build a sermon on the Scriptures. The New Testament had been available since 1526, but the clergy had complained that the mere text was no great help. Olavus apologized for the hurried nature of his work, and promised that another Postil would be prepared, suited for Swedish conditions, and more complete than this emergency effort. As mentioned, the translation was practically literal. Only here and there, where Luther treated the abuses too rough-handedly for "simple clergy," Olavus deleted or modified. The work, however, is Luther's, not Olavus', and the homiletical work of Olavus is to be sought rather in the Postil of 1530.

The Swedish clergy had been commanded to preach, and the New Testament had been given them as their source and textbook. They had replied that they did not know how to interpret the Scriptures. The Preface to the Postil of 1530 declared, "Certainly it would be best if one read the Scriptures themselves, if the intelligence allowed, yet where it does not, we have to creep until we learn to walk. We hope we have, in this Postil, however simple it is, invalidated their excuse, so that our parish preachers cannot say that they do not understand the text, and thus know not what to preach. Here the meaning is expressed so simply, that even if one read from the book to the people it would not be without fruit."[13] In these words are suggested the main characteristics of the book—Scriptural, simple and clear, practical. Almost invariably the sermon is thus constructed: the text, a paraphrase of the contents, an application of its "teaching." Sometimes the paraphrase is preceded by

[13] *Works*, III, 5.

a short explanation of the "occasion" of the text. Usually the application consists of two or three points, and is shorter than the paraphrase which is the body of the sermon. The sermons cover the Church Year with its principal holidays. Beside the foremost holidays, the following days are treated: Candlemas, Annunciation, St. John the Baptist, Visitation, Our Lady (Virgin's Death), St. Michael, All Saints. One sermon is given as a model for the Days of the Apostles, two sermons for the "days of holy men who were not apostles." Especially in these saints' festivals Olavus endeavored to point out the Scriptural as opposed to the traditional significance of the holiday. Polemics entered rarely into the collection, though it was not altogether excluded. Thus, it was advocated the prayer days should be abolished, if they could not be transformed so as to be celebrated more acceptably to God (Sermon fifth Sunday after Easter); the celebration of the day of the Virgin's death was wholly without foundation in Scripture (Sermon on that Day); compulsory confession at Easter was an erroneous practice (Sermon on Maundy Thursday); true service to God consists in fulfilling the commands of God, not the regulations of men (Sunday after Ascension); true fasting must come from an inner desire, not an outward force (Sermon on Ash Wednesday); confession to God is of greater importance than confession to man—the latter is voluntary (Fourth Sunday in Lent; in spiritual things there can be no commercialism (Tenth Sunday after Trinity). But these criticisms were not the rule. Usually they occurred as natural examples of the Truth, to which special days or seasons called attention. The Postil was throughout constructive.

Ecclesiastical Transformation in Sweden 185

It would be difficult to conceive of a simpler exposition of Scriptural texts than this one, whose purpose was to serve untutored clergy and, still more, untutored laymen. The words of Olavus in the Preface indicate that the Postil would probably be read to the congregation word for word, at least where the clergy could not formulate their own sermons. Over and over again, like a trained schoolmaster, he therefore repeated the few fundamental truths that every Christian should know. We do not find here the passion, the personal experience, the thunder and lightning of a Luther, who expressed *himself* in every sermon. Olavus rarely appeared in his sermons, but was intent on having his readers, as children in a schoolroom, see and learn what was written on the board before them. The writing was clear: God had had compassion on the misery into which man had come through sin; He sent Christ to bear the guilt and punishment of human sin; the believer in Christ receives the Holy Spirit which leads him out of sin into a fellowship with God wherein it is his delight to do the commands of his Lord. The sin of man, the mercy of God in Jesus Christ, the duty of the redeemed to love their fellowmen—of these truths Olavus never tired to preach. They, together with the paraphrase of the text, were the sum and substance of his sermons in the Postil of 1530.

True to his convictions, Olavus Petri sought to bring the Scriptures to the people. The translation of 1526 had only partially brought the desired effect, and that among a restricted group of the clergy. A further approach was now opened through the preaching of the clergy, who, as far as Olavus was concerned, should teach the Scriptures. His Postil offered all the texts in Swedish. These, with the paraphrase in the sermon, would do much to inform the congregations. He also urged the preachers, in the Preface to the Postil, to read a half or a whole chapter from the Swedish New Testament each holy day "to prolong their sermon, so that the people might hear the whole of the Gospels, to the end, one after another, and thus in time accustom themselves to the Word of God, so that finally there might not be much need of the Postil, for the Scriptures themselves would be used."[14] The purpose of the Postil was nothing else, consequently, than a beginner's book in the Scriptures, both for clergy and laity. Furthermore, containing, as it did, forms for the opening and closing of the service, various prayers and admonitions, and a Catechism for the instruction of the people in the fundamentals of the Christian religion, the Postil was in reality a handbook and guide for the homiletical and catechetical duties of the Swedish preacher. Added to the Handbook of 1529 and the Swedish Mass, it completed the constructive labors of Olavus to build up a new faith and new forms in the place of that which was declared false; or, as Olavus would say, the new was the old purged of its human inventions and ancient errors.

The Catechism appended to the Postil had a practical purpose. The preacher was enjoined to read "The Ten Commandments, the Credo, and the Lord's Prayer, every holiday, after the sermon, for the people, so that they can learn them correctly." This was not sufficient, however, for "occasionally he ought to explain them according to the contents of the Cate-

[14] *Works,* III, 8.

chism."[15] Following the sermon for the fifth Sunday after Easter—one of the Prayer Days—we find the rubric "On the Prayer Days the people should be taught the Commandments, the Credo, and Pater Noster, with their meaning."[16] The Catechisms of Luther had appeared in 1529, and Olavus made use of the explanations as material from which the clergy could better teach their people the meaning of the first steps in Christianity. The clergy, too, were to admonish their parishioners to teach their children in the home, and when they became of age to send them to school, for "Christianity cannot be maintained unless children are given schooling and knowledge." For Olavus, Christianity and knowledge of the Scriptures were inseparable.

Even before this date, Olavus had interested himself in the spreading of elementary Christian knowledge among the people. His earliest work, *An Useful Teaching* (1525-26), was built on the tenets that the Church through the centuries had come to consider the foundation stones of the Christian religion. It is possible that Olavus was the translator of a Rostock edition of *Kinderfragen* (a German reworking of a Catechism of the Bohemian Brethren), which appeared in Swedish in 1526.[17] Avowedly he was the translator of another German textbook, catechetical in content though not in form. Johann Toltz had printed his *Handbuchlein für junge Christen*, in Wittenberg in

---

[15] *Ibid.*, p. 8.
[16] *Ibid.*, p. 216.
[17] *Een skön nyttugh underwisningh* (A Fine Useful Teaching) included in the works of Olavus, though its translator is uncertain (*Works*, I, 141ff.).

1526,[18] and Olavus translated it, with insignificant changes, into Swedish, in 1529, calling it *A Brief Introduction into the Holy Scriptures."* [19] In concise, clear form the work defined Law, Gospel, Faith in Jesus Christ, the Sacraments, Righteousness, Fasting, Prayer, the Old Adam and the New, the Freedom of the Will, the Church, True Pastors, Marriage, the Saints, etc. The forms and thought of the schoolteacher of Plauen were very congenial to the schoolmaster of Strengnäs, and often in the works of the latter we find definitions and expressions that resemble those of the former. In Sweden as in Germany the work was popular—a second edition of the Swedish translation appeared in 1538. As its Swedish title suggested, it was intended by Olavus to help the reader to understand the Scriptures.

A second group of homiletical works by Olavus Petri contain those sermons which were prompted by special events or conditions in the Church or State of Sweden. First of these was the Coronation Sermon.

On January 12, 1528, Gustavus Vasa was crowned king of Sweden, in the Cathedral of Uppsala. The sermon was preached by Olavus Petri, who made use of the opportunity to instruct the king and people concerning their respective privileges and duties.[20] The king was reminded that he had his office for the sake of the people, and the people did not exist for

---

[18] F. Cohrs, *Monumenta Germaniae Pedagogica*, XX, 243ff. A Rostock edition appeared February 16, 1526.

[19] *Een liten ingong i then helga scrifft* (*Works*, II, 371ff.). A Danish translation of Olavus' work is known from 1529, wherefore some have thought Olavus' translation to be earlier than 1529. *Cf.* Klemming, *Sveriges, Bibliografi*, pp. 206ff.; S. Ek, in *Samlaren*, 1918, p. 2, note 2.

[20] *Works*, I, 315ff.

his sake. He was a servant of God, so that "all honor and reverence which he received he should transfer to God"; his office was one that could rightly be filled only through the wisdom and love of God. "Silver and gold, horses and trappings, castle and fortress" might be in his possession, but ought not to be objects of confidence and trust above God. The king's sovereignty was confined to things temporal, but "since the soul is better than the body" it behooved him to care for the spiritual welfare of his people, even "keeping an eye on bishops and priests who are in his land, when they are negligent in those things commanded them." If necessary the king should endure martyrdom for his people, but to "suffer persecution for the sake of righteousness is great grace before God." His address to the king, the preacher concluded thus: "Thus, mighty Lord, Your Grace has now heard the rule according to which he should conduct himself, and when it is so followed, fortune and happiness will be Your Grace's lot; and God will be with you." Not less direct was the admonition to the people. They were by Scripture commanded to obey the authorities, give them "tax and due, fear and honor," and in all things not contrary to God, be subservient to their ruler. The Scriptural command extended to all in the kingdom, though in Sweden one party had "drawn away with privileges and liberties from the obedience to the ruler and established a new realm by itself, as if it had nothing to do with the king." But Scriptures gave "neither pope nor bishop nor prelate" any such immunity from the temporal sovereign. Sweden ought to be thankful for a Christian ruler, and each one should now fulfill his duty, so that freedom and Christian government might dwell in the land. It was a clear lesson presented to both king and subjects, by a fearless preacher, who based his teachings on the authority of Scripture, whence he drew his power and commission. Gustavus was not apt quickly to become a martyr for his people nor consider himself merely a servant, but he perceived that the preacher had moral sanction as well as moral courage, which were not to be despised. The political theories represented in the Coronation Sermon will be dealt with in another connection.

Later in the same year (1528), previous to the annual meeting of the clergy in their respective dioceses, Olavus found occasion to impress upon the clergy and the congregations the rightful relationship that should exist between them.[21] On the basis of Scripture, he proved that bishops and priests, "which are one and the same," were ordained to preach. "That (preaching) is the main thing in this office, so that if this ceases, then the whole office ceases." Administration of the sacraments was important, but subordinate to the function of preaching. Preaching was the written letter, the sacraments were its seal. Finally, it belonged to the clergy to set their people an example of Christian daily life and virtues. The corresponding obligations of the laity were to heed the preaching of the clergy and care for the clergy's support. Olavus made clear, though, that the clergy were to be obeyed and supported by virtue of the preaching of the Word of God, and not for the maintenance of a whole system of man-made practices. In the closing part of the treatise, conditions contrary to those described as rightful were mentioned and remedies suggested. Preachers who were too old to learn to

[21] "A Christian Admonition to the Clergy" (*Works*, I, 353ff.).

Ecclesiastical Transformation in Sweden

preach should either quit the ministry or engage personally someone to preach for them, "for here must needs be preaching." The laity were exhorted to show the fruits of the Gospel in other ways than denial of dues to the clergy. The decisions of Vesterås in 1527 had overturned the traditional relationship between clergy and people as far as finances were concerned, and had not improved the relationship in spiritual matters. Olavus realized the situation full well. His "Admonition" was timely and to the point. The conditions he described would require many years and much training ere his ideal could be approached.

Years of hard experience intervened between the first and second admonition that Olavus directed to his fellow preachers. In 1535 he addressed the evangelical preachers through a sermon based on the commission of the disciples in chapter ten of the Gospel of Matthew.[22] A comparison of this sermon with that of 1528 reveals changes that had taken place both in the life of the country and of the Reformer during this period. The "evangelical cause" had made progress, but still in 1535 Olavus bade his friends pray that "it might go through with fruit." It was "God's cause," and "it needed God's deeds, not only those of man, if it were to have success." The people were described as "scattered sheep without a shepherd" and their children were not in schools. "Many are found who seek the milk and the wool, yea even the meat, of the sheep, but they are very few who care for the salvation of the sheep." The preachers were reminded that their aim was to break down the devil's kingdom, and establish the Lord's. Their duties were not easy.

[22] "An Admonition to All Evangelical Preachers" (*Works*, III, 473ff.).

"There is no mystery about the wolf persecuting the sheep, but it is a mystery when the sheep takes courage to become a messenger to the wolves in the hope of being able to convert them from their cruel nature to humility, so that they shall cease being wolves and become sheep." The transformation in the religious life had not been without perils, and the evangelical preachers had had to consider the condition of the traditionalists. Unfortunately some had taken upon themselves to criticize everything, without themselves being better; in fact "they are four times worse." Seemingly more of these were on the evangelical side, and the Gospel suffered from their recklessness. The preachers were advised to study and master the Scriptures, for the gift of the Spirit was no substitute for personal faithfulness in study and work. "He who will not faithfully use those gifts which he has received, to the praise of God, certainly is not deserving to receive more." Persecution was not to be feared as much as success. The entire discourse was an earnest plea to the faithful preachers of the Gospel to fulfill their duties humbly and trustingly, despite persecution, difficulties, and seeming impossibilities. In the background we can discern that Olavus was not satisfied with conditions, either among the old or the new party. The latter, indeed, caused him more concern, for the friends of the evangelic movement did it more harm than the enemies. The old hierarchy had lost its power, but its place had not yet found educated, capable, Christian men, who would be more concerned about building up than tearing down. To counteract the baneful influences of the Church's loss of prestige and power, Olavus fully and directly pictured the true disciples and apostles who might hope for the enduring blessing of God in their work. However great the lack of true evangelic shepherds, there could not be a lack, in 1535, of understanding of the type of preacher that the Gospel demanded.

The disappointment that found expression in 1535 in the writings of Olavus increased rather than decreased, until in 1539 a certain tone of pessimism, even of bitterness, was audible. The "Sermon against the Terrible Oaths,"[23] of 1539, not only had political consequences, but revealed a different temper than that of ten years previous. "It must be admitted that the devil never before has reigned so openly and visibly in the world as he now does in these terrible oaths and blasphemies of God." The awful swearing that he daily heard about him had become to Olavus a sign of the perversity of his generation, and he believed that "the extreme punishment of God" was imminent because of the universal blasphemy of God's name. No sin could be called greater than to wish harm upon a fellowman through invoking the holiest names and symbols of the holy God. Beside it, the sins of the papacy were small, for its practices at least aimed to honor His name. Christians by name and profession did not hesitate to swear by the name that formerly Christians would die to keep holy. Preaching could not remedy the grievous sin, for they who persisted in the practice considered themselves good Christians. Olavus then turned to the authorities. Why did they permit misuse of the name of the Highest Ruler when they were careful to punish breaches of honor against their own name? It was the duty of the ruler to punish the practice, for he had his office from God

[23] *Works,* IV, 375ff.; *cf.* Olavus' reference to the same sin in his legal writings, pp. 306, 308, 336.

and was answerable to God. "And the ruler must himself cease from such oaths, otherwise he can do little to remedy the matter." A French king, Louis, had known how to set an example—"would to God that all Christian princes were of like mind—but now it is not so. Instead they contribute to the practice by themselves setting an example." The results were everywhere apparent. Children followed in their elders' footsteps and learned of them to swear. Treaties and contracts between individuals and states meant little or nothing, because the oaths by which they were sealed had lost all force. Even the relationship between king and people suffered, for it depended on godliness. These were sharp words, and direct in their aim. It was the same Olavus who had preached to the same king at Uppsala in 1528, only that now Gustavus felt strong enough to go his own ways and brooked no opposition. This sermon became one of the charges against Olavus in the trial of the same year that almost brought his days and work to a sudden end.

A group of works of a homiletical or devotional character, which came from the printer anonymously, have been attributed to Olavus Petri by reason of the style and character of the contents. Two were in verse, a third in prose.

The Soul's Consolation and Healing, Though at All Times Useful, yet Most So in the Hour of Death[24] was printed in Stockholm in 1537. It professed "God's own apothecary—which is the Holy Scriptures," as its source, and proclaimed as its aim the healing of the soul, which should be cared for equally as well as, or better than, the body, which man did not hesitate to

[24] *Works*, III, 347ff.

find remedies for in times of need. The need of the soul was especially apparent in the hour of death, when three forces above others attacked it—the burden of sin, the fear of death, the dread of hell and eternal condemnation. From "God's apothecary" the author drew forth an abundance of Scripture passages, relating to one or other of these three experiences. The dying should find comfort against the qualms of conscience by faith in the atoning death of Christ. "God has accepted the death of His Son as a complete penance and compensation for all your sins." Against the fear of death, faith in the promise and resurrection of Christ should be the defense. "God himself came from heaven to become a mortal man in order that the mortal nature of man, by personal union with the immortal nature of God, might, by God's infinite power, be exalted to immortal life." Only a true confidence in Christ could allay the fear of hell. In the hour of death, the death of Christ and his words from the Cross gave great solace to the believer. The treatise closed with an exhortation to the living to prepare for death before it came suddenly upon them. The booklet is an evangelical *Ars Moriendi,* with precedents both in Roman and evangelical literature. Unlike the Roman, this *Ars Moriendi* referred the reader (or him who read for the dying) solely to the Word and its promises.

"*Tobie Comedia,* Stockholm, 1550," [25] read the title page of a Biblical drama that has been ascribed to Olavus. It has the flavor of a medieval miracle play, as well as its dramatis personnae—the angel, the devil, the faithful father, the mistrusting wife, the virtuous son. The play is a dramatization of the apocryphal

[25] *Ibid.,* p. 395.

Book of Tobias. The god-fearing and generous father, Tobias, loses his sight and with it his friends and means, even the good-will of his wife. The virtuous son is sent to collect a loan, and finds the Angel Raphael as a companion, who secures a wife and riches for the young Tobias, and sight and a Job's restoration for the old Tobias. The miraculous agency is a fish; it causes the defeat of the devil and the opening of the eyes of Tobias. The interest of the story, in its naïve and quaint narration, is sufficient to carry the reader over the uneven and monotonous couplets. But the author made no pretense of being a poet. In the very opening he revealed his identity—a preacher. Man, he admitted, soon tires of one kind of sermon, and it is both necessary and wholesome to have recourse to another. Even in heathen times wise men had seen the possibility of using the stage as a means of moral instruction, and Christianity in Sweden as elsewhere had used "ballads, rhymes, and comedies" to teach spiritual truths. "He who had liking for rhymes and verse, he may read this Comedy," for in it were many good examples of Christian virtues. "But he who has more love for simple speech, let him read the Book of Tobias itself in the Bible"—the main thing was the emulation of the example.

After the death of Olavus, another versified Biblical narrative was printed in Stockholm (1556), whose authorship was not given, but has generally been ascribed to the Reformer. Its title was, *The Suffering and Resurrection of Our Lord Jesus Christ, as described by the four Evangelists—Item how one should in a godly manner contemplate this suffering and resurrection of our Lord. A brief instruction in verse form.*[26] The fourfold division of the book followed the title's suggestion of the contents—the death of Christ, the resurrection of Christ, contemplation of the death, contemplation of the resurrection, of Christ. The first two parts remind us of the *Parabolae* which appeared in the 1536 collection of hymns. In both cases the verse is a rhymed paraphrase, closely following the Biblical text. An internal proof of the authorship of Olavus presents itself in the third part, where, among the lessons to be learned from the suffering of Christ, especially that one is stressed which would forbid the misuse of the name of Him who suffered much for man. The thought is identical with passages in the sermon against swearing.[27] The work is itself a sermon, similar in its construction to the sermons of the Postil—a paraphrase of the text, followed by applications based on it. As described in the title, it is an instruction, or sermon, presented in rhyme, or verse. As in the *Comedy*, the form was the rhymed couplet, and here as there, the instruction, not the verse, was the dominant factor.

From the pen of Olavus we know two fragments of works on "Saints" and on "Angels," the one being the conclusion, the other the beginning, of sermons on the Scriptural teaching in regard to these subjects.[28]

The name of Olavus was given in a booklet of 1558, printed in Stockholm, with the title *Concerning the Most Vital Events and the Age of the World*. It is an eschatological study, following the traditional theory of the age of the world—four thousand years

---

[26] *Works*, IV, pp. 443ff.
[27] *Cf.* pp. 506, l. 28, p. 508, l. 13, and pp. 376, 380, 381, 382, 385.
[28] *Ibid.*, 579ff.

before Christ, and, until the end, two thousand years after. The author names the principal events from the beginning to the birth of Christ, and "for the simple folk" mentioned the most important name or event of each thousand years. The end of the world was near, and Christ could come at any time, for the last period was to be "shortened." The treatise has much in common, especially in its first part, with Andreas Osiander's *Vermutung von den letzen zeiten/ und dem Ende der Welt/aus der heiligen Schrift gezogen,* which was printed in Nürnberg in 1545.[29] The extent of the relationship between the two cannot be determined, but in view of other bonds between Swedish and Nürnberg Reformation literature, it is not improbable that some connection exists. That Olavus was inclined to eschatological thought the accusers at his trial bore witness, and his "Sermon against Oaths," in 1539, revealed his faith in the near approach of the end of the world.

In connection with the treatment of one book of Olavus published in 1535, and another unpublished until recent times, we would endeavor to summarize the theological thinking of the Swedish Reformer. The unpublished work (until 1898) was also unfinished at the time of Olavus' death. It has the title, *Concerning the Noble Creation of Man, His Fall and Restoration,*[30] and is in many respects an elaboration of Olavus' first work, *An Useful Teaching.* To it was to be appended an exposition of the Ten Commandments, the Twelve Articles (Creed), Christian Prayer, Our Father, and the Sacraments. The book of 1535 was called *"A Short Book in Which It Is Explained*

[29] A copy of this work is in the Royal Library, Berlin.
[30] *Works,* III, 513.

How Man Attains to Eternal Bliss/if It Takes Place Through His Merit or Through the Pure Grace and Mercy of God," [31] and has been called the most mature exposition of the dogmatic standpoint of Olavus.[32] These two writings are doubly valuable as sources for knowledge of the religious principles of the Reformer—less than any other, they depend on other sources either for their content or their form; more than any other, they are free from all polemics, and seem to have been written in the stillness of thought directed to the subject matter and not distracted by opposition.

Man was created in the image of God; not in a physical sense, for God is a Spirit, but in the endowment of holiness, righteousness, goodness, wisdom, and power, man was made to resemble his Maker.[33] The deed whereby man sinned was not so criminal in itself, but it represented in man a lack of reverence, faith, and obedience in God, whose Majesty he no longer honored.[34] God could not remain God, if he allowed this sin to go unpunished. Had the penalty been commensurate with the sin, hell would have been the immediate reward, but the Eternal Christ was present even then to make the verdict more lenient.[35] The consequent punishment was intended not for man's destruction, but for his betterment.[36] Creation itself shared in the doom,[37] and earth became a place of misery, Paradise being transformed into thorns and thistles.[38] Despite the aim of the punishment—the

---

[31] *Works,* II, 449ff.
[32] *Ibid.,* p. XVII (Westman); also J. E. Berggren, in Uppsala Univ. *Årskrift,* 1899, p. 43.
[33] *Works,* III, 519.
[34] *Ibid.,* p. 539.
[35] *Ibid.,* p. 540.
[36] *Ibid.,* p. 541.
[37] *Ibid.,* p. 546.
[38] *Ibid.,* p. 554.

correction of man—humanity finds no happiness, for it would gladly be free from the punishment of sin, but not from sin itself.[39] The sin of Adam and Eve is repeated in the life of every individual, for man has God's will in the Law, which no man has ever completely obeyed.[40] The Law cannot therefore save man, for even its most zealous followers, the Jews, have failed to keep it perfectly—it was given not to save man, but to keep man mindful of the extent of his apostasy from God.[41] Righteousness comes not by the Law.[42]

Ultimately, the salvation of man is to be sought in God's election of men to salvation.[43] To effect such a salvation, he gave His Son—through Him the world had been created, through Him it was to be restored.[44] The humiliation of Christ—incarnation, suffering, and death—was the compensation for the punishment of man.[45] When man accepted Christ as his Saviour, the merits of Christ transformed his standing before God—he received the forgiveness of sin, and was righteous before God. "Righteousness and the forgiveness of sins were one and the same thing."[46] This changed relationship to God depends entirely on man's fellowship with Christ, a fellowship effected through faith in the promise of Word and Sacrament. When we believe, "we have Christ, and when we have Him, then we have the forgiveness of sins and righteousness that is in Him."[47] Salvation consists in the forgiveness of sins, made possible through God's work in Christ.

Man accepts salvation through faith. But since

[39] *Ibid.*, p. 555.
[40] *Works*, II, 459.
[41] *Ibid.*, pp. 462, 465.
[42] *Ibid.*, p. 466.
[43] *Ibid.*, p. 467.
[44] *Ibid.*, p. 468.
[45] *Ibid.*, p. 470; *cf.* III, 572.
[46] *Ibid.*, p. 471.
[47] *Ibid.*, p. 473.

faith is a faith in God, it must be based on what is truly the promise of God—the Word of God.[48] Faith is false if it have a false foundation, wherefore the consequence of false teaching is fatal. Any teaching derived elsewhere than from the Word is uncertain.[49] That faith is also false which does not bear the fruits of faith, which are visible in a new life. For when man truly believes in Christ, it is an act of thanksgiving and of love to Him whose sacrifice has saved him, and such gratitude and love find expression in devotion to His will, in fulfillment of His commandments. Thus the newly awakened love to God does what the previous fear and dread of God could not accomplish— transforms the heart, so that its desire is in the Law of God. Previously, God was a Judge, now He is a Father.[50] Forgiveness of sins is followed, or accompanied, by a forsaking of sin, and a life in righteousness.

Faith comes by preaching, or the proclamation of the will and mercy of God. Preaching includes the proclamation of the sacraments of Baptism and the Lord's Supper, as well as the Word. But not all believe that hear. Belief depends on the presence or absence of the Holy Spirit, who is present in Word and Sacrament for those foreseen by God to receive Him. Those who receive the Spirit also receive Christ Himself.[51] This is the new, or second, birth, whereby men become the children of God, and enter into the life abundant with the fruit of faith.[52] And thereby man is restored to the original place in God's plan, where he stood before the Fall, in which he lives to the honor and

[48] *Ibid.*, p. 474.
[49] *Ibid.*, p. 475.
[50] *Ibid.*, p. 476-477.
[51] *Ibid.*, pp. 479-480.
[52] *Ibid.*, p. 488.

praise of the Creator, his whole life being dictated by the will of God.[53] Flowing from the new love man has found to God, is a love to fellowmen. Not only is such love a commandment to be fulfilled, but a means whereby man may express his love and gratitude to God, for all love to man should be on account of God and to His honor.[54] In his new relationship to God, man learns rightly how to treat himself. He is to subdue the sinful nature within himself, that the life of the Spirit may have fuller place. To this end fasting and discipline may be necessary, but it is the lower nature, not the body, that should be castigated.[55]

In the whole process of salvation, the Spirit of God, not man, is the moving power. No place in the system is found for reward, even for the good deeds that are the result of faith. All is the work of God. The righteous man receives salvation and eternal bliss, not as a reward, but as a natural consequence of his righteousness, which is itself a gift of God. Good deeds testify to the presence of a righteous life, evil deeds to an evil life. The testimony convicts or saves, because it reveals the nature of the heart.[56] If the heart is turned to God in faith, it is righteous, and then turns to man in love. "Faith receives, love gives." [57]

By the preaching of His Word, the Holy Spirit assembles the faithful throughout the world into a spiritual fellowship, whose Head is Christ, and distributes spiritual gifts whereby the Church is built up in faith and virtue. The ministry is the office through which God reveals the same truths as formerly He revealed in the Word; the latter is the norm of the

[53] *Ibid.*, p. 492; *cf.* III, 573.
[54] *Ibid.*, pp. 494-495.
[55] *Ibid.*, pp. 497-498.
[56] *Ibid.*, pp. 502-504.
[57] *Ibid.*, p. 508.

former.[58] The Church is a spiritual fellowship; its treasures and duties are spiritual.

The dogmatic position of Olavus was definite and comprehensive. He had thought through the whole doctrine of the Church, not in a profound or philosophic manner, but practically and logically. On the fundamental question of religious authority that underlay the Reformation he was at one with Luther. The Scriptures, interpreted by their own light, were the source of religious knowledge and the inspiration of spiritual life. As the Christian Church had originally grown out of Scriptural revelation, so it must ever continue to be renewed and to grow out of the same root. The Roman Church was a human institution which corresponded very little with the Christian Church. The Word of God through the Law revealed to man his abnormal condition, through the Gospel it offered him restoration to man's normal estate. Olavus Petri had solved the mystery of predestination no more than had Luther, but on the testimony of the Word both accepted the Pauline teaching. Christ was God's means of satisfying, on the one hand, the Divine justice, and on the other, of drawing men to Himself and salvation. By the office of preaching, in Word and in Sacrament, the invitation was given to men to find forgiveness of sin, and life eternal. The Holy Spirit enabled them to believe, and through faith all the riches of the Christian life and heavenly kingdom became theirs. This world stood under the ban of sin, and would continue so, until the Day of Judgment, but it was the duty of the faithful to transform social life as much as possible by their life of love. Olavus time and again stressed the life that the redeemed

[58] *Works*, III, 574-575.

must manifest. The Church was the fellowship of the faithful, and was to be the witness of God until He returns to judge the wicked, and establish the everlasting kingdom of the righteous.

In the earliest of the writings of Olavus, *An Useful Teaching,* he had shown a clear understanding of the tenets that became the ever-recurring doctrines of all his teaching and writing. Indeed, the whole system that we have found in the book of 1535 already had been expressed in 1526 in the first book.[59] From the three foundation truths—the spiritual character of the Church, the Scriptural authority as absolute, and the salvation of man by faith in the free grace of God in Christ Jesus—all the structure of Olavus' dogmatic thinking had its development. With Peder Galle and Paulus Eliae he discussed the questions of the temporal power of the Church, the primary duty of the clergy, the authority of Scripture versus authority of the Church, the place of good deeds in the plan of salvation, the freedom of the will, the value of the sacraments, and similar doctrines. In every case his stand was but an application of the fundamental doctrines alluded to. The works on Marriage, on Monastic Life, on Human Statutes, were equally the logical consequence of his stand. The same system is everywhere apparent in the Postil, even in the hymns. From beginning to end, the works of Olavus Petri showed a remarkable consistency and definiteness in subject matter. Speculation played no part in the system, and little of philosophy was there. True to his principle, he built his thought on Scripture, and was not at all inferior to Luther in the definiteness of

[59] *Works,* I, 24-33, 43-50.

his faith. In the systematic presentation of his thought, Olavus was kin rather to Melanchthon than Luther. He was not the discoverer of new phases of spiritual truth, but the fearless, consistent, clear-minded teacher of what he himself was convinced was the truth.

The literal interpretation of Scripture was for Olavus the accepted method. With Luther, he doubted the authenticity of the Book of Revelation—it was not a book with which one could defend a doctrine.[60] The apocryphal books could not be placed on a level with the canonical books.[61] One passage of Scripture should be interpreted in the light of the whole, not as an isolated oracle,[62] and its meaning should be understood in the light of its historical setting.[63] It should never be forgotten that "in Scripture we seek nothing else than our salvation,"[64] wherefore Scripture should be considered in the light of its purpose.

Not unnaturally the thought of Olavus was colored by the teaching of the medieval Church and the nature of his times. God was the Most High Majesty, whose honor had been violated by the disobedience of his subjects.[65] He had chosen those who were to be saved from the beginning.[66] His wrath over sin was so terrible that only eternal punishment could pay the

[60] *Ibid.*, p. 213.

[61] *Ibid.*, p. 303.

[62] *Ibid.*, p. 536; *cf.* II, 512-514, where James' seeming contradiction to Paul is treated.

[63] *Works*, II, 505.

[64] *Works*, I, 200; *cf.* pp. 294-295.

[65] *Works*, III, 539; *cf.* IV, 391; *cf.* J. A. Eklund, *Andelivet i Sveriges Kyrke*, I, for the influence of Germanic conceptions on Christian thought in the Germanic countries.

[66] *Works*, II, 467.

penalty of sin, and His might was great enough to prolong hell eternally.[67] What man could not eternally recompense, Christ being "such an Exalted Person" was able to repay in a short period of suffering.[68] Clearly, Olavus of Sweden followed in the footsteps of Anselm of Canterbury. But when he entered the field of the Christian faith and Christian life he was in a new and brighter sphere. His description of man's relationship to Christ is equal to the best.[69] And the oft-repeated admonition to show the fruits of faith in Christian virtue belongs to the noblest features of Olavus' teaching. The Church should be a community of good works.[70] Our love to God He directs upon our neighbor.[71] The man who fulfills his obligations to his neighbor is more acceptable to God than he who seeks refuge from his fellows in a monastery.[72] Olavus' conception of Christianity was everywhere ethical.

In his attitude toward the Roman Church, on the one hand, and to Luther, on the other, Olavus marked the path which became the way of the Swedish Church out of medievalism into the modern centuries. Christianity for him did not mean dependence on Rome. The missionaries who brought the Faith to Sweden, "Ansgar and Sigfrid with others, brought Christ's holy Gospel, the pure and precious Word of God—and taught us to hold firmly to the Word and promises of God, to trust in the death and suffering of Christ who has reconciled us to our heavenly Father whom we

[67] *Works*, III, 554.
[68] *Ibid.*, p. 572.
[69] *Works*, I, 28-30; II, 476-477; III, 572-573.
[70] *Works*, I, 44.
[71] *Ibid.*, p. 272.
[72] *Ibid.*, p. 506.

had angered and who has secured for us eternal life, and in this faith to have brotherly love among each other and do each other good."[73] This was the true Faith, which later doctrines and practices of Rome had sullied and obscured. For Olavus, the Reformation meant the sweeping away of these "human institutions," that the Word and its preaching might again have sway, as in the days of Ansgar and Sigfrid.[74] As the Word had established Christianity in Sweden, so it should reestablish the true Faith. Even the doctrines of the Church Fathers were to be judged by the Word;[75] only so much of the past need be kept as was in accord with Scripture. Authority for a reformation in the Church of Sweden was not derived from a Council. "We have the Word of God before us, that shall be our norm."[76] On the other hand, Luther was to be considered as a counselor, not a new pope, and his counsel was subjected to the same principle as all the teaching of all others—insofar as he showed the way to a more Scriptural presentation of Christianity he was a trusted guide. "We have Christ for a master, Him we shall heed, in His name we are baptized, what He commands that we shall do."[77]

No clearer statement can be found of the doctrinal nature of the Swedish Reformer and the Swedish Reformation. Christ was enthroned as the supreme authority. His Word was given in the Scriptures. His believers were the Church. The sum of Christianity was faith in His Word and emulation of His life. A reformation in the Church meant no break or innovation, but rather a reassertion of the true nature of

[73] *Ibid.*, p. 339.
[74] *Ibid.*, p. 340.
[75] *Works,* I, 211, 234.
[76] *Works,* II, 400.
[77] *Works,* I, 168.

Christianity with a practical appliction of the principles derived from the Scriptures. The Church of Sweden was a part of the communion of Christians; it was neither Lutheran nor Roman. For the sake of the weak, practices of the past were to be tolerated until the illumination of the Word would automatically disperse the shadows of lingering errors. It was the fortune of the Swedish Church to have in its earliest Reformation period a man who saw the consequences of his teaching, and pictured a full canvas of the true character of a Christian community. That the reality did not correspond fully to the ideal was not the fault of Olavus Petri. His merit was to have given his Church and nation an ideal.

CHAPTER VII

THE LEGAL AND HISTORICAL WORKS

THE first Swedish work of jurisprudence, and the first critical Swedish history, have Olavus Petri as their author. As secretary of the City Council (*Rådet*) in Stockholm between 1524-1531,[1] and chancellor for a few years to the king, the faithful and studious preacher of St. Nicholaus Church also found time and occasion to interest himself in the laws of his country and city, as well as to collect material for his *Chronicle*. His legal notes and his historical work were not printed until long afterwards—the one in 1619, the other in 1818—but circulated in manuscript until the centuries reached a stage of development closer to that of the mind of Olavus than his own times had attained.

"The Commentary on the Municipal Law" was not an independent work, but a series of notes and comments written in the margin and between the sections of the manuscript copy of the current law in Olavus' possession.[2] That it is the writing of Olavus, the style of the language and the points of contact with the *Chronicle* testify. To a large extent the annotations consisted of explanations of words and phrases in the law book. But the notes also described characteristics

---

[1] The Minute-Book is still preserved. Its contents are printed in the *St. Eriks Årsbok*, 1908-1915.

[2] *Works*, IV, 315ff.; *cf.* C. G. E. Bjorling, "*Vår äldsta lagkommentar*," in *Lund Univ. Årsskrift*, 1896, pp. 1ff.; also Schück, *Svensk Litteraturhistoria*, I, 493.

of the people, and suggestions for the benefit of the judge. Comparisons were made between the various codices of law in Sweden, as well as with civil and canon law. The longest "note" is in the form of a preface, in which it was declared that the purpose of written law was found in its acting as a norm for the ruler and a source of information for the ruled. Both the ruler and the ruled should be guided by it. The reason for the rise, and the fall, of canon law was also briefly explained.

More important were the "Rules for the Judge,"[3] which were likewise inserted in the law manuscript. For the last three hundred years they have found a place in the editions of the Swedish law.[4] Not only for Olavus but for succeeding generations they expressed characteristics essential to a Christian judge. As he had instructed the occupant of the royal chair, so Olavus impressed the occupant of the judicial, that his office was a trust from God, in whose place he functioned, to whose judgment he was responsible. The judge must know the law, even as a preacher must know the Scriptures. His constant aim should be the welfare of the community—his office was created for the community, not the community for him. Personal gain had no place in his judicial decrees; the judgment that was based on bribery, direct or indirect, brought its punishment both to judge and community. His competence was of greater importance than the law itself. "A good and honest judge is better than good law," for even a good law was invalidated by a dishonest judge. Mercy must be found in the tribunal, otherwise "the highest justice was the highest injustice." Where the written law in its application might

[3] *Works,* IV, 301ff. [4] *Ibid,* p. xi.

hinder the welfare of the land, it had to yield to what was of greatest benefit. The judge was referred to the popular proverbs which in themselves were maxims of law, viz. "The envious shall not testify," "One shall not correct evil with double evil," "All is not true that is probable," "What one likes one easily bears witness to." Not the letter, but the sense, of the law should be considered in judging. Poor and rich should suffer alike, if the crime were the same. Anger did not become a judge. "All punishment should be for improvement." Torture should never be resorted to when a charge could not be substantiated by testimony, and no one should be judged by confession secured by torture. The intention of the defendant, not the manifest deed alone, should be taken into consideration, for not all crimes were intentional. In general, the judge was not only to pronounce judgment, but ever to seek to help, and to act to the best welfare of both the accused and the community.

In these concise, almost proverb-like, statements, Olavus furnished the judges with guidance in their high calling. He was, indeed, far ahead of his time in his insistence on consideration of the intention of the criminal, in his advocacy of the abolishment of torture, and in his conception of the meaning of punishment. In his capacity of secretary to the Stockholm Council, Olavus had experience in the process of the law of his time. Hardness even to cruelty marked those days, when the gallows were an everyday sight, and the ax fell often as a consequence of small offenses. Justice was difficult and slow, and often followed a line of gold. Reforms were not easily effected in this branch of the government, least of all such reforms as Olavus urged. The century passed before any other treatment of the law of the country was produced.

A Swedish Chronicle[5] was the most elaborate work that Olavus attempted. At the time of its composition it met only a cool response. The king denounced both it and its author, and those interested in history turned from him to a contemporary chronicler for the story of Sweden's glorious past. The *Chronicle*, however, circulated widely in manuscript, and in time came to its rightful honor as the most valuable history of the century. It was, in fact, the first history of Sweden written with truth as its guiding principle.

Olavus openly admitted the purpose of the *Chronicle* in its opening words: The lives of the forefathers should be recounted as a guidance and warning for the children. "It is better to learn wisdom through the misfortunes of another than of ourselves." With such a motive, the chronicler could not be content with a narration of events and deeds, but should seek their roots and causes, for the instruction could be of benefit only if it taught how to anticipate evil and make possible good. The Swedish and Danish Chronicles were not commendable because they had forfeited truth for national glory. The present chronicle was to include what seemed most in accord with the truth. On the whole, the reader was warned, he would find mostly turbulence and strife, with many examples of the turning of the wheel of fortune.

The history of Sweden, Olavus argued, could be written only for the previous three hundred years, the period following the establishment of Christianity in

[5] *Ibid.*, Introduction, by J. Sahlgren; *cf.* L. Stavenow, *Olavus Petri som historieskrifvare;* Schück, in *Illus. Sv. Litteraturhistoria*, pp. 294ff.

the land. The origin of the nation was uncertain, though presumably the Swedes were part of the northern Germanic race settled in Germany, England, and Scandinavia. The language, legal methods, and similar customs favored this theory. The story of the Goths who emigrated from Sweden and gave rise to the Goths of Continental Europe, Olavus considered mostly fable, and in the legends of the raids and life of the Vikings he found little that could throw glory on his nation. "It would be greater honor for us if our ancestors had always been peaceful and gentle, remained at home and been contented with what God had given them, and not robbed and plundered others."[6] The pre-Christian inhabitants had a religion similar to that of other German tribes. Thor, Odin, and Freja, corresponding to the Roman Jupiter, Mercury, and Venus, were the principal deities, with Uppsala as the chief center of worship, where living sacrifices were made in national assemblies every ninth year. Gods corresponding to the Roman Cires, Neptune, and Saturn seem also to have been worshiped. The title of the Swedish king—King of Gotha and Svea—indicated that the kingdom had not always been one, and it was known that southern Sweden had often been shifted between Sweden and Denmark. Formerly, probably four hundred years ago, there had been a lively commerce with England, of which the presence of much English mintage testified. This was practically all that could be said of the heathen period of Sweden's history, which had left no historical records save some few Runestones scattered here and there in the land.

Still Olavus endeavored to glean the truth from the

[6] *Works*, IV, 10.

untrustworthy Swedish and Danish Chronicles, and beginning with the time of Christ he gave from these sources what seemed to him most likely. He even devoted some space to the contemporary doings of the Goths and Visigoths, as his story progressed, yet with little faith in any relationship between their history and that of his country. The ravages of the Vikings on the other hand, he reluctantly laid to the account of the Swedes. Not only kings and wars engaged his attention. The condition of the peasantry was described at a certain period, and the system of coinage was explained.[7] The reason for the slow advance of Christianity was found in the paucity and methods of the missionaries. "Idolatry needs be taken off the heart first, rather than off the altar."[8] At the time of the coming of the first missionaries the language was so similar that English and German preachers could be understood.[9] The origin of written law was explained, and extracts from the law book included in the narrative.[10] Naturally, the history of the Church received attention, record being made of the first connections with Rome, the work of English missionaries, the founding of the bishoprics.[11] As the events gave occasion, the founding of Stockholm was noted, the life at a royal court pictured, the development of national law noted. The life of Birgitta received some attention, but her revelations were characterized as "most likely" being dreams.[12] As evidence of oppression suffered under foreign kings, a letter of the men of Uppland to the provinces of southern

[7] Ibid., p. 37.
[8] Ibid., p. 39.
[9] Ibid., p. 40.
[10] Ibid., p. 44.
[11] Ibid., p. 54.
[12] Ibid., p. 113.

Ecclesiastical Transformation in Sweden 215

Sweden was inserted,[13] while for records of extranational events, the reader was referred to the chronicles of other countries.[14] Certain happenings gave rise to quite a long discussion on the advisability of having many or few armed forts in a kingdom.[15] An important state document was incorporated in the relation of an agreement between Sweden and Denmark.[16] The founding of the University of Uppsala was entered in its place in the story.

The Chronicle was a cultural history in a sense that few histories of the time were. It represented the many-sided interests of its writer, who was at home in the fields of social and religious as well as political history. But the foremost aim was never lost sight of. History should instruct. "If Chronicles are to be read merely out of curiosity, or to pass time, they are better left unread." [17] The Past should yield examples for the benefit of the Present and Future. The examples that Olavus found in the annals of his people and asked them to ponder were mostly in the realm of the relationship of people and ruler, and of nation and nation. He had not much sympathy for wars of which the preceding centuries had been filled. Neither Sweden nor Denmark should boast of their victories, for "harm and destruction have been the lot of both." [18] A nation often feels the loss of its men incommensurate with the gain won through killing enemies. "The peace that has to be obtained through wounds

[13] *Ibid.*, pp. 125-126; *cf.* pp. 160-161, 212-213.
[14] *Ibid.*, p. 146.
[15] *Ibid.*, p. 156.
[16] *Ibid.*, pp. 181-182; *cf.* pp. 222-223.
[17] *Ibid.*, p. 15.
[18] *Ibid.*, p. 36.

and dead men is dearly paid for."[19] Nor does a people gain by revolt against its ruler. "The subjects cannot be considered as having the right to kill their princes and kings, however iniquitous these are."[20] Those who have rebelled against their rulers have suffered dearly.[21] On the other hand, the rulers are not without responsibility, for they must answer to God for their misdeeds.[22] As the subjects are forbidden to rebel, so the ruler is forbidden to give them reason for rebellion."[23] The rule of the sword is of double effect—what is won through the sword is usually lost through the sword.[24] Even one of the most courageous patriots of the fifteenth century received a dubious verdict from Olavus, who would not decide whether or not his great patriotic deeds could outbalance the fact that he was in revolt against the lawful authority.[25] Contracts were ever to be held sacred. "One is bound to keep faith and be true even toward enemies."[26] Where such good faith was lacking, oaths were of little benefit. On the contrary, the greater the oaths and promises, the less they were usually observed.[27]

Not always was the teaching merely general in its application. Olavus found examples from former years that could be of advantage to contemporaries he had in mind. King Magnus Barnlock lived in the grateful memory of his people, who had given him his nickname because he was concerned about preserving to the peasants their possessions. But "there are not many in the world who can be called Barnlock. Barn-

[19] *Ibid.*, p. 51.
[20] *Ibid.*, p. 52; *cf.* p. 153.
[21] *Ibid.*, pp. 173, 197.
[22] *Ibid.*, p. 59.
[23] *Ibid.*, p. 82; *cf.* p. 88.
[24] *Ibid.*, p. 57.
[25] *Ibid.*, p. 169.
[26] *Ibid.*, p. 67.
[27] *Ibid.*, p. 99.

raiders have always been more common in the world."[28] Likewise toward churches, rulers were formerly more liberal and just, wherefore they enjoyed the blessing of God. "But in respect of those who want to snatch everything to themselves, without regard to right, God knows the art whereby they who were forced to give become no poorer, and they who take to themselves become no richer."[29] Gustavus Vasa felt the sting, and Olavus had to suffer the king's vengeance.[30]

To Olavus himself history had one great significance —it revealed the judgment of God upon wickedness and the blessing of God upon righteousness. As means of punishment God used wicked rulers[31] and catastrophes of Nature.[32] Broken contracts, rebellion, avarice, pride, anger, and envy were the roots of the tree whose fruits were war, desolation of city and country, misery in untold forms, and inglorious death. The virtues of godliness included peacefulness and contentedness, endurance of evil government, obedience and honesty, patience and faith. It was a strictly religious view of history. Olavus did not perceive the working of political, economic, and social forces that underlay the motives and movements of the centuries he surveyed. For the emergence from the ceaseless Danish wars of a national spirit and an independent country he had no feeling. He admittedly strove to see the causes and origins of events, but in reality he was content with an explanation of the *occasion* of an historical

[28] *Ibid.*, p. 84.
[29] *Ibid.*, pp. 83-84.
[30] Gustav I forbade its publication, and endeavored to suppress the Ms. copies of the *Chronicle* (Hildebrand, *Sveriges Historia,* IV, 348).
[31] *Works*, IV, 78.
[32] *Ibid.*, p. 114.

occurrence. To the deeper strata of continuous cause he did not penetrate. Each event and person was judged as an isolated entity before an absolute norm. That norm forbade rebellion, discountenanced war, almost denied the right of resistance. Olavus Petri was not far from the realm of pacifism. Not only principle directed him to his conviction, but weighing the gains of generations of bloodshed, he wondered what his country had profited by the law of the sword.

Also the political thought of the author of the *Chronicle* was strictly religious. The king was God's representative, and ruled through His pleasure. Because he was accountable to God, he was not to be judged by the people. God had permitted him to come to the throne, therefore the people were subject to his rule. They were to suffer misrule as a punishment for sin, and to bear the judgment until it pleased God to remove the burden, which it was His, not their, prerogative to accomplish. Rebellion became revolt both against ruler and God, and the lot of the nation was made still more miserable. Wrong could not be remedied by wrong, but by humility and faith.

The merits of the *Chronicle* are not in its political theories, or in a historical conception of the events and conditions it recorded, but in its character and materials. It is critical toward tradition and legend. The contemporary Johannes Magnus went another way, taking and embellishing all the possible and impossible facts of tradition that might glorify the age of the Gods and Vikings, and embroidered a fascinating fabric to stimulate the pride and emulation of his countrymen. For a century his method became the dominant one, as opposed to that of the austere and conscientious Olavus. The *Chronicle* was remarkable in what it omitted. But also its contents were important. The presence of letters and documents in a history, as proof for the truth of the work, was an omen of a new age in historical writing. So also the reference to coins, language, customs, philology, laws, and the like marked an advance over former methods.[33] But above all, the criterion of truth in a work of history was a vital innovation. Olavus not only preached it but practiced it, and nowhere more commendably than in treating matters that involved patriotic or religious prejudices. His attitude toward the Roman Church in his *Chronicle* is remarkably free from partisanship, even if it be granted that such an attitude was prompted by a fear of Protestant extremes.[34] Judged by the standard of the twentieth century, the *Chronicle* may not be called an historical work. But the sixteenth century knew no evolutionary theory either in biology or history, and the Renaissance idea of biography was then little understood in Sweden. Judged by its own century and precedents, the *Chronicle* was a masterly compilation, conceived in the spirit of truth, executed by a mind with many interests, and directed to a correction of life and morals among high and low.[35]

[33] Probably in preparation for his *Chronicle* Olavus gathered the material on Runestones and their reading, which is preserved from his time. It represents the first known attempt at a scientific treatment of this subject. Also, there is preserved from Olavus a list of the cities and ecclesiastical institutions of the Sweden of his day. See *Works,* IV, 553ff.; *cf.* Schück, in *Samlaren,* 1888, "Några Småskrifter af Olavus Petri."

[34] *Cf.* Stavenow, *op. cit.,* p. 17.

[35] "For centuries the most important historical work in the Swedish language" (Hildebrand, *Sveriges Historia,* IV, p. 348).

CHAPTER VIII

THE SUBORDINATION OF CHURCH TO STATE
OLAVUS PETRI AND THE EVANGELICAL MOVEMENT
1531-1552

THE five years, 1526-1531, had brought an unprecedented output of Reformation literature, and in the life of Olavus it was the period of literary production. Previous to 1526 but eight insignificant books had been printed in Swedish.[1] In the first four years of his activity Olavus produced double the number existing before him.[2] At the same time he was secretary in the City Council and preacher in the St. Nicholas Church. His efforts toward Church reform were not without opposition, even in Stockholm, the most friendly of all places in Sweden to the new order of things. Early in 1525 (February 11) he had married, as he noted in his autobiographical record, *"Meam Christinam."* The step caused disturbance, *"omnibus papistis reclamantibus eo quod fuerim diaconus."*[3] If we can trust a description of his brother, Laurentius Petri, who in 1566 put into writing his memories from these earliest Reformation days in Sweden, "Master Olof in the basket" was not the subject only of commendation. In their bitterness against the religious changes, the burghers of the old faith turned upon

[1] Holm, *Olavus Petri*, p. 83.
[2] Schück, *Olavus Petri*, p. 52.
[3] *Works*, IV, 562.

"the preachers, who had brought them about through the Word of God. He was considered best and most pleasing to God who could shout loudest against the 'Lutherans,' 'heretics,' 'faith-wreckers,' 'traitors,' and could blaspheme as best he could invent."[4] But gradually the opposition was suppressed, though not eliminated, and by 1531 the evangelical party was supreme, so that Swedish Mass, Swedish preaching and singing, and a strong evangelical sentiment characterized the community.

Who the leaders in this movement were considered to be, a letter of Paulus Eliae, the Danish monk, reveals: "Olavus Petri, Laurentius Andreae, the comfort and adviser of Olavus Petri, and Master Sven of Skara, my old schoolmaster—apostate Christians, traitors to God and the Holy Church."[5] The former Skara schoolmaster referred to was then dean (*domprost*) in Skara, but between 1524 and 1527 had acted as chancellor to Gustavus I, while Laurentius Andreae was secretary in the Privy Council. The two had been classmates in Skara, and with Olavus undoubtedly formed a powerful trio in the counsels of the king. It is natural to assume that the king's German secretary, who was also pastor in the St. Nicholas Church (1524-1527), had influence in matters that affected both Church and State.[6] Not without reason the en-

[4] Holm, *op. cit.*, p. 47.

[5] Uno von Troil, *Skrifter och Handlingar til Uplysning i Svenska Kyrko och Reformations Historien*, I, 150 (April 28, 1528).

[6] In this group is undoubtedly to be found the translators of the 1526 Testament. Especially Sven was a gifted student, probably the foremost humanist in the evangelical circles. He maintained friendly relationships with the Catholic party, and his real evangelical position is difficult to define. See biographical sketch by Lektor F. Ödberg, in *Vestergötlands Forminnesförenings Tidskrift*, 1897, häfte 8-9.

emies of the king believed that he was being guided by advisers who were anything but Roman in their sympathies. The strongest as well as the clearest-minded of these advisers was the one of whom we know the least, namely, Laurentius Andreae. Outside of a little book on the relationship of faith and good works, issued in 1528,[7] no literary productions bear his name. But it is certain that he was the guiding hand in the 1526 Translation of the New Testament. His greatest achievements lay in the realm of the translation of policies into actions, and to him more than to any other adviser belongs the credit of having helped the king to victory in the ecclesiastical transformation of 1521-1531. Yet toward the end of that period the ways of king and chancellor began to part, and in 1531 Olavus succeeded to the post, while Laurentius drew further into the background, until in 1532 he wrote to Sven, then bishop of Skara, that he was "now almost entirely separated from His Majesty's service."[8]

The withdrawal of Laurentius Andreae from the service of the king represented a disagreement between the two in the matter of policy toward the Church. Gustavus had succeeded in breaking down the opposition of the Church to his government, and throughout the struggle had considered the bishops' temporal authority as the source of peril for a national State. Once the power that had formerly been theirs had come into his hands, he showed himself reluctant toward the assumption of that power by an evangelical episcopacy. He was determined to break the

[7] "Underwisning om Troona och godha gerningar," in *Skrifter och Handlingar til Uplysning i Swenska Kyrko och Reformations Historien,* Tredje Delen (Uppsala, 1791), pp. 1-16.

[8] Ödberg, *op. cit.,* p. 35.

power of the churchmen as a political force. Laurentius Andreae had hitherto been one with the king in the attack on the Roman episcopacy, but he was not in accord with the policy of complete subjection of Church to State. The king's indifference toward the archbishopric of Uppsala and the confirmation of the bishops-elect [9] seemed proof that he would as soon as not see the elimination of the episcopal system. That far Laurentius and Olavus would not go, for they perceived that it involved the existence of the Church itself. But Gustavus would no longer follow counsels when they meant a check on himself, and ere long Laurentius Andreae yielded and withdrew from the position of secretary in the Privy Council. Olavus, in 1531, accepted the seal, but in 1533 resigned it.[10] He, even less than Laurentius, would place himself at the unconditional service of the king, and the king found him as unwilling to weave according to his pattern "as a frisky cow to spin silk." [11] Various secretaries followed who were more pliable in the king's hands, until in 1539 foreign men were imported who were completely subservient to the royal will.

Eventually the archdiocese had received its bishop in Laurentius Petri, but him as well as the other bishops the king clearly gave to understand that the Crown was superior to the Staff. The archbishop was allowed to provide his diocese with incumbents, except in the case of more important positions, when the king's consent should be obtained. The schools ought to be supervised better than had been the case, and

[9] See *supra*, 58-59.
[10] *Works*, IV, 562.
[11] In *KÅ* 1909, pp. 74-75.

though the Scriptures should be taught, knowledge *"pro utilitate rei reipublices"* ought to be found there. And "in no case shall any reformation be undertaken, before the archbishop has first consulted us as to the method and nature of the changes," for "hasty reformation is followed by bitterness."[12] With the bishops and the various dioceses the king entered into detailed contracts, specifying whence the incumbents should receive their support, and providing that the Crown should not be deprived of any possible source of revenue.

The period was not one of happiness either to the friends of the new or the old order. Olavus in his *Admonition to all Evangelical Preachers* of 1535 gave vent to the disappointment of his group. In common with the king, he stressed the need of improvements in the schools. The Reformer realized that the lack of evangelical preachers of ability and character would imperil the cause of a true Church, and for the training of future leaders schools were necessary. But the economic condition of the Church made the improvement of the schools impossible, unless the Crown intervened. And Gustavus' wishes were not followed by grants. Olavus complained that supporters of the evangelical movement were its worst enemies, because of their actions. The king, in 1536, again had to warn his representatives not to violate the Vesterås agreement of 1527 by making it an occasion of despoiling all Church property.[13] But Gustavus himself set a bad example. Even international relations cast reflections on the religious matters. While the king was

[12] *GR* VIII, 324-325 (Nov., 1533).
[13] Thyselius och Ekblom, *Handlingar Rörande Sveriges Inre Förhållanden under Konung Gustaf I*, II, pp. 80-82.

engaged in war with Lübeck, many of the German burghers of Stockholm, together with leaders of the Swedish party, had plotted his downfall. The fact that the most eager of the Reformation advocates were to be found among these rebels did not place the evangelical party in a better light before the friends of the old customs.

The progress of the reformation of the inner life of the Church went on very slowly. In 1536 parts of the Old Testament in Swedish were issued from the press, presaging the coming of the whole Bible in the vernacular. These books included the *Psalms, Proverbs, Ecclesiastes, Sirach's Book* [14]; possibly Olavus had a hand in this work. This year, too, produced another enlarged edition of the Hymn Book. The following year brought a third edition of the Swedish Mass, remarkable especially because of its permission of certain rubrics in Latin [15]—a compromise with the opponents of the Swedish Mass. On the other hand, the archdiocese synodical circular of 1535 prescribed the reading of masses as in medieval days, and the first Swedish Mass in the northern communities, such as Skellefteå, 1536, and Umeå, 1537, "were not very welcome." [16] A few years later the king accused the nobility in the southern provinces of letting the evangelical cause go "by wind and wave," complaining that they had not in the preceding years fulfilled the

[14] Isak Collijn, *Sveriges Bibliografi Intill År 1600*, Band II, h. 1, pp. 43-48; *Works*, IV, 511ff. The translation of the Psalter literally follows Luther's Translation of 1524. Also the other books were a faithful translation of Luther's version. *Cf.* A. E. Knös, in *Uppsala Univ. Årsskrift*, 1861, p. 98, "*Om Revision av Svenska Bibelöversättningen*."

[15] *Works*, II, 443.

[16] K. B. Westman, *Kultreformproblemet i den Svenska Reformationen*," in *Hist. Tidskrift*, 1917, p. 7; Anjou, *op. cit.*, p. 133.

decisions of the kingdom in regard to the Church.[17] When one of the evangelical preachers, Magister Claus, had preached the truth in these parts, trouble had followed, and the king had had to protect his rights.[18] Even in Strengnäs it was difficult to find capable evangelical preachers "to keep up the Swedish Mass" and the preaching.[19] On the whole, the picture suggested by Olavus in his *Admonition* of 1535 seems not to have been overdrawn.

The royal policy by no means meant a retreat from the evangelical position, but its goal meant a subjection of the Church which the evangelical leaders refused to sanction. Thus the king lost their guidance and good-will at the same time that he was attacked by the "papists,"[20] as the opposition now began to be called. His adherence to the Reformation program was manifest in the choice of the two bishops who succeeded to Vesterås and Strengnäs. Peter of Vesterås and Magnus of Strengnäs were the last of the pre-Vesterås (1527) churchmen, and when the former died in 1534 and the latter was driven from his office in 1536 because of Roman views, two convinced evangelical bishops took their places, Henrich in Vesterås, in 1535, and Bothvid in Strengnäs, in 1536. So also his repeated commands to the nobility and his representatives in the region of Vadstena showed his purpose not to tolerate a renaissance of the Roman party. He had experienced that as soon as he turned his attention from this region, the evangelical preachers and school teachers were oppressed by the Vadstena

[17] Thyselius, *op. cit.*, pp. 110-112 (Feb. 28, 1539).

[18] *Ibid.*, pp. 86-87 (March 30, 1537).

[19] *Ibid.*, pp. 93-4, Letter of Bishop Bothvid to the king's chancellor, May 20, 1538.

[20] Anjou, *op. cit.*, p. 135.

monks and the Linköping bishop's party.[21] But when his lieutenant, Måns Johanson, evidently in accordance with the royal policy, issued an order compelling the introduction of the Swedish Mass, he received a sharp letter from the king asserting that no man's salvation depended upon the language of the Mass, but upon proper instruction in religious matters—until the people were better informed, the old order was to be less severely dealt with.[22]

Sooner or later the relationship between the king and his former advisers was bound to come to an issue. The rapacity of the king in despoiling the treasures of the Church had won their disapproval as well as that of the Roman adherents. The minuteness with which he specified the income of the clergy brought complaints that the work of the Church was being hampered. With good grounds the evangelical party hoped that some of the confiscated Church goods might be used for the improvement of the schools. These were in a deplorable condition; in 1538 one of the councilmen in Stockholm sent his children across the kingdom to Skara, to Bishop Sven's School, "since the schools have practically died out" elsewhere.[23] Gustavus had, indeed, granted some support to students at foreign universities, so that alone at Wittenberg about forty Swedish students were enrolled between 1527-1539.[24] And he had tried to secure teachers from Germany, but was unsuccessful, because of the reputation of the country as "barbarian," and of the king as a hard master.[25] But, in general, the

[21] Thyselius, *op. cit.*, pp. 110-111.
[22] *Ibid.*, pp. 118-119 (May 31, 1539).
[23] Ödberg, *op. cit.*, I, 8-9, p. 43.
[24] Anjou, *op. cit.*, II, 103.
[25] Ödberg, *op. cit.*, p. 40; Thyselius, *op. cit.*, pp. 103-108.

royal policy toward education was one of the weakest
parts of the new regime. The reputation of Gustavus
abroad as a hard ruler was but an echo of sentiment
at home. Even in the pulpits he was decried as a
tyrant. Parts of Olavus' *Chronicle* had come into his
possession, and its comparison of former and later
kings was not lost to his attention. It was in 1539
that Olavus became most direct, and Gustavus felt the
sting of his "Sermon on Oaths."

Something of what mood the king was in was
revealed in a letter to Archbishop Laurentius Petri in
April, 1539.[26] He was clearly vexed with the emphasis
the archbishop and others placed on ceremonies and
the Mass. "Your yourself know that the people are
quite ignorant (*"grofft"*) and have very little understanding in these matters, and trouble is the result.
You ought to know full well, if you seek examples in
the Scriptures (which I take for granted that you
read more than we), that you will find that Christ
and His disciples preached before they held masses."
So the archbishop was instructed to procure "good and
Christian preachers" who could teach the people "faith
and the fruits of faith." Afterwards it would be time
to reform ceremonies. The archbishop had seemingly
complained that it was not in his power to provide
preachers, for the king evasively replied that he had
not put any hindrance in the way. Laurentius further
received a sharp reproof because he had not more often
consulted the king in matters relating to the Church,
though he should have known that the king was concerned about the "clear and pure Word of God," and
"had we not done more for it than yourselves, one
might question if the matter peradventure had come

[26] *GR* XII, 184-188.

so far, as it now is." For his request for more support, Laurentius received stones instead of bread. "Were the will good, and the greed not too great, there would be means enough." "You are to be preachers, not lords." "You need not think that we shall let it occur again, that bishops shall have the sword." And even if things were tolerable in Uppsala, the archbishop need not feel content, for he was to concern himself for the diocese and the whole kingdom. Furthermore, Gustavus took it ill that "for several years, here in Stockholm and probably elsewhere, we have been much attacked from the pulpits." Instead of teaching, the preachers were yelling about tyranny and cruelty. "In the most recent print, about oaths," the government had been charged as the cause of all evil. "And such preaching and prints we consider to be more an occasion to rebellion and disturbance than any Christian instruction." As a result, any further reformation or any printed matter should not be permitted without the knowledge and sanction of the king. And unless the Word and Gospel be more acceptably proclaimed "by you and your advisors" than to date, the king was dubious of his next step. The letter closed with an afterthought to the effect that the archbishop was to have strict supervision over the preachers he sent out, so that they knew what they were to preach, and the older men were to be preferred in the parish churches to the younger men who were more apt to cause trouble.

It was probably the most remarkable letter ever received by a Swedish archbishop from his king. The position of the king was clear. The Church was to be a teaching institution, subject to the State and forming a moral support of the State. A reformation of ceremonies was desirable, but not of primary importance. The letter itself was a declaration of the king to be *summus episcopus* in his kingdom. Archbishops as well as lower officers were to preach the Gospel. But they were so to preach as to enforce royal authority, not undermine it. The branding of Olavus' latest sermons as "rebellious," was ominous of what was to follow before the year was gone.

Yet one thing stood in the way of the realization of this policy. Gustavus needed subordinates pliable to his will. For several years he had searched Germany for a secretary and for teachers. Finally he succeeded. In 1538 an adventurer by the name of Konrad von Pyhy, with some knowledge of law, but with a mysterious past and not much stability of character, was attracted to Sweden and installed as chancellor to the king.[27] He filled the three requirements then demanded by the office—he was something of a jurist, could write German, and would obey the king. He was followed in 1539 by a more honorable and respected countryman, a nobleman of Rügen, George Norman.[28] The latter had studied in Wittenberg, was a Master of Arts, and on Luther's recommendation, left a position at Greifswald to become tutor to Prince Eric. But the king found other uses for his talents. Supported by von Pyhy and Norman, he proceeded to a reorganization of State and Church which would more effectively meet the needs of administration at the same time that it centralized in his hand the powers of government.[29]

The archives for the latter half of 1539 are scanty,

[27] Termed chancellor in Dec. 14, 1538 (*GR* XII, 121).
[28] *Cf. Sveriges Historia,* IV, 225ff.
[29] *Ibid.,* pp. 234ff.

partly because of the illness of the king, a fact which may have influenced somewhat the course of events.[30] But from two letters of the bishop of Linköping to the bishop of Skara,[31] we learn that a meeting *ad corrigendos inveteratos errores et mores nondum castigatos"* had been called at Uppsala, and that in the fall the meeting had been held. It marked the final break in the relationship of the king to the former leaders of the transformation in the Church. The exact resolutions of the meeting are unknown, and the fact that the bishop of Linköping wrote that no innovation would be made in the ceremonies in his church until the Recess had been finally issued by the king indicates that they were not immediately decreed. More important was the fact that Laurentius Andreae and the German representatives of the king had come to open disagreement on a question touching the unity of the universal Church. Evidently the point of dispute was the episcopal organization of the Swedish Church, and its relationship to the State. To the decisions of the Council the representatives were forced to accede. The use that the king made of his victory appeared December 8, 1539, when George Norman was proclaimed *ordinarius* and *superattendent,* with power to exercise the jurisdiction of the king "over bishops, prelates, and all other clergy and their subordinates, in matters of religion." [32] In reality, thus, the independence of the Church was denied, and the bishops and archbishops reduced to offices of supervision. In this manifesto the king called himself "the highest protector of the holy Christian faith throughout the

[30] Hildebrand in *Sveriges Historia.*
[31] Hildebrand and Alin, *Svenska Riksdagsakter,* I, 244.
[32] Thyselius, *op. cit.,* pp. 122-126.

whole realm." He had won his goal, and his power over the Church was to be exercised by a superintendent and his assistant.

The document of December 8 was dominated by one thought—evangelical preachers had made use of their position to undermine obedience to royal authority. Both subtly and openly they had taught and preached from the pulpits nothing less than treason. This was given as the motive for the establishment of a superintendency, to the end that the preaching would be conducive to the maintenance of order, as well as of the Word. The ordinarius should examine the preachers, to learn if they were of the right convictions, and at stated times should conduct visitation, through which, among other purposes, the loyalty of the clergy should be ascertained. The fear that Gustavus had felt fifteen years earlier toward the Roman prelates he now felt toward evangelical preachers. Then those had threatened the State, now these seemed to threaten his and his heirs' kingship. As then the result had been the dispossession of the power and position of the Roman leaders, so now it led to a trial where Olavus Petri and Laurentius Andreae were accused of treason. The unhappy event —a spot on the otherwise brilliant record of national achievements rendered by Gustavus Vasa to his country—took place in the native city of Olavus, in the castle of Örebro, at New Year's, 1539-1540.

The accusation was drawn up by von Pyhy in German (then the language of the chancery) and freely blended fact and fable.[33] What was said in one of the charges was probably true of many—though the alleged fact had taken place "several years ago" it had

[33] H. Lundstrom, in *KÅ*, 1909, pp. 54-84.

not come to the king's attention before "this year" (1539). In brief, the king's accusations were the following: He had long had cause against them, but on account of the people had shown forbearance. When the king had wanted to resign the rule over the kingdom, Laurentius and his party had persuaded him to remain, because they were themselves in mortal peril. It was Laurentius who had persuaded the king to allow the Gospel to be preached and papistic superstitions to be suppressed, promising that he would so order it that no tumult should ensue. But disturbance did follow, and Laurentius had led the king into deep waters, but then left him to his fate. Laurentius had been in compact with the German burghers of Stockholm and the Swedish mint-master, Anders Hansson, and had twitted the king that with his evangelical following he was as strong as His Majesty. The accused had encouraged inciting preaching against the old Church and profited by the despoliation of altars and churches. They had wanted the city to have power over the castle, had introduced innovations into the court, and deprived the king of certain incomes from the city. Their unwise counsels had plunged the king into a war with Lübeck, and they had recommended incapable secretaries to the king. Master Olof, who was versed in "all free arts and faculties, namely, theology, *iuro divino et civili, in medicinis* and several others," had not been satisfied with these attainments, but with Anders Hansson had practiced the arts of treason, and "that highly praised art called the course of the heavens or astronomy." Also, Olavus had written "chronicles and histories" further to impress his learning on the people. Their interest in astronomy had given Olavus and Anders a difficult

problem a few years previous, until they found that
the sign in the heavens could be interpreted as an
omen of punishment, because the government had
erred. This the king had just found out. The preachers had been enjoined to teach the Catechism and
respect of authority to the people; instead they
preached on texts from the Apocalypse. Laurentius
had even made bold to reprimand the king for his
greed of money and advised him that "good friends
were a better and more useful asset to the king than
much money." Olavus, whom Laurentius had recommended as his successor, had been as capable as "an
ass in playing the lute." Only recently had Gustavus
found men who could serve the kingdom efficiently.
In Wittenberg it was customary for authors to seek
approval of their books before they were printed, but
here Olavus circulated chronicles intended to subvert
the government, and in his printed sermon on oaths
had insulted the authority. Both of the accused had
had knowledge of treason, but had not revealed it;
rather they had sought to protect the traitors.

The accusation was, in a sense, a review of the
reign of Gustavus, but hardly such an one as he
himself would have cared to have considered official.
In a fit of anger, seemingly, he recalled the adversities
of the past twenty years and hurled them at the two
defendants. Into the fabric the German chancellor
had not been slow to weave a few threads. As a legal
document the charge had little worth. Historically, it
presents the weakest phase of the king's character,
which allowed him to thrust aside his most capable
friends and advisers when they checked his further
advance. The most fatal charge against Laurentius,
even though it is presented in figurative language, was

his desertion of his master in deep waters. He had refused to go the whole way in destroying the power of the Church—to the king that meant a treasonable desertion, for after 1530-1531 he had been alone in his policy. Olavus had injured the royal dignity by his sermons and his *Chronicle;* it is possible, too, that he had had knowledge of the sedition in Stockholm during the war with Lübeck, though absolutely no evidence exists that he favored or aided it. In a word, the king was not in a mood to be blocked in his policy of subordinating the Church to the State. Recent events, most recently the Uppsala Council, had irritated and annoyed him. In the German chancellor he found both a means to his goal and encouragement in his procedure. He wanted evangelical as well as Roman adherents to respect his authority and rule, and he knew that the strength of the former party was in Laurentius Andreae and Olavus Petri.

The charge was treason, and by the Royal Council, in which sat the brother of Olavus, Archbishop Laurentius Petri, the two were condemned to death.[34] It is doubtful, however, that the king ever expected to go that far. He wanted to make an example rather than execute the accused. The sentence was changed without difficulty, and fines were imposed instead of the death penalty. The friends and parishioners of Olavus in Stockholm paid his fine, while Laurentius, after paying his, withdrew in solitude to Strengnäs. From his king, whom he had helped to a position of power and authority, Laurentius deserved a better reward. By his Church, whose character he had bravely defended and helped to shape, he has hardly been appreciated because of the silence of the records

[34] *KÅ*, 1909, p. 84; Thyselius, *op. cit.*, pp. 134-137.

and of his own unobtrusive nature. He was one of the men who make nations and institutions for coming generations rather than names for themselves.

The king's supremacy was no longer disputed, and Norman had but to execute the royal will. Together, king and ordinarius conducted a visitation in Vestergötland in the spring of 1540, which netted the royal treasury a rich harvest of silver and treasure that in the king's opinion was not needed in the churches. The extent to which the confiscation went is suggested in a complaint from these parts of the kingdom a couple of years later, "that it was soon as pleasant to go in a desolate forest as in a church." The visitation also produced another fruit—a program for the reorganization of the Church under the king.[35] In each province a conservator was to be appointed—a layman, who was to be responsible for the rights and goods of the Church and the clergy. Besides him, two seniores should be named, who were to conduct visitations, and, as clergy, be entrusted with the non-material part of the Church's work. The seniores were subordinate to the conservator, who in turn reported to the ordinarius, or superintendent. When matters of general importance arose that affected the life of the whole Church, a synod should be provided for, wherein the clergy could consider and decide on the four great departments of the "spiritual Church," viz. doctrine, ceremonies, education, and charity. This provincial administration of the Church was parallel with a contemplated organization in the State,[36] whereby each province should have its lieutenant, sub-chancellor, four councilors, and one secretary.

[35] Thyselius, *op. cit.*, pp. 126-134.
[36] *Sveriges Historia*, IV, 234ff.

With such a system, the king hoped to exercise a close supervision over the different parts of the kingdom, and himself hold the reins of government. The process might be called one of "germanization" of State and Church, and von Pyhy and Norman were the king's tutors. The independent Swedish peasantry, however, soon raised a storm that overthrew the king's paper structure.

Since the meeting in Uppsala the further reformation of ceremonies had engaged the mind of the king and his German counselor. The archives speak of a royal proclamation that was issued by the king from Örebro, directed against "sundry false and perverted doctrines and opinions" in the Church.[37] Its contents are not preserved, but probably they were similar to an elaborate program that soon appeared under the title of *Articuli Ordinantiae*.[38] The king's Instructions outlining the new provincial organization, issued April 9, 1540, referred to "the Four Articles on which our spiritual Church's Ordinance is founded and built," and which were soon to be printed. They were, however, neither printed nor ever enforced, but their nature illustrates the mind and policy of the king. The Ordinance followed closely the Bugenhagian *Kirchen Ordnung* that had been adopted in Denmark, June 14, 1539. Variations and omissions from this plan were influenced by local conditions, Melanchthon's *Loci Communes*, the Wittenberg, and the Pommeranian Ordinances. The *Loci* furnished guidance in regard to preaching, while Norman's native Church became in some respects a model for organization. The

[37] Thyselius, *op. cit.*, p. 167.
[38] *Cf.* Ahnfelt, "Articuli Ordinantiae," *Tidskrift för teologi*, 1892, pp. 352-422.

king's Four Articles related to Doctrine, Ceremonies, Schools and the Care of the Poor. These fundamental departments of the "spiritual Church" received attention in the Ordinance. Provision was made for daily matins and vespers; the Litany was to be sung by choir boys before the beginning of the mass; daily mass was to be permitted but the people should be encouraged to go to Communion; a knowledge of the primary truths of the Catechism was to be a prerequisite for participation at the Lord's Supper; the number of holidays was specified. On the main festive days Latin Mass was to be permitted, and special music and ceremonies and preparatory services were suggested, in order that greater reverence might be won among the people. Extreme Unction was abolished, while Confirmation was yet a subject for greater consideration. The Ordinance also provided instructions for marriage, church discipline, schools, legacies, the care of the poor, the number of *necessarii personae i*n a church. Fasting was not prohibited as a "discipline." Preaching should continually seek the instruction of the people, while inculcating respect for the government was strongly urged.

The *Articuli Ordinantiae* make apparent that the king was not averse to a progressive cleansing of the Church from Roman practices as long as such a change was prepared by instructive preaching, but that he was intent on supplanting the bishops by gathering the control of the material Church into his own hands. In the proposed Ordinance the seniores were on equality with the bishops. The office of the latter was made superfluous, while that of the former was subordinated to the lay conservator. To avoid trouble the present bishops retained their name, but Gustavus appointed no new bishops in his reign, and after 1540 only those retained the title who bore it in that year. The episcopacy was to be permitted gradually to die out. Bishops and clergy were to preach and teach, the government would rule.

The religious education of the nation received in 1541 a mighty stimulus in the printing of the Swedish Bible. Though its publication may have been hastened by Norman, work on its preparation had gone on long before the coming of the German secretaries. The individual books which were ready in 1536 testified to that preparation, and in the Introduction to the Book of Sirach then printed a promise was given that the whole Old Testament would come. The same Introduction gave as the norm for the Swedish work "the most recent German translation, whose authors doubtless have gone through carefully all the translations, and rendered the most correct and clear readings." [39] A letter of the archbishop to Norman toward the end of 1540 told of the progress and authors of the translation.[40] Laurentius Petri thanked the superintendent for the loan of some books which had been useful for reference and correction. He and "others who are in this work" had enjoyed the use of the books "almost a year." The translation had progressed as far as the Psalter. Manifestly, then, a commission had been at work for some time; the archbishop seems to have been the responsible head. The books which had been printed in 1536 were further revised,[41] probably with the help of some of Norman's literature. Who the collaborators of the archbishop were is unknown, but

[39] *Works,* IV, 552.
[40] Thyselius, *op. cit.,* pp. 240-241 (Nov. 12, 1540).
[41] A. E. Knös, *"Om Revision av Svenska Bibelöversättningen,"* in *Uppsala Årsskrift,* pp. 96ff.

quite certainly Olavus was prominent among them.[42] In 1541 the work was completed and printed by Richolff in Uppsala. In the Preface, "the interpreter" asserted that he had attempted to render the most accurate meaning. He has not "so much followed the Latin Bible as the German of Dr. Martin Luther, as well in Introduction, Glosses, Notes, Concordance, and Order, as in the Text itself. Because said German Bible is not only much clearer and understandable than the Latin, but it also draws much closer toward the Hebrew Text." The translation is not a work for "the wise, who seem to think themselves in no need of such," but for the simple folk who seek for the truth in the Word, but cannot read the Hebrew and Greek languages. The Swedish Bible of 1541 was of national significance. Each parish was assessed an annual tithe for the printing of the book, and each church in the kingdom was presented with a copy.[43] The translation of 1526 had been the work of a party, that of 1541 represented the official Church. The king had affirmed that in the realm the "pure and true Word of God" should be preached. In the translation of 1541 the evangelical Church received a translation at once the finest literary work of its time and the most effective religious means for the establishment of the "rediscovered Faith."

The changes in the Swedish Mass as it appeared in revised form 1541 [44] were significant of the tendency of the evangelical movement to assimilate the heritage of the old in the development of the new. The

[42] In May, 1538, he had issued a receipt for money to be used for paper for the printing of the Old Testament (Thyselius, *op. cit.*, p. 240).

[43] Anjou, *op. cit.*, pp. 125-126.

[44] *Cf.* Quensel, *op. cit.*, II, 54-67; Brilioth, *op. cit.*, pp. 411-413.

Confiteor at the opening of the service was made optional, both as to language and form—it became the confession of the pastor instead of the congregation. Introitus and Graduale might be in Latin or in Swedish, so also the Credo. The Epistle and Gospel could be the pericope selections, instead of the hitherto prescribed lectio continua. Nunc Dimittis fell away from the Communion rubrics, and the Benediction was accompanied by the sign of the Cross, thrice repeated. Most important of all, the preaching service was combined with the Mass, the sermon, with its introductory and concluding prayers, being inserted between the Gospel lectio and the Creed. The Mass had thus again come to be the principal service, incorporating in itself the preaching service, which, a decade before, had assumed an independence that might have led it into the prominence it found in the Calvinist branch of the Church, where the Communion service became a subordinate one. But the deciding influences in the Swedish Reformation issued from Wittenberg, or from native conservatism. For both the desire to conserve the old and the *Deutsche Messe* of Luther were formative in the Mass of 1541, which represented a compromise, or rather a union, of the medieval, age-old form of the Mass and the evangelical preaching and teaching service. Of course, the Mass as a sacrifice was banished, together with the prayers and phrases that flowed from such a conception, but the framework of the Mass was kept and the center of gravity moved from the sacrament to the sermon. Consequently the result in the Swedish Church was a middle course between the Calvinist and the Roman services. The former subordinated the sacrament to the sermon, the latter the sermon to the sacrament. The Swedish

Church theoretically placed both on the same level. Practically, the sacrament suffered, because of the irregularity of attendance at communion. In the greater stress on song the Mass of 1541 was an advance on previous forms; in the use of Latin, it was reactionary. Its German-Swedish character would lead us to suppose that both Norman and Laurentius Petri were responsible for this revision of Olavus' original Swedish Mass.

Gustavus Vasa had almost reached a point of undisputed supremacy in nation and Church by 1542, when once again he was forced to realize that his countrymen had an innate love of independence. His centralization of the government, with its consequent supervision and regulation of the most minute details, was new to the conservative Swedish peasantry, which was accustomed to a large amount of local liberty and freedom of action. At most it had known a strong nobility, which often had oppressed it, but in that case the cause was nearer, and therefore both more easily understood and withstood. With greater difficulty could an invisible, distant power be conceived, whose lieutenants pretended to have power to regulate details of trade and labor and everyday life, forbade use of woods and streams, levied tax upon tax, and stripped churches of gold and silver and fabrics. The grumbling was greatest in the southern part of the kingdom, in Småland. Dalarne and the northern provinces seem to have learned respect for authority by the bitter experiences of former years. But in the south, trouble had long been brewing. In 1537 the king had made a gesture of threatening power, but to no effect. The confiscation of church goods in the Visitation of 1541 did not improve matters. Nor was

Ecclesiastical Transformation in Sweden 243

the new German regime much liked. Finally, in May, 1542, the smouldering fire burst into flames. A peasant, Nils Dacke, assumed the leadership. The discontent was widespread and Dacke was a capable inciter. So successful was this peasant general that when winter made further military operations difficult, the king had to enter into a truce with him. Dacke, however, knew how to gain power better than how to use it, and the king used strategy and eloquence when these were of more effect than arms. He pictured certain phases of the "old" order of things, for which the peasants contended, in a manner that made them understand that the old was not in every respect superior to the new.[45] By the summer of 1543 the insurrection was broken, Dacke killed, and the king again master in his country. Even more certainly than before the fact was established that the national power had come to take the place of provincial freedom and unregulated local independence.[46]

At the fateful Örebro Council in 1540 Gustavus had persuaded the Council to recognize the divine nature of kingship, whereby the crown should be inherited by his sons and descendants, instead of being bestowed by election, as the Swedish custom had been. Early in 1544 the estates had been assembled to ratify this measure and to decide on necessary reforms in the Church. By this date the German chancellor, von Pyhy, had managed to earn the king's displeasure. Especially a costly embassy to France, that ensnared the Swedish king in the French king's war with the emperor, had caused Gustavus to lose confidence in von Pyhy. The uprising in Småland and Pyhy's

[45] Thyselius, *op. cit.*, pp. 185-186.
[46] *Sveriges Historia,* IV, 264-286.

private life—he was accused of bigamy—put the king
in a bad mood and the chancellor's counsels were no
longer needed. The elaborate system for the provincial administration fell of its own weight, and the king
took the government into his own hands again. At
Vesterås, in 1544, he presented the matters that in his
opinion were in need of reformation. During the
Dacke uprising his letters breathed a spirit of
impatient bitterness toward the "papists" and their
ceremonies. He seemed intent now to make use of
his victory to rid the Church of their influence. Consequently, the decisions of Vesterås [47] marked the
furthest advance of his measures against the old
cult. As so many times before, it was ordered that
"the Word of God and the Holy Gospel should be
used in the Christian congregation." The worship of
"deceased saints," the making of pilgrimages, the use
of consecrated water or salt, of incense, or of the monstrance, were categorically forbidden. So also private
masses were no longer to be permitted, nor should
ceremonies be held over the dead. Images were to be
removed from the churches. The number of holidays
was diminished; the people were admonished to be in
the church during services, and often to go to Communion. Other resolutions demanded the payment of
church tithes, the sending of children to school, the
support of students. In regard to discipline, it was
urged that absolution be secured from the pastor or
punishment would follow; swearing and drinking and
guild gatherings for pleasure were forbidden. Disloyalty to the king might result in ban. The estates
promised obedience to Gustavus and his successors;
he, in turn, promised to rule righteously.

[47] *Svenska Riksdagsakter*, I, 390-391.

These were the last reforms made in the reign of Gustavus (who ruled fifteen years longer), and they indicated how far the religious transformation had proceeded under his government. The power of the opposition was definitely broken. And when the king appointed ordinarii in the various dioceses, besides the bishop, the function of the episcopacy as an independent authority of the Church ceased. Bishop Jöns Magni in Linköping resigned from his office in 1543,[48] and the following year even the bishop of Skara laid down his staff, though he continued to exercise the greatest authority in his diocese.[49] At the death of the king in 1560, only the archbishop, Laurentius Petri, remained of the consecrated bishops. On him alone depended the connection of a future episcopacy with the historic line of Sweden's bishops.[50] Gustavus almost succeeded in the elimination of both the political and spiritual power of the class he believed incompatible with the welfare of the nation. In 1555 and 1557 he divided the largest and most influential dioceses, further to weaken their independence. The transfer of property from the Church to the State went steadily on. Gradually the Chapters disintegrated, the property formerly under bishops and cloisters and parishes became Crown possessions, the Church tithes were turned into other channels, and the clergy of the kingdom became, in the majority of cases, functionaries of the State.[51] The king had

[48] Anjou, *op. cit.*, p. 136.

[49] Ödberg, *op. cit.*, pp. 58-60.

[50] It is not impossible that the ordinarii were consecrated. By the people they were called "bishops." But the intention of the king was to permit the institution to disappear with the name (*cf.* Anjou, *op. cit.*, pp. 137ff.).

[51] *Sveriges Historia*, IV, 336-345.

taken upon himself the care of the Church as a whole, but it was an undertaking too great for his resources. Again in 1546, the complaint of the deplorable condition of the schools was heard.[52] The scarcity of pastors was general. Church discipline and the ecclesiastical organization had no certain foundations. Clearly, Gustavus had not solved the problem of the character of the Evangelical Church. He had broken the power of the old and done away with most of its forms, but future generations had to give the new its rightful position in the State.

After the dark days at Örebro, at New Year's, 1539-1540, Olavus Petri had returned to Stockholm, and continued his work as pastor. In 1539 he had been ordained "presbyter" or priest, by Bishop Bothvid of Strengnäs; in 1543 (April) the king commissioned him pastor of *Ecclesia Stockholmensis*. As further evidence of Olavus' restoration to favor in the king's eyes might be noted the fact that in 1542 he had been appointed inspector of the city school. Of his family life or pastoral work in Stockholm we know little, for the autobiographical records are meager.[53] Two children had been born to him, Elizabeth and Reginald. In 1543 Elizabeth was married to Dominus Erick Petri. Reginald, as his father before him, sought higher education in Germany. He had probably had some schooling previously in Uppsala, for in 1542 he was entered at Rostock as *"Reinoldus Holmensis Upsaliensis."* [54] He also kept his father's surname; in the summer of 1545 he was at Leipzig as *"Ragnaldus Olavi Phace Suecus."* [55] In 1550-51 he studied at Witten-

[52] Ödberg, *op. cit.*, p. 56.
[53] *Works*, IV, 160ff.
[54] *Mat. Univ. Rostock*, II, 104.
[55] *Mat. Univ. Leipzig*, I, 653.

berg, with a subsidy from Gustavus.[56] Thus he followed his father's footsteps of thirty years earlier date. Nor does the father fail to note that when Reginald visited Sweden in 1549 he had been *promotus Magister*. Sadness entered the daughter's home in 1549 and 1550, when the pestilence took away the three children. Olavus also noted the death, in 1548, of Michael Langerbeyn, his fellow preacher in Stockholm. The longer (and later) version of the autobiographical notes states that Olavus had been vice-pastor for Michael since 1543, on account of the latter's age and infirmity. It also calls Michael the "father-in-law" (*socer*) of Olavus. Though this is improbable, it is not impossible that Olavus may have been his brother-in-law. Certainly the two were close friends, and the friendship had been of long standing, for both were from Strengnäs diocese and both had memories from German universities, while since 1526 Michael had taken an active part in the furthering of the Reformation teaching.[57] Together the two had preached and worked in Stockholm from 1543.

In relationship to his king, Olavus showed himself as fearless a preacher after Örebro as before. In 1544 the king had received information that Olavus had preached boldly concerning the government. Gustavus contented himself this time with the order that Master Olof should be seriously admonished so to preach as to inculcate reverence for the powers that be, and "not always to beat on the authorities' shield as his custom is." He suggestively added, however, that if no improvement was noted in the preaching, it would

[56] Annerstedt, *op. cit.*, p. 54.
[57] See G. Carlsson, "Nicolaus Stecker," in *KÅ*, 1922, pp. 84-86.

be necessary "to think otherwise in the matter." [58]
From these years comes evidence that Gustavus had
wanted Olavus, who he knew could write history, to
record the reign which he felt was worthy of record—
his own. In 1545 Olavus was requested to bring the
work, which the king hoped was ready, relating to
the "terrible and unchristian tyranny" of Christian II
in Sweden, from which Gustavus naturally felt he had
delivered his country. The letter indicates that the
king had "previously negotiated" with Olavus in this
matter.[59] But, as far as we know, Olavus never wrote
the history of his king. Later the archbishop was
asked to rewrite his country's history, but the work
was not a success. In the rhetorical panegyric of Peder
Swart the king finally found what he thought a record
of his reign should contain. Olavus Petri was
unskilled as chancellor. Still less was he at home in
the art of flattery and royal eulogy. His standard for
governments was too ethical and ideal and ascetic to
allow him to feel that the rule of Gustavus Vasa fulfilled all the commandments.

Once more before his day's task was completed
Olavus Petri was to be a prophetic voice in the guidance of the course of the Swedish Church. In February, 1548, the king had requested an opinion from
his Council as to the attitude of the country to the
decisions of the Council of Trent. The members of
the Council had replied that the decisions of the
Council of Trent should be judged by the Word of
God before they could be accepted. As for Sweden,
they were convinced that the affairs of the Church
had been ordered in accordance with the expressed

[58] Thyselius, *op. cit.*, p. 242.
[59] *Ibid.*, p. 262.

Ecclesiastical Transformation in Sweden 249

commandments of the Word and the conditions of the nation. They were willing to defend the king before the world in his measures against bishops, "who had wanted to make out of an ancient and free kingdom a diocese and episcopal realm for their own sole benefit." [60]

A year later the government was confronted by the necessity of formulating a policy with reference to the Interim. In March, 1549, the king wrote to George Norman to come to him at Gripsholm Castle, along with Master Olof in Stockholm," that they might discuss the question.[61] Probably as a result of this conference, a meeting was called at Uppsala, attended by the archbishop (called then "bishop") of Uppsala, Bishop Bothvid of Strengnäs, two representatives from the bishop of Vesterås, and four pastors from Uppsala and Stockholm, among them Olavus Petri. From this meeting, held during 1549, emanated a solemn protest against the Interim. The Interim was declared to be a "return to papistry." The papal authority rested on "human commandments and statutes," and no "true Christian" could acknowledge it. To return to papal subordination, now after the Truth had been reestablished, would be a "sin against the Holy Spirit." Rather than accept the Interim, the alternative of death would be preferred.[62] During the winter of 1549-1550 the question was proposed at representative gatherings in the provinces, whether or not the country wished to return to Roman rule. The answer was decidedly in the negative, from nobility, clergy, and peasantry. Everywhere the people were

[60] *Svenska Riksdagsakter*, I, 570-571.
[61] Thyselius, *op. cit.*, p. 329 (March 12, 1549).
[62] *Svenska Riksdagsakter*, I, 588-590.

committed to the evangelical cause.[63] The royal policy had become a national conviction.

April 19, 1552, Olavus Petri's life came to an end. He was hardly sixty years of age when his work was done. And in the church where he had labored over a quarter of a century, in the St. Nicholas or *Storkyrkan*, he was entombed. Ten days after his death, Laurentius Andreae died, in Strengnäs. The two leaders of the Swedish Reformation disappeared from the scene the same month. With the death of Gustavus Vasa, in 1560, the first phase of the Reformation was closed.

Almost one hundred years were to pass before the new order of things in the Church could become definitely established. By 1552 the Roman Church had ceased to exist in Sweden. But as yet the relationship toward the doctrines of Calvin had to be determined. Then was to follow a period of reaction under John III, when Rome's power was again to assert itself. By 1593 the Church could definitely declare itself for Lutheran doctrines and confessions, so that in 1630, when Gustavus Adolphus moved into Germany to settle the fate of the Protestant Church, he came as a king from a united land and Church. The Treaty of Wesphalia in 1648 determined the fact of a Church separated from Rome. Then, in Sweden too, the Church had come into its own, and its position as a National Evangelical Church was assured.

It is not too much to claim for Olavus Petri that he was the prophet of the Swedish evangelical communion. In the days of disintegration and destruction of the old, he saw clearly the character of a new church. His writings reveal an understanding of the fundamental principles of the Christian community,

[63] *Ibid.*, I, 598-600.

and his endeavor was to put first things first. The extreme measures adopted by Gustavus Vasa toward the material organization of the Church, time and wiser decisions could remedy. But had the period of the transformation lacked the spiritual truth and wisdom and candor of Olavus Petri, it would have lacked a soul, and the Reformation would have destroyed spiritual as well as material treasures. Olavus Petri knew the power of destruction. He preferred the power of construction. The heart rather than the altar must witness the first reformation. He set himself to the task of making available the treasures of Scripture, liturgy, and song of the Christian Church to his fellow countrymen. He pointed out more insistently the things that should be kept than the things that should be abolished. Patiently, fearlessly, humbly, faithfully he used every mode of expression in his power to build up the true invisible realities of Christian religion. The further history of the Swedish Reformation, and of the Swedish Church, was a realization of the ideals presented by Olavus Petri long before that Church understood the nobility and fullness of those ideals. He taught the Swedish people to read, but more than that, he taught them the relationship of the Book to their life in home and Church and State.

BIBLIOGRAPHY

The following constitutes a partial list of the books used in the writing of this treatise. Some of the principal sources, such as the *Tideboken,* The New Testament in Swedish, 1526, the Ratschlag, and the early hymn books, are not included here, as their complete titles are given in the course of the narrative. Only those books are cited which have furnished quotations or important facts for these pages. Together they form a select bibliography for the study of the relationship between the Swedish and German Reformation.

AHNFELT, O., *"Articuli Ordinantiae,"* in *Tidskrift för teologi.* Sthm., 1892.

Album Acad. Vitebergensis, I.

ANDERSSON, A., in *Skrifter utgifna av Svenska Litteratursällskapet,* XI, 3. Uppsala, 1893.

ANJOU, L. A., *Svenska Kyrkoreformationens historia.* Uppsala, 1850.

ANNERSTEDT, C., *Uppsala Universitets Historia,* I. Uppsala, 1877.

BAGGE, J. F., *Beskrivning om Upstaden Örebro.* Sthm., 1785.

BANG, A., CHR., *"Dokumenter og studier vedrörende den lutherske Katekismus' historie i Nordens Kirker,* I," in *Univ. Program.* Christiania, 1893.

BECKMAN, J. W., *Den Svenska Psalmboken.* Sthm., 1866-1872.

BERBIG, GEO., *Quellen und Darstellungen aus der Geschichte des Reformations jahrhunderts.* Leipzig.

BERGGREN, J. E., *"Olavus Petri's reformatoriska grundtankar,"* in *Uppsala Universitets Årsskrift,* 1899.

BJORLING, C. G. E., *"Vår äldsta lagkommentar,"* in *Lund Univ. Årsskrift*, 1896.
BRILIOTH, Y., *Nattvarden i Evangeliskt Gudstjenstliv.* Sthm., 1926.
BRUNN, CHR., *Psalmeboger fra Reformationstiden,* I, II. Kbhn., 1865.
CARLSON, G., *"Nicolaus Stecker,"* in *Kyrkohistorisk Årsskrift,* 1922.
COHRS, F., *Die Evangelischen Katechismusversuche vor Luthers Enchiridion,* in *Monumenta Germaniae Paedagogica,* XX-XXIII. Berlin, 1900-1902.
COLLIJN, ISAK, *Sveriges Bibliografi Intill År 1600,* Band II, h. 1. Uppsala, 1927.
DANIEL, H. A., *Codex liturgisches Ecclesiae Lutheranae.* Leipzig, 1848.
EHRENCRON-MÜLLER, *Författar Lexicon,* III. Kbhn.
EK, S., *Våra Första Psalmböcker* in *Samlaren,* 1918.
EKLUND, J. A., *Andelivet i Sveriges Kyrka,* I, II. Uppsala, 1911, 1913.
ENDERS, E. L., *Briefwechsel,* I. 1884.
ENGELSTOFT, C. J., *Nyt historisk Tidskrift,* II. Kbhn., 1848.
Flugschriften aus der Reformationszeit, I-XVIII, in *Neudrucke deutscher Litteraturwerke des XVI und XVII Jahrh.* Halle, 1877-1902.
FOERSTEMANN, C. E., *Liber Decanorum Facultatis Theologicae Academiae Vitebergensis.* Leipzig, 1838.
—— *Neues Urkundenbuch zur Geschichte der evangelischen Kirchenreformation,* I. 1842.
FRIEDENSBURG, W., *Urkundenbuch der Universität Wittenberg,* I. Magdeburg, 1926.
GEFFCKEN, J., *Die Hamburgischen Niedersachsichen Gesangbucher des 16 Jahrh.* Hamburg, 1857.
GR=Gustavus I:s Registratur, I-XXIII. Sthm., 1861-1905.
HALLMAN, J. G., *The tvenne bröder Olavus Petri och Laurentius Petri Phase, till lefverne och vandel beskrifne.* Sthm., 1726.
HALLMAN, L., *Det Gamla och Nya Strengnäs.* Strengnäs, 1853.
HSH=Handlingar rörande Skandinaviens historia, utgifna

af Kungliga Samfundet för utgifvande af handskrifter rörande Skandinaviens historia, XIII-XVIII. 1828-1833.
HEINEMANN, OTTO, Johannes Bugenhagens Pomerania. Quellen zur Pommerschen Geschichte. Stettin, 1900.
HEISE, A., Ny Kirkehistoriske Samlingar, V. Kbhn., 1869-1871.
HILDEBRAND, E., och Alin, O., Svenska Riksdagsakter, I. Sthm., 1887-1888.
HILDEBRAND, E., Sveriges Historia, IV. Sthm., 1920.
HILDEBRAND, H., Sveriges Historia, I. Sthm., 1905.
Historisk Tidskrift. Sthm., 1881ff.
HJÄRNE, H., "Reformationsriksdagen i Vesterås," in Ur det förgångna. 1912.
HOFBERG, H., Nerikes Gamla Minnen. Örebro, 1868.
HOLL, KARL, Gesammelte Aufsätze zur Kirchengeschichte. Tübingen, 1923.
HOLM, R., Olavus Petri. Sthm., 1917.
HOLMQUIST, H., Svenska Reformationens Begynnelse, 1523-1531. Sthm., 1923.
HÖFLING, J. W. F., Liturgisches Urkundenbuch. Leipzig, 1854.
KARLSON, K. F., Blad ur Örebro Skolas Äldsta Historia. Örebro, 1871.
KLEMMING, G. E., Sveriges Bibliografi, 1481-1600. Uppsala, 1889.
KLIEFOTH, TH., Die ursprungliche Gottesdienstordnung in den deutschen Kirchen lutherischen Bekenntnisses. Schwerin, 1847.
KNÖS, A. E., "Om Revision av Svenska Bibelöversättningen," in Uppsala Univ. Årsskrift, 1861.
KÅ=Kyrkohistorisk Årsskrift. Uppsala, 1900ff.
KÖSTLIN, JULIUS, Osterprogramm der Univ. Halle-Wittenberg, 1887.
LIEDGREN, EMIL, Svensk Psalm och Andlig Visa. Sthm., 1926.
LBH=Linköpings Bibliotheks Handlingar, I, II. Linköping, 1793-1795.
LINDERHOLM, E., Gustav Vasa och Reformationen i Sverige. Uppsala, 1917.

LINDQVIST, N., *Reformationstidens Bibelsvenska.* Sthm., 1918.
LUNDSTROM, H., *Undersökningar och Aktstycken. Bidrag till Svenska Kyrkans Historia.* Uppsala, 1898.
────── "Rättegången," in *Kyrkohistorisk Årsskrift,* 1909.
LÖHE, W., *Sammlung liturgischer Formulare der evangelisch-lutherischen Kirche,* III. Nordlingen, 1839.
MANDEL, H., hrsg. "Theologia Deutsch," in *Quellenschriften zur Geschichte des Protestantismus,* heft 7. Leipzig, 1908.
MARTIN, C. R., *Sveriges Första Messa, med Jämförelser och Belysningar.* Uppsala, 1901.
Matrikel Univ. Greifswald, I.
Die Matrikel der Univ. Leipzig, I. Leipzig, 1895.
Matrikel der Univ. Rostock, hrsg. von E. Schafer. Schwerin, 1919.
MÖLLER, W., *Andreas Osiander, Leben und ausgewählte Schriften.* Elberfeld, 1870.
MULLER, KARL, *Kirchengeschichte,* II, 1. Tübingen, 1922.
ÖDBERG, F., *Om magister Sven Jacobi,* in *Vestergötlands Fornminnesförenings Tidskrift,* 1897, häfte 8-9.
QUENSEL, OSCAR, *Bidrag till Svenska Liturgiens Historia,* I, II. Uppsala, 1890.
RE=Realencyclopädie für protestantische Theologie und Kirche. Leipzig, 1896-1909.
REUTERDAHL, H., *Svenska Kyrkans Historia,* I-IV. Lund. 1838-1866.
RICHTER, E. L., *Die Evangelischen Kirchenordnungen des 16 Jahrhunderts,* I. Weimar, 1846.
RIEDERER, JOH. BARTH., *Abhandlung von Einführung des teutschen Gesangs in die evangelisch-lutherische Kirche überhaupts und in die nürnbergische besonders.* Nürnberg, 1759.
ROHDE, E., *Svenskt Gudstjenstliv.* Sthm., 1923.
RUNDGREN, C. H., "Laurentius Andreae," in *Svenska Akademiens Handlingar ifrån år 1886,* Part VIII. 1893.
Samfundet St. Eriks Årsbok, 1908-1915.
Samlaren=Skrifter utgivna af Svenska Litteratursällskapet. Uppsala.
SCHÜCK, H., "Våra äldsta psalmböcker," in *Samlaren,* 1891.

—— *Striden mellan Olavus Petri samt Peder Galle.* Samlaren, 1886.
—— *"Våra Äldsta Reformationsskrifter och Deras Författare,"* in *Historisk Tidskrift*, 14. 1894.
—— *Några Småskrifter af Olavus Petri.* Samlaren, 1888.
—— *Olavus Petri* (3d ed.). Sthm., 1911.
—— *Svensk Litteraturhistoria.* Sthm., 1890.
SECHER, C. E., *Povel Eliesens Danske Skrifter.* Kbhn., 1855.
STAVE, ERIK, *"Om källorna till 1526 års öfversättning av Nya Testamentet,"* in *Skrifter utgifna af Kong. Humanistiska Vetenskapssamfundet i Uppsala*, III. Uppsala, 1893.
STAVENOW, L., *"Olavus Petri som historieskrivare,"* in *Göteborgs Högskolas Tidskrift.* 1898.
STEFFEN, R., *"Våra första reformationsskrifter och deras författare,"* in *Samlaren* (extra häfte), 1893.
STIERNMAN, A. A., *Alla Riksdagars och Mötens Besluth*, I. Sthm., 1728.
SWART, PETER, *Konung Gustaf I:s Krönika*, utg. av Nels Eden. Sthm., 1912.
THYSELIUS, P. E., och Ekblom, V., *Handlingar Rörande Sveriges Inre Förhållande under Konung Gustaf I*, I, II. Sthm., 1841, 1844.
TROIL, UNO VON, *Skrifter och Handlingar til Uplysning i Swenska Kyrko och Reformations Historien*, I-IV. Uppsala, 1790-1791.
TUNBERG, S., *"Vesterås Riksdag 1527,"* in *Uppsala Univ. Årsskrift.* 1915.
WACKERNAGEL, K. C. P., *Das Deutsche Kirchenlied von Martin Luther bis auf Nicholaus Herman und Ambrosius Blaurer.* Stuttgart, 1841.
WESTMAN, K. B., *"Kultreformproblemet i den svenska Reformationen,"* in *Historisk Tidskrift*, 1917.
—— *Reformationens genombrottsår i Sverige.* Sthm., 1918.
WEICHMANN-KADOW, C. M. VON, *Joachim Slüters ältestes rostocker Gesangbuch vom Jahre 1531—nach dem original drucken wortgetreu herausgegeben.* Schwerin, 1858.

WA=Luther's Werke. Kritische Gesammtausgabe. Weimar, 1883ff., especially Vols. I, VI, X, XII, XIX, XXX.

Works=Olavus Petri Samlade Skrifter, utg. af Sveriges Kristliga Studentrörelse under redaktion av Bengt Hesselman, med litteraturhistoriska inledningar av Knut B. Westman och J. Sahlgren, I-IV. Uppsala, 1914-1917.

INDEX

Åbo bishopric, 5, 173
Alexander III, 4
Älfsborg, 4
Anders Hansson, 233
Annates, 9, 10
Anselm, 206
Ansgarius, 4, 82, 132, 207
Aristotle, 64, 68-69, 70
Articuli Ordinantiae, 237-238
Augsburg, Diet of, 58

Baptism, ritual for, 170-171
Bell tax, 56-58
Bible, Swedish translation of, 18-19, 102-103, 125, 225, 239-240
Birgitta, St., 5, 79, 123, 214
Bohemian Brethren, 187
Bologna, University of, 64
Böschenstein, 70
Bothvid, bishop of Strengnäs, 226, 246, 249
Brandenburg *Ratschlag,* 113, 114, 116, 117, 122, 131, 133-134, 137, 145
Brask, Hans, bishop of Linköping, 6, 8, 11-17, 19, 22-28, 30, 34, 35, 38-41, 65, 125
Bremen, 4
Bugenhagen, 237
Burial, ritual for, 175-176

Calvin, 250
Canon Missae, 149-150
Carlstadt, 148
Casimir, Markgraf of Brandenburg, 112-113
Caspar, Johannes, 66

Charles V, 112
Christian I, 3
Christian II, 3, 5, 16, 30, 39, 57, 77, 123, 248
Christina, wife of Olavus Petri, 220
Christina Laurentii, mother of Olavus Petri, 63
Claus, Magister, 226
Cologne, University of, 65
Conradus Rogge, bishop of Strengnäs, 77, 80
Copenhagen, 26, 123, 124, 125

Dacke rebellion, 243
Dalarne, 4, 14, 17, 20, 24, 28-33, 35, 36, 38, 39, 43-45, 48, 57-58, 242
Danish *Chronicles,* 212
Danish *New Testament* in, 105, 108
Danish *Psalmbook,* 159
Dantzig, 39
Denmark, 2, 3, 12, 31, 36 Note, 51, 53, 60, 91 Note, 125, 213, 215, 217, 237
Döber's *Evangelische Messe,* see *Nürnberg Messe*

Enchiridion Geistlicher Leder und Psalmen, 156
Engelbrekt, 2, 62, 216
England, 60, 213, 214
Erasmus, 70, 71, 97, 102, 106, 107, 123, 127, 128
Erfurt, University of, 64
Erfurter Enchiridion (1524), 161, 162; (1525) 162

Index

Eric, Magister, 19
Eric of Pommerania, 2
Eric, Prince, 230
Eric Trolle, 3
Eskil, St., English missionary, 77

Finland, 5, 28-29, 54-55
France, 243
Francesco de Potenza, 9
Frederick, king of Denmark, 124
Furnschilt, 113

George, Duke, letter of, 23
George, Graf von Wertheim, 113
German soldiers, 6; burghers in Stockholm, 53, 85; Peasants' Revolt, 17, 60, 126
Germany, reputation of Gustavus Vasa in, 227
Goths, 213, 214
Gottland, 38
Greifswald, University of, 64, 65, 66, 230
Gripsholm, monastery, castle, 19, 20, 35, 249
Gudmund Pedersson, 17
Gustav Trolle, archbishop of Uppsala, 3, 7, 9, 30, 65, 77
Gustavus Adolphus, 250
Gustavus Vasa, founder of Swedish State, 1, 2; hostage to Denmark, 3; at head of revolt, elected king, 4; relations with Rome, 7-10; Council at Vadstena, 1524, 11-12; relations with Brask, 13-18; Council at Stockholm, 1525, 14-15; advocacy of Bible translation, 18-19; Council at Vadstena, 1526, 19-20; Council at Stockholm, 1526, 21-22; plan for disputation, 23-24, 115; defense of policy, 25-27; opposition, 27-29; Diet at Vesterås, 29-38; last letter to Brask, 39-40; results of Vesterås, 40-42; Council at Uppsala, 1528, 43; coronation, 44, 188-190; peace in Dalarne, 44-45; Church Council at Örebro, 1529, 45-47; uprising in Småland, 48-51; Diet at Strengnäs, 1529, 51-52; dictatorial policy in Church, 52-56; bell uprising, 56-58; election of archbishop and royal wedding, 58-60; relation to *Ratschlag*, 117; attitude toward Swedish hymns, 161; criticized by Olavus Petri, 194, 217, 224; break with Reformers, 222-223, 225, 226, 231-232; independent policy in Church, 227-230; German secretaries, 230ff.; accusation and trial of Laurentius Andreae and Olavus Petri, 232-235; reorganization of Church, 236-239; Dacke rebellion, 242-243; Diet at Vesterås, 1544, 243-244; attitude toward bishops, 245-246; success and failure, 246; last dealings with Olavus Petri, 247-249; death, 250.

Hamburg, 4, 156
Handbook, see *Manual*
Handbüchklein für junge Christen, 187
Helsingland, 57-58
Henrich, bishop of Vesterås, 226
Holger Karlsson, 50
Humanism, 221 Note, 123
Hymn Books (1530, 1536), 159-169, 225

Il Principe, 123
Indulgences, 74, 114
Ingemar, bishop of Vexiö, 5, 54
Institutio principis christiani, 123

Interim, 249

Jakob Ulfsson, 64
Jemtland, 44
Johannes Beldenack, 78
Johannes Magnus, papal nuntius, archbishop-elect of Uppsala, 7, 8, 9, 10, 13, 18-19, 22-23, 65, 218
John III, 250
John von Hoja, 49
Jönköping, 48
Jöns Boethius, bishop of Vexiö, 54, 58, 60
Jöns Hansson, 25
Jöns Laurentius, dean at Uppsala, 16
Jöns Magni, dean, bishop, of Linköping, 54, 58
Jöns Nilsson, 30

Kalmar, 4
Kalmar Recess, 2
Kalmar Union, 2, 78
Kinderfragen, 187
Klug's *Gesangbuch*, 162
Knut Michaelis, 14, 21, 24
Knutsson, Karl, 3

Laurentius Andreae, archdeacon at Strengnäs, 7; chancellor, 8; letter to monks at Vadstena, 10; at Council of Vadstena, 1524, 11-12; at Diet of Vesterås, 1527, 33; regarding consecration of bishops-elect, 43; president at Church Council at Örebro, 1529, 45, 47; reputation, 50; regarding archbishopric of Uppsala, 58; education, 65; early life, 78-79; attitude toward Lutheran Reformation, 82-83; New Testament translation, 86, 93, 104-109; relationship to king, 221-223, 231-236; death, 250

Laurentius Petri, archbishop of Uppsala, 59, 63, 220, 223-224, 228, 235, 239, 242, 245, 248, 249
Leipzig, University of, 64, 65, 66, 67, 246
Linköping, bishopric, 5, 38, 41
Lübeck, 4, 6, 20, 21, 28, 29, 31, 44 Note, 56, 62, 224, 233, 235
Lund, archbishopric, 4
Luther, at Wittenberg, 67-76; *Betbuchlein*, 88, 97, 98, 110-111, 124; Bible translation, 97, 98, 99, 100, 106, 107, 225 Note, 240; *De Servo Arbitrio*, 128; *Letter to the German Nobility*, 130; *Von Ehelichem Leben*, 135-136; *Von Menschenlehre zu meiden*, 145; *Formula Missae*, 150, 157; *Deutsche Messe*, 150, 157, 241; Hymns, 162; *Taufbuchlein*, 170-171; *Traubuchlein*, 173-174; *Catechism*, 182, 187; *Postil*, 182-183
Lutheranism, 7, 10, 11, 13, 16, 23, 31, 44, 48, 79

Machiavelli, 123
Magnus Barnlock, 216
Magnus Harraldson, bishop of Skara, 5, 9, 18, 20, 28, 29, 43, 49-51, 65, 125
Magnus Sommar, bishop of Strengnäs, 5, 9, 43, 59, 79, 226
Måns Brynteson, 20, 21, 28
Måns Johanson, 227
Manual, 164-165, 169-177
Manuale Åbo, 173
Manuale Lincopensis, 173
Marriage, ritual for, 173-174
Mårten, bishop of Åbo, 54, 55
Mass, German, 148
Mass, Latin, 51, 149-150, 161, 179, 238
Mass, Swedish, 49, 51, 57, 59, 148-159, 164, 179, 180, 225, 226, 227

Matts, bishop of Strengnäs, 5, 9, 77-78
Melanchthon, 69-70, 205, 237
Melchior Hoffman, 26
Michael Langerbeyn, 66, 247
Michaels, Magister, 21
Monasteries, 12, 14, 35, 36-37, 41, 46, 55-56, 84, 137-140

Nerike, 57
New Testament in Swedish, 22, 86-87, 95-110, 161
Nicholas Benedicti, dean of Strengnäs, 79
Nicholas Ragvaldi, archbishop of Uppsala, 2
Nils Andreae, archdeacon of Vesterås, 54
Nils Arvidson, 48
Nils Olson, 25
Norman, George, 230, 231, 236, 237, 239, 242, 249
Norrland, 41
Norway, 14, 21, 22, 44-45, 60
Nürnberg, 112, 113, 141, 145-146, 151, 157, 198
Nürnberg Enchiridion (1525) 162, (1527) 152-159, 162
Nürnberg *Messa* (Döbersche), 151-159, 164 Note, 172

Öland, 5 Note
Olavus Brunes, 67
Olavus Magni, 7, 29, 84
Olavus Petri, at Örebro, 62; at Uppsala, 63-65; at Wittenberg, 67-76; ordained deacon, 77; teaching at Strengnäs, 7, 79-83, 99; acquaintance with king, 7; secretary in Stockholm city council, 53, 84, 209-211; preacher at St. Nicholas, Stockholm, 8, 84-85, 220-221, 246, 247; marriage, 15, 148; *An Useful Teaching*, 86, 87, 91-99, 187, 198, 204; *New Testament in Swedish*, 99, 100-110; disputation in Uppsala, 116; *Reply to Twelve Questions*, 116, 117-122, 130, 131, 145; *Minor Reply to Paulus Eliae*, 116-117, 132; *A Little Book Concerning the Sacraments*, 117, 133-135, 169; *Reply to an Unchristian Letter*, 122, 126-130, 167-168; *A Short Instruction Concerning Marriage*, 135-137; *A Little Book in which the Monastic Life Is Described*, 137-140; *Concerning the Word of God and the Commandments and Statutes of Men*, 140-145, 165-166; *Why the Mass Should Be in Swedish*, 148, 180; Hymns, 165-169; *Manual*, 169-177; *Postil* (1528), 178, 182-183; (1530), 178, 183-186; *Catechism*, 186-187; *Five Useful Teaching*, 187; *Brief Introduction into the Holy Scriptures*, 188; *Coronation Sermon*, 188-190; *Christian Admonition to the Clergy*, 190-191; *An Admonition to All Evangelical Preachers*, 191-193, 224, 226; *Sermon against the Terrible Oaths*, 193-194, 228; *The Soul's Consolation and Healing*, 194-195; *Tobie Comedia*, 195-196; *The Suffering and Resurrection of Our Lord Jesus Christ*, 196-197; *Concerning the Most Vital Events and the Age of the World*, 197-198; *Concerning the Noble Creation of Man*, 198ff.; *How Man Attains to Eternal Bliss*, 198ff.; theological thought of, 199-208; *Swedish Chronicle*, 209, 212-219, 228, 233, 235; *Commentary on the Municipal Law*, 209-210;

Index

Rules for the Judge, 210-212; chancellor to the king, 223; trial, 232-235, 246; family, 246-247; last services, 248-249; death, 250; estimate of, 250-251
Olof, archbishop of Trondhjem, 20, 22, 24, 45, 104-106
Ordinantia, see Vesterås *Ordinantia*
Örebro, 62-63; Church Council at (1529), 45-48, 145, 169, 170, 172, 175, 179; Royal Council at (1539), 232, 237, 243
Osiander, 113, 141, 143, 198
Östergötland, 5 Note, 20, 48
Otto, bishop of Vesterås, 5, 65

Paris, University of, 64
Paulus Eliae, 117, 122-133, 138, 145, 204, 221
Peder, bishop of Vesterås, 9, 54, 59, 60, 226
Peder Galle, 59, 115, 117, 118-122, 131, 138, 145, 204
Peder Helsing, 38
Peder Jakobson, bishop-elect of Vesterås, 5, 9, 14, 22, 24-25
Peter Olaffson, 63
Peter Swart, 6, 7, 34, 59, 83, 91 Note, 99
Petrus Brask, 66
Petrus Magni, bishop-elect of Vesterås, 9
Petrus Schwenn, 66
Pommeranian Ordinances, 237
Prague, University of, 64
Preaching, 178-186, 190-191
Preaching Brethren, 17
Prussia, 22, 27, 36 Note, 157
Pyhy, Konrad von, 230, 231, 232, 234, 235, 237, 243-244

Ratschlag, see Brandenburg *Ratschlag*
Regensburg, 112

Reginald, 246
Reinhart, 123
Richolff's press, 86, 89, 95, 240
Rostock, 45; University of, 64, 65, 66, 67, 246
Rostock *Gesangbuch,* see Slüter's *Gesangbuch*
Roth, Stephan, 182
Rothenburg, 113
Rügen, 230
Runestones, 213, 219 Note
Russia, 28-29

Sachsen-Lauenburg, 58
Schleupner, 113
Schools, 55, 63, 224, 227, 245
Seven Penitential Psalms, 88, 90, 155
Sigfrid, St., English missionary, 82, 132, 207
Skara, bishopric, 5, 9, 45
Skellefteå, 225
Skeninge, Council of, 4
Slüter's *Gesangbuch,* 152-159, 162, 163, 164
Småland, 5 Note, 20, 48, 242
Söderköping, 13, 27, 29, 31
Speratus' *Gesangbuch,* 162, 163
Spires, 112
Stecker, Nicolaus, 85, 221
Sten Sture, 3, 14, 64
Stöckel, 113
Stockholm, 3, 4, 35, 53, 84-85, 148, 149, 214, 220, 225, 229, 235, 247, 249; Council (Jan. 1526), 14; (Aug. 1526), 21
Strengnäs, bishopric, 5, 44, 62, 84, 226, 247; Diet of (1523), 7, 44; (1529), 51-52; city, 7, 76-77, 226
Sven, dean, bishop, of Skara, 54, 56, 58, 60, 221, 227, 231, 245

Tausen, Hans, 125
Theologia Germania, 72-74

Index

Thomas Aquinas, 64
Thuro Benedicti, 66
Tideboken, 89-91
Toltz, Johann, 187
Torgams, 59
Trent, Council of, 248
Tuna, 45
Ture Ericsson, 27
Ture Jönsson, 12, 20-21, 28-29, 31, 34, 35, 38, 41, 49-51, 125
Tyge Krabbe, 51, 124, 125

Umeå, 225
Uppland, 48, 49
Uppsala, archbishopric, 4, 41, 54-55, 58-59, 223, 249; disputation at, 23-24, 116; University of, 63-65, 215, 246; Council at (1528), 43; (1531), 57-58; Church Council at (1539), 231, 235, 237

Vadstena, Convent at, 5, 10, 41, 46, 79, 226-227; Council at (1524), 11; (1526), 19

Venatorius, 113
Vesterås, bishopric, 5, 17, 45, 226; Diet of (1527), 31ff., 32-34, 122; *Recess*, 36, 42, 43, 48, 50, 224; *Ordinantia*, 37, 42; Diet of (1544), 244
Vestergötland, 5 Note, 20, 27, 48-49, 236
Vestmanland, 57
Vexiö, bishopric, 5
Vincent, bishop of Skara, 5, 65
Vincent Lunge, 44-45
Visiting of Sick, ritual for, 171-172
Volprecht, 113

Walther's *Gesangbuch*, 162
Wilhelm, Graf von Henneberg, 113
Windesheim, 113
Wittenberg, University of, 65, 66, 67, 68-70, 72, 74, 76, 85, 227, 230, 246-247; *Hymnbook*, 161; *Ordinance*, 237
Worms, Edict of, 112